MERRY GENTLEMEN

MERRY GENTLEMEN

A Bacchanalian Scrapbook

*Being a curious, diverting and instructive
miscellany of the Bacchanalian arts and sports,
with notes, quotes and comments;
the whole having been gathered together
for your especial entertainment*

by

ROWLAND WATSON

MCMLI
T. WERNER LAURIE LIMITED
LONDON

Printed in England by
W. S. Cowell Limited
at their press in
the Butter Market, Ipswich
for the publishers
T. Werner Laurie Limited
187 Piccadilly, London, W.1
1951

THE ENGLISHMAN'S NEED
OF DRINK

There is no nation yet known in either hemisphere where the people of all conditions are more in want of some cordial to keep up their spirits than in this of ours.

JONATHAN SWIFT (1667–1745)

TOTAL ABSTINENCE

I do not believe in total abstinence, nationally. I am inclined to fear lest a total abstaining nation should become a gluttonous, grasping, selfish, tyrannical, morose, and intolerably conceited nation; but I do believe in the practicability of a traditionally hard-drinking nation—we have been drinking hard for twelve hundred years— growing gradually less drunken, and I hope to have ere long occasion to show that the habits tend very conspicuously indeed in the direction of moderation in the use of strong drink.

GEORGE AUGUSTUS SALA (1828–96)

For my old friends Beulah and Ralph Cockrill

who grow younger in their retirement

at Leigh-upon-Mendip

FOREWORD

During the many years I spent in search of unusual material for *A Scrap-book of Inns*, I put on one side some passages which throw light on the drinks and drinking customs of our ancestors, in the hope that a selection of these would make a fit companion volume and another study of social life from an odd angle.

Again, for the most part, I have avoided the familiar. The novelists have not been included and there are no drinking songs. The picture presents much merriment and in parts, the grim and sordid. For this reason, I have tried to strike a balance with the section entitled *The Warning*.

To quote from the sub-title of *The Rambler's Magazine*, 1783, this book is 'calculated for the entertainment of the Polite World, and to furnish the Man of Pleasure with a most delicious banquet of Amorous, Bacchanalian, Whimsical, Humorous, Theatrical and Polite Entertainment'.

ROWLAND WATSON

ACKNOWLEDGEMENTS

I have pleasure in thanking the following for allowing me to use copyright matter:

Miss Eleanor Farjeon for *A Nursery in the Nineties:* Mr Jethro Bithell for his translations of Emile Verhaeren's poems: Dr Martin Shaw and the Oxford University Press for *Up to Now:* my good friend the late Reginald L. Hine, who was pleased I wanted to quote from *The Story of Hitchin Town:* Messrs John Murray for *The Bancrofts: Recollections of Fifty Years:* Messrs Methuen & Co. Ltd. for *Old Country Life* and *The Vicar of Morwenstow,* both by the Rev. Baring Gould and *The Parish Clerk* by the Rev. P. H. Ditchfield. (It will be noticed that some of the most entertaining passages in this book were written by clergymen): Messrs Gerald Duckworth & Co. Ltd. for *Round About the Upper Thames* by Alfred Williams: *The Times* for *Another Little Drink* and for a letter from Mr Walter Seeley, who has also kindly given his consent: The *Evening News* for the story about Sir Norman Birkett: The Proprietors of *Punch* for two articles from early numbers: *The Pennant,* the house magazine of Messrs Benskin's Watford Brewery Ltd, for *Conversation Piece* by P. L. J. Millen.

I am also grateful to the Librarian and staff of the Fulham Library, who have always been anxious to help me.

My special thanks are due to E. H. W. Meyerstein. For thirty years we have regarded our libraries as belonging to each other.

ROWLAND WATSON

CONTENTS

BACCHUS – page 13

Enigma on a Corkscrew—Kinds of Drunkards—An Oration in Praise of Drunkenness—Husband and Wife—Dram Drinking—Liberty to Drink—The Smallest Beer—In Praise of Ale—Claret—Cider—Smoking and Drinking—Hoisting Sail—The Captain's Feast—The Consul Entertains—Family Prayers—The King's Health—The Jolly Toper—Illicit Distilling—Home-made Wine—Another little Drink—The Old Masters—Drinks of all Nations—Drinking Cups—Pledging—Reeling Home

TIPPLING – page 48

A Drinking Match—Manchester Hospitality—A Feast at Huntington—A Letter to a Gentleman wherein is described the Humours of a Drunken Rencounter—Drunken Schoolmasters—The Quakers' Tavern—Candidate for Parliament—My Wife's Relations—A Sussex Tradesman—The Parsons' Corkscrews—Election Expenses—Thieves—The Gout—The English—The Women of Edinburgh—The Clerical Dispute—Dealer in Foreign Spirituous Liquors—Bishops in Taverns—Gluttony—A Public House Trick—An Irish Wake—The Tavern Carouse—Drunken Edinburgh Lawyers—Brooks's Club—A Marine—The Knighthood—The Sixty-sixth Regiment of Foot—A T.B.—The Judge Pronounces—The Tea Drinkers—The Horse Guards—Medenham Abbey—Do I at last see you sober!—Seeing London—Trinity College, Dublin—The Lawyer's Word—Doctor and Patient—A Drink on Stage—The Pint Back Stage—Low Life in London—The Artist's Model—The Roving Irish—The Carlyles' Servant—The Servants' Hall—A Sailor Ashore—Ratcliffe-Highway—The Tap of Temperance—Tom Archer from Drury Lane—Jack on the Stage—The Stick of Whiskey—The Country Doctor—Religious Ceremonies—The Village Songster—Barnes!—Jumping out of Bed—Blowing out the Candle—The Benevolent Clergyman—A Man about Town—A City Chop House—Ratcatcher Joe—The Parish Clerk—Was I Here?—The Stock Speech—Father and Children—The Cabby—The Home Coming—The Servant Problem—The Teetotaller's House—The Lucky Chimney Sweep—Peasants—Conversation Piece

NOTABLE DRINKERS – page 127

William Butler, Physician—Ralph Kettle, D.D.—Francis Bacon—Thomas Hobbes—Henry Martin—Sir John Denham—Andrew Marvell—Louis François Roubiliac—Joseph Nollekens—James Boswell—The Duke of Norfolk—John Hamilton Mortimer—Sir John Danvers—Richard Brinsley Sheridan—George Frederick Cooke—John Philip Kemble—Richard Porson—Edmund Kean—William Pitt—Robert Burns—George Colman—Lord Byron—Charles Lamb—John Mytton

ALCOHOLIC QUESTIONS AND ANSWERS – page 162

Red Noses—Drink and Suicide—Over the Left Thumb—Drink and Speech—Drink and Violence—Drunkenness or Fornication—The Fumes of your Liquor—The Water Drinker—Drinking and Blindness—The Publican's Dilemma

CONTENTS

THEY ALSO SERVE – page 172

THE WARNING – page 204

NIPS – page 228

LIST OF ILLUSTRATIONS

LIST OF ILLUSTRATIONS

Bacchus

ENIGMA ON A CORKSCREW

Though I, alas! a pris'ner be,
My trade is others to set free:
No slave his lord's behest obeys
With such *insinuating* ways.
My genius, piercing, sharp, and bright,
Wherin the men of *wit* delight.
The clergy keep me for their ease,
And turn and wind me as they please.
A new and wondrous art I show,
Of raising *spirits* from below;
In *scarlet* some, and some in *white*,
They rise, walk round, yet ne'er *affright*.
In at each mouth the spirits pass,
Distinctly seen, as through a glass;
O'er head and body make a rout,
And drive, at last, all secrets out;
And still, the more I show my art,
The more they open every heart.
Although I'm often out of *case*,
I'm not asham'd to show my face;
And the plain squire, when dinner's done,
Is never pleas'd till I make one.
I twice a day a hunting go.
Nor ever fail to seize my foe;
And, when I have him by the poll,
I drag him upwards from his hole;
Though some are of so stubborn kind,
I'm forc'd to leave a limb behind.
I hourly wait some fatal end,
For I can *break*, but never *bend*.

KINDS OF DRUNKARDS

He is foxt, hee is flawed, he is flustered, hee is suttle, cupshot, cut in the leg or backe, hee hath seene the French king, he hath swallowed an haire or a taverne-token, hee hath whipt the cat, he hath been at the scriveners and learn'd to make indentures, hee hath bit his grannam, or is bit by a barne-weesell, with an hundred such-like adages and sentences.

PHILOCOTHONISTA OR THE DRUNKARD OPENED DISSECTED AND ANATOMIZED
Thomas Heywood, 1635

The first is Ape drunke, and he leapes, and sings, and hollowes, and daunceth for the heauens: the second is Lion drunke, and he flings the pots about the house, calls his Hostesse whore, breakes the glasse windowes with his dagger, and is apt to quarrell with any man that speaks to him: the third is Swine drunke, heauy, lumpish, and sleepie, and cries for a little more drinke, and a fewe more cloathes: the fourth is Sheepe drunke, wise in his owne conceipt, when he cannot bring foorth a right word, the fifth is Mawdlen drunke, when a fellow will weepe for kindnes in the midst of his Ale, and kisse you, saying: By God Captaine I loue thee, goe thy waies thou dost not thinke so often of me as I do of thee, I would (if it pleased God) could I not loue thee so well as I doo, and then he puts his finger in his eie, and cries: the sixt is Martin drunke, when a man is drunke and drinkes himselfe sober ere he stirre: the seuenth is Goate drunke, when in his drunkennes he hath no minde but on Lechery: the eighth is Foxe drunke, when he is craftie drunke, as many of the Dutch men bee, will neuer bargaine but when they are drunke. All these *species* and more I haue seene practised in one Company at one sitting, when I haue been permitted to remaine sober amongst them, onely to note their seuerall humors. Hee that plies any one of them harde, it will make him to write admirable verses, to haue a deepe casting head, though hee were neuer so verie a Dunce before.

PIERCE PENILESSE HIS SUPPLICATION TO THE DIVELL
Thomas Nashe, 1592

AN ORATION IN PRAISE OF DRUNKENNESS
SPOKEN AT OXFORD, 1700

This Dome, this *Lycæum*, is only Consecrated to such, whose smiling Aspect bespeaks them Friends to the Good-natur'd God of Wine, whose sacred Rites I esteem, and whose eminent Perfection, *Drunkenness*, I intend to make the Subject of my ensuing Discourse. Nor must the Philosophers or Divines here exert their Austerity, or interpose with their Maxims of Decency and good Manners. I acknowledge myself of no Sect but that of *Epicurus*, whose drunken Atoms reel'd into Order, and fram'd a World infinitely beautiful. A World that produces Ten Thousand Pleasures, but none so great or agreeable as those that proceed from the soft Enchantment of the *Vine*, a Plant that has greater Power over the Minds and Nature of Mankind, than the subtile Draughts of *Circe* or *Medea:* You smile, and think me in the Condition I would persuade my Audience to be. But, Gentlemen,—you are mistaken, I am sober, to my own Misfortune; and soberly, I desire, I exhort you all to be drunk: Sobriety makes a Man revengeful, or fit to ruin the Common-Wealth: In Drunkenness, the Injur'd forgets his Sentiments of Passion, remembers neither the Blows of his Enemies, nor of Fortune, is as great as an Emperor, and if he speaks a little Treason, or so, never acts any against the Government. 'Tis Wine that enlivens the Conversation, makes the Soldier bold and daring, refines the Politicks of the Statesman, and makes the Casuistical Divine most Orthodox in his Opinions. If we look back into the Primitive History of the first Ages, into the Originals of Nature, from the very first Structure of the World, we shall find that Drinking to excess has been a Custom approv'd of by all Nations. Our Great Grand-mother *Eve* was certainly drunk with the Grape, before she lusted for the Apple; and if she had had any Conscience, she might well have been contented with the first, without coveting the latter. The Confusion of *Babel* was a parcel of Drunkards, who fell out among themselves, when they had taken a Cup of the Creature; and they separated themselves into several Troops and Companies, in order to raise that agreeable Plant which gave them so comfortable a Liquor. But why do I dwell upon a Truth that is notorious to all manner of People, or endeavour to convince the World of the Antiquity of Drunkenness, which now stretches itself through all the Universe? The Custom of Nations is the Law of Nations, and the wise *Athenians* obliged their Common-wealth to submit to such Customs as were of three Years standing, as if enacted in the most solemn manner. But Drunkenness has possest the World, and been a practical Virtue these Three Thousand Years and upwards, and only younger than the Divine ones are. I see, Gentlemen, you begin to change your Sentiments, and this Assembly must acknowledge, that Drunkenness may justly challenge a Priority in Practice, before all other Virtues whatsoever. The Annals of our Fore-fathers can produce no Custom so primitive, or fitter to be imitated by Posterity. The Custom of Drunkenness we receiv'd from our

15

Fathers, to whom the same Virtue was transmitted from their Ancestors, and made Illustrious by the Tradition of so many Ages. I am of Opinion, that if the *Jews* had been as careful in collecting Transactions of this Nature, as recording to Futurity the respective Births of their Sons and Daughters in some Folios of Bulk and Piety, this sage Practice would appear much ancienter than the Books of *Moses;* and even to extend itself backwards to the Patriarchs of the Antidiluvian World. *Noah,* the *Janus* of Antiquity, pass'd away the melancholy Hours of Confinement in the fine wooden World of his own Structure, with a consoling Bottle; and in Gratitude to the Juice, with which they made the Patriarch so merry, during the most dreadful Convulsions of Nature, upon his happy Descent from that floating Castle, he planted a Vine, and drank heartily thereof: He bless'd his Sons, and his Blessings are as permanent as the Heavens. To enumerate all the Merits of Drunkenness, would exceed the Limits of my intended Harangue; I shall only insist upon the Prudence of those good Patriots, who with great Wisdom first instituted to the great *Bacchus,* Mysteries celebrated by the greatest part of mankind; and however the Names and Appellations of such Tracts, or drunken Ceremonies may differ, yet the Fact and Practice is the same in all the polite Governments of *Europe; Spain, France* and *Italy,* have their Carnavals; the drunken *Mahometan* his Days of Excess before the *Biram;* the *Protestants* and *Lutherans* their Holy-days; and this Reverent City, what the Learned call their *Act.* These are Times dedicated to Drinking, and all the Irregularities that attend the Wanton Fumes inspired by the God of Wine; such Hours slide away with Pleasure, indulge the wearied Senses, soften the Soul with extreme Delight, and flatter the Mind with endearing Thoughts of Happiness: The Melancholy are not entertain'd upon these occasions with other Objects than such as are likely to dispel the dismal Clouds of Miseries, such as render the Soul serene and gay. Superstition, and the dull Religious, meet in these Rencounters with no Hobgoblings or dancing Fairies; no Stories of Purgatory, or the Punishments of the Dead, the Priests impose no longer on Mankind, nor amuse the People with empty Representations of what they give no Credit to themselves. Me-thinks I see some among you inclin'd to contradict my Assertions, and ready to run upon Invectives against the celebrated Rites I have been discoursing of; but let me tell you, besides the Injustice you do the generous Liquor of the Grape you speak against a Truth confirmed by common and daily Experience, by the Use of the Ancients, and the Practice of the Moderns. To Satisfy you of the stupendous Effects of Drunkenness, and its unlimited Power and Advantages to all Orders of Men, reflect upon those

Scenes which a thousand times have been obvious to your Eyes; look upon that sober Mechanick, how dull, how heavy is the Animal, scarce by his Intellects to be distinguish'd from the Inhabitants of the Desarts, the Beasts of the Fields, or Fowls of the Air! but when Wine ferments the grosser Particles of his Brain, and lends its kind Assistance, he then proves himself a Rational Creature, turns Politician, argues upon the Right of Empire, makes War and Peace, beats the *French* with his Stratagems, rallies the *Germans*, and laughs at the slow Portuguese; he turns a State-critick, and harangues his Audience upon the most important Affairs. The same Divinity encourages the Youth of this University, obliges them to lay aside their Modesty, so injurious to their Fame; they find Rhetorick, Divinity, Physick, Philosophy, Law, and all other Sciences in a Bottle; they take their Degrees without the usual Formalities and Expence; boldly set up for Doctors, and preach upon the nicest Points of Knowledge with the utmost Assurance imaginable; They expect to be made Deans and Bishops, and think their Parts give them a just Title to so eminent a Station: Nor does the Young only reap the Benefits that proceed from the Force of Wine; the Old, whom Age and Diseases have render'd almost incapable of Action, or partaking in the Pleasures or Business of the World, find themselves vigorous and lusty by drinking full Bumpers of that sparkling Juice: from thence they find their Nature and Inclinations chang'd, as well as Strength renewed. They dance away the Laziness of Age, make Love as if they had recover'd Time, and had never seen above Twenty Winters, when their hoary Heads confess their Years, and stupify the World with so powerful an Alteration: But what is equally surprizing, their Temper is chang'd, their darling Humour, Avarice, is lost, and their Hearts become unbounded, and free as the God by whom they are possess'd. Wine gives all Things, it makes the Dull Ingenious, the Modest Bold, the Fearful Brave; refines the Judgment of the Doctors, and makes their Opinions most Canonical. It must be confess'd that the Notion of Liberty is deeply imprinted in our Hearts, there being certainly nothing more advantageous, nothing more beneficial, more pleasing and agreeable to Human Reason. 'Tis Liberty that by its Origin and Excellency imparts to us a great Resemblance, and, as it were, unites us with the Divine Nature itself: For the Gods, tho' they enjoy immense Pleasures, yet their highest Excellency consists in having their Will unlimited by any superior Power. You that are Enemies to Drunkenness, consider seriously the Course of all Sublunary Things; consider whether 'tis not the Drunkard, that before all others can boast of this Liberty, and acts as uncontroulable as the Gods themselves. If such an one affronts his Friend or his Neighbour, the Civil Magistrate, or the Government, 'tis imputed to Wine; the considerate World say, *The Man was not himself;* he escapes public Justice and private Revenge, and that Liquor that renders him happy in his Thoughts, makes him also secure, and protects him in his Person. If the Drunkard commits a Murther, he will be hang'd when he is sober; so that he has all the Reason in the World to repent of, and avoid Sobriety: If this seems a Paradox, I beg the Favour you would try the Experiment, and put such a Crime in execution. If an honest Gentleman is a little too much heated with the Fumes of Wine, and plays the Hero in the Streets, affronts the Men, ruffles the Women, roars like a Lion, and becomes as mad as the Tigers that draw the God he pays obedience to; such a Person meets with all the Civility imaginable, every one is ready to flatter him, to speak the softest Words, and use the tenderest Actions in order to reduce him to Reason; but when he returns to his Senses, when the next Morning has dissipated the divine Fumes of the last Night's drinking, what Plagues must the poor sober Mortal undergo? His Spouse who addrest herself within some few Hours so kindly, raves like a Fiend, the Tune is now altered, she breaks out—Is this the Course you take? Must I be always a Slave to your Humour? Is this the Effect of a Gentleman-like Education? Is it thus you provide for your Family? What occasion is there for more Arguments to prove what in itself is so apparent, and beyond contradiction? That there is no Comparison in Happiness betwixt a Sober and a Drunken Man, no more than betwixt the most Miserable and the most Happy, since the first linger away their Lives in perpetual Drudgery, in Slavery and Obligations; the last enjoy all the Sweets of an unbounded Liberty; those have their Chains, whilst these are as unconfin'd as the greatest Monarchs, and scarce inferior to the Celestial Beings. What Lustre has a Crown, and what Pains do Mankind take to extend an Arbitrary Sway over their Fellow-Creatures? Ambition has very often carried Mankind from the Paths of Justice; and how many Thousand have been sacrificed for the attaining the Royal Dignity? Now if I can make it appear by undeniable Instances, that a Drunkard does not only fancy himself a King in his own Conceit, but acts, is respected and attended as such, and purchases this Sovereignty only with a few Bottles, which is sometimes obtained by the Great by Perjuries and Bloodshed; you must confess that he is as happy, if not much happier, than a King. What can appear more like a great Prince, than to see a Drunkard seated in an Elbow-Chair, majestically spewing, while one Servant holds the Bason, and another fetches him Cordials, and a third pities his Condition, and uses the softest Expressions to divert his Master's Peevishness or Fury?

The Royal Drunkard uses his Hands and Feet very briskly, and upon the least occasion his Domesticks feel their Sovereign's Resentment. 'Twas in these Pleasures *Heliogabalus* spent his imperial Hours, in drinking the most noble and generous Wines, and eating the greatest Rarities that Art or Nature could produce. He neglected the other Advantages of Empire, and sought a more pleasing and solid Satisfaction in the Enjoyment of Wine and good Company. Drinking largely got *Prometheus* his Reputation, and *Anacreon* was as famous for a Bottle, as he was soft and pleasing in his Poetry. Let us Drink then, my Friends, for to morrow we may die. Pray how do you like these Assertions? You seem to approve them well enough; but you will be better pleas'd, when I assure you, that those who take delight in Drinking, commonly make a graceful Appearance both in their Bodies and Faces. Perhaps you will answer, How can Drunkards seem agreeable? Well—I wonder at you; for if we measure Beauty, either by Bulk or Complexion; the Drunkard in either of these makes a most glorious Figure. Without surveying the whole Frame of his Body, pray take notice of his Belly, how plump and round it is! Of what a magnificent Circumference! How strong and large are his Legs, fit and proportioned to support the noble Structure above! Next, pray view his Face, how round, how smooth his Cheeks, like those the *Painters* give to Infant Angels, or the illustrious Son of *Semele*, as purple as his Wine, and always smiling like the God of Love! The Drunkard's Voice is hoarse and manly, not like the squeaking Trills of an *Eunuch*, but like the martial Kettle-Drum; and gentle Sleep concludes the Story, assists the God of Wine, and renders himself obedient to the Divine Boy, when the Thunder of *Jove*, nor the Arrows of *Cupid* can't command him. Oh! charming Virtue, Drunkenness! Mistress of all Pleasures, that conquers all Things, all the Race and Generations of Men! What Hero of Antiquity can the Fables of the *Greeks*, or the Histories of the *Romans* produce, that hath held, and yet does, so many Nations and so great Personages in Chains? In vain does *Hercules* boast of all his Victories, of his *Hydra*, and *Amazonians*, and the hellish *Cerberus*. Wine has overcome more Ladies and greater Monsters than e'er the Son of *Alamena* could subdue. All Empires and Kingdoms submit themselves to Drunkenness; she makes them stagger with the Power of her Breath; she Reigns imperially in *Germany* and *Denmark;* lords it over *Poland, Sweden* and *Norway;* among the *Dutch* she is a Stadt-Holder, and even extends her Dominion to this University, reigns over the Doctors, Fellows and Students.—But hold! perhaps you'll affirm, that only the Thinking of strong Liquors has had the same effect upon me, as the Drinking of them occasions in others; and that I am too tedious and prolix in a Matter obvious in itself to the meanest Understanding: I shall therefore trouble my Audience no farther than only to add, that 'tis highly reasonable, that a Custom establish'd and continu'd since the beginning of the World to this Day, ought to be preserv'd inviolable; that a Custom fram'd and cemented by Nature, supported by Reason, and practised with Success, ought to be deliver'd down to Posterity, be maintain'd with Honour, and had in Veneration by all succeeding Ages.

AMUSEMENTS SERIOUS AND COMICAL, CALCULATED FOR THE MERIDIAN OF LONDON.
Thomas Brown, 1700

HUSBAND AND WIFE

Hear then, ye Wives, who to a *Male* incline,
Nor blush to heighten your Repast with Wine;
And let the Spouse agreeing in the End,
Drink moderate, and social Glasses blend:
For Nature, when she moulded *Woman's* Frame,
Gave Moisture to her Womb, her Temper, Flame;
And these exalted by the *Vinous* Heat,
A proper Mixture for a *Male* complete.
Nor yet too frequent to the *Liquor* press;
The Juice is noxious taken to excess:
It floats in heavy and unactive Streams,
And damps the native Heat with sickly Streams.
Nature oppress'd in her Foundation fails,
Too gross from thence to form the vig'rous *Males*.
Remember how once *Bacchus* fluster'd came,
And hot with Wine compress'd the *Cyprian* Dame:
Folding the Goddess in his drunken Arms,
Glowing he kiss'd, and rioted in Charms:
The crude warm Seed thus immaturely wrought,
A foul, obscene disfigur'd Daughter brought;
The *Gout* her Name, of pale and squallied Face;
Limping she walk'd, and hobbled in her Pace.
Let Prudence then thy flowing Cup restrain,
And golden *Moderation* hold the Rein.

CALLIPAEDIA: OR THE ART OF BEGETTING BEAUTIFUL CHILDREN
Claudius Quillet. Translated by Mr Sewell. Third Edition. 1733

20

DRAM DRINKING

Sir,

I have the misfortune to be married to a poor sickly creature, who labours under a complication of disorders, and which nothing can relieve but a continued course of Strong Liquors; though, poor woman! she would not else touch a Dram for the world. Sometimes she is violently troubled with the tooth-ach, and then she is obliged to hold a glass of Rum in her mouth, to numb the pain: at other times she is seized with a racking fit of the cholic, and nothing will so soon give her ease as some right *Holland's Gin*. She has the gout in her constitution; and whenever she feels a twitch of it, the only thing is sheer Brandy, to keep it from her head: but this is sometimes too *cold* for her, and she is forced to drive it out of her stomach with true *Irish* Usquebaugh. She is never free from the vapours, notwithstanding she is continually drinking Hartshorn and Water: and ever since she miscarried, she is so hysterical in the night-time, that she never lies without a Cordial-Water bottle by her bedside. I have paid the apothecary above fifty pounds for her in one year; and his bill is laced down with nothing but Drops, Peper-Mint Water, and the Cordial Draught repeated.

Her very diet must always be made *heartening*; otherwise it will do her no good. Tea would make her low-spirited, except she was to qualify every dish with a large spoonful of Rum. She has a glass of Mountain with Bitters an hour before dinner to get her an appetite; and her stomach is so poor, that when she is at table, she must force every bit down with a Glass of Madeira. We usually have a tiff of Punch together in the evening: but the acid would gripe her, and the water keep her awake all the night, if it was not made *comfortable* with more than an equal portion of Spirit.

But notwithstanding the grevious complaints she hourly labours under, she is very hale; and her complexion is, to all appearance, as healthy and florid, as a milk-maid's: except, indeed, that her nose and forehead are subject to red pimples, blotches, and breakings out, which the apothecary tells me are owing to a kind of a *phlogistic* humour in her blood. For my part, considering the quantity of combustibles she continually pours down, I should imagine the fire in her stomach would kindle a flame in her countenance; and I should not wonder, if she looked as horrible, as those who hang their face over a bowl of Burnt Brandy at Snap-Dragon.

I am, Sir, your humble servant,
TIMOTHY NOGGAN.

THE CONNOISSEUR. 30 January, 1755

LIBERTY TO DRINK

There has been in all governments a great deal of absurd canting about the consumption of spirits. We believe the best plan is to let people drink what they like and wear what they like; to make no sumptuary laws either for the belly or the back. In the first place, laws against rum, and rum and water, are made by men who can change a wet coat for a dry one whenever they choose, and who do not often work up to their knees in mud and water; and, in the next place, if this stimulus did all the mischief it is thought to do by the wise men of claret, its cheapness and plenty would rather lessen than increase the avidity with which it is at present sought for.

THE EDINBURGH REVIEW
The Rev. Sidney Smith, 1819

THE SMALLEST BEER

He observed that the howses that had the smallest beer had most drunkards, for it forced them to goe into the town to comfort their stomachs; wherfore Dr Kettle always had in his College excellent beer, not better to be had in Oxon; so that we could not goe to any place but for the worse, and we had the fewest drunkards of any howse in Oxford.

AUBREY'S BRIEF LIVES
Ralph Kettell, third President of Trinity College, Oxford (1563-1643)

IN PRAISE OF ALE

Ale is rightly called Nappy, for it will set a nap upon a mans threed bare eye when he is sleepy. It is called *Merry-goe-downe*, for it slides downe merrily; It is fragrant to the *sent*; It is most pleasing to the *taste*; The flowring and mantling of it (like Chequer worke) with the Verdant smiling of it, is delightfull to the *sight*, it is *Touching* or *Feeling* to the Braine and Heart; and (to please the senses all) it provokes men to singing and mirth, which is contenting to the *Hearing*. The speedy taking of it doth comfort a heavy and troubled minde; it will make a weeping widow laugh and forget sorrow for her deceased husband; It is truly termed the spirit of the Buttry (for it puts spirit into all it enters); It makes the footmans Head and heeles so light, that he seems to flie as he runnes; It is the warmest lineing of a naked mans Coat (*that's a Bull*); It satiates and asswageth hunger and cold; with a Toaste it is the poore mans comfort, the Shepheard, Mower, Plowman, Labourer and Blacksmiths most esteemed purchase; It is the

A GIN BOTTLE

Tinkers treasure, the Pedlers Jewell, the Beggers Joy, and the Prisoners loving Nurse; it will whet the wit so sharp, that it will make a Carter talke of matters beyond his reach; It will set a Bashfull suiter a woing; It heates the chill blood of the Aged; It will cause a man to speake past his owne or any other mans capacity, or understanding; It sets an edge upon Logick and Rhetorick; It is a friend to the *Muses*; It inspires the poore Poet, that cannot compasse the price of *Canarie* or *Gascoigne*; It mounts the Musitian above *Eela*; It makes the Balladmaker Rime beyond Reason, It is a Repairer of a decaied Colour in the face; It puts Eloquence into the Oratour; It will make the Philosopher talke profoundly, the Scholler learnedly, and the Lawyer Acute and feelingly. *Ale* at Whitsontide, or a Whitson Church *Ale*, is a Repairer of decayed Countrey Churches; It is a great friend to Truth, for they that drinke of it (to the purpose) will reveale all they know, be it never so secret to be kept; It is an Embleme of Justice, for it allowes and yeelds measure; It will put courage into a Coward, and make him swagger and fight; It is a seale to many a good Bargaine. The Physitian will commend it; the Lawyer will defend it, It neither hurts, or kils, any but those that abuse it unmeasurably and beyond bearing; It doth good to as many as take it rightly; It is as good as a paire of Spectacles to cleare the eyesight of an old parish Clarke; and in Conclusion, it is such a nourisher of Mankinde, that if my mouth were as bigge as Bishopsgate, my Pen as long as a Maypole, and my Inke a flowing spring, or a standing fishpond, yet I could not with Mouth, Pen, or Inke, speake or write the true worth and worthiness of *Ale*.

DRINKE AND WELCOME
John Taylor, 1637

CLARET

At Londonderry I experienced the same cordial and generous reception in private life which had marked my stay at Belfast; but I was here led to observe, for the first time, the hard-drinking which prevailed in the interior. At the table of Mr Rice, Sir John O'Neil, and the Belfast society in general, it was the custom to put a bottle of wine at each person's elbow, and let him fill as he pleased; but here were particular meetings, where bumpers were drunk for the evening out of half-pint goblets,— which were without a stand, in order to compel the bibber to empty their contents at a draught. This race of convivialists (who, from their strong heads and capacious entrails, were denominated by their brother Bac- chanals—the 'six-bottle men') were chiefly composed of old fox-hunters and country 'squires; and, like certain plants, seemed only to be kept alive

24

by perpetual soaking. But these persons were not to be stigmatized as drunkards: their drink was claret, a light wine (wanting its modern spirit, brandy); and possessed of a more than ordinary deadness of constitution, habit had rendered this extraordinary means of vivification harmless. Those who suffered from their system were strangers who had not been schooled in it (and in this way the old saying of 'killing with kindness' was very literally verified); but it was a surprising event indeed if one of the 'initiated' could not, after making a cellarage of his stomach, and stowing away his half-dozen, maintain the perpendicularity of his attitude with the most mathematical precision.

I visited a 'six-bottle club' but once, and from the headache it cost me, was wise enough ever afterwards to decline an *encore*; but I remember very well being invited to one which held its orgies at a sea-side hamlet, and was very generally attended, with the following highly cheerful inducements: 'Will you come over to us, Mr Bur-nard, for a wake? You'll be mightily plased with the fillows you'll mate there, and plinty of variety: for one Sunday night you'll see as merry a set of divils round the table as your heart could desire; and the nixt, more than half will be under the sod, and a set of frish faces will pop into their places.—Will you come, Mr Bur-nard?'

RETROSPECTIONS OF THE STAGE
John Bernard, 1830

CIDER

When I took my Yorkshire servants into Somersetshire, I found that they thought making a drink out of apples was a tempting of Providence, who had intended barley to be the only natural material of intoxication.

The Rev. Sydney Smith (1771–1845)

SMOKING AND DRINKING

In this year also, William Breedon, parson or vicar of Thornton in Bucks, was living, a profound divine, but absolutely the most polite person for nativities in that age, strictly adhering to Ptolemy, which he well understood; he had a hand in composing Sir Christopher Heydon's Defence of Judicial Astrology, being at that time his chaplain; he was so given over to tobacco and drink, that when he had *no* tobacco (and I suppose too much drink) he would cut the bell-ropes and *smoke* them!

HISTORY OF LILLY'S (WILLIAM LILLY 1602–81) LIFE AND TIMES, 1715

Another waste of time that I would warn against is smoking, the idlest of all amusements, and the stupidest of all kinds of intoxication. I have heard indeed an excuse alleged for it, by an old smoker, that it is good for the memory; and as a proof of it, the advocate remarked, that if a man be ever so drunk, he is reminded by it to drink again.

MEMOIR OF JOSEPH BRASBRIDGE
Second Edition, 1824

HOISTING SAIL

We hoist sail; and, with Essex on the left hand, and Kent on the right, we come to the Buoy in the Oaze—a thing as strange to me as was the rest of their dialect. Hither many of our seamen's wives follow their husbands, and several other young women accompany their sweethearts, and sing *Loth to depart* in punch and brandy; so that our ship was that night well furnished, but ill manned, few of them being well able to keep watch had there been occasion. You would have wondered to see here a man and a woman creep into a hammock, the woman's legs to the hams hanging over the sides or out at the end of it. Another couple sleeping on a chest; others kissing and clipping; half drunk, half sober or rather half asleep; choosing rather (might they have been suffered) to go and die with them than stay and live without them. Here I could relate several amorous songs, some from the men to the women, others *contra*, showing them 'loth to depart'.

Claret and brandy, punch and good ale abound
Wishing us safety to the pleasant Downs.

THE CAPTAIN'S FEAST

We are past the Rock of Lisbon, but could not discover it by reason of the fog. This day our noble Captain feasted the officers of his small squadron with a piece of pork boiled in a dish; a gigget of excellent mutton and turnips; a piece of beef of eight ribs, well seasoned and roasted; and a couple of very fat green geese; last of all, a great Cheshire cheese: a rare feast at shore. His liquors were answerable, viz. Canary, sherry, Rhenish, claret, white wine, cider, ale, beer, all of the best sort; and punch like ditchwater; with which we conclude the day and week in drinking to the King and all that we love; while the wind blows fair.

THE CONSUL ENTERTAINS

I was invited to dinner with our Captain, and our Doctor, our Purser, Captain Mauris, and Captain North, to our Consul's on shore, where we had a prince-like dinner; and every health that we drank every man broke the glass he drank in; so that before night we had destroyed a whole chest of pure Venice glasses; and, when dinner was ended, the Consul presented every one of us with a bunch of beads and a handful of cross, for which he sent to Jerusalem on purpose, as he told us afterwards.

THE DIARY OF HENRY TEONGE, 1675–79

FAMILY PRAYERS

This evening, between nine and ten o'clock, when I had began prayers with my family, I was so overpowered with the effect of some perry which I had taken, not knowing how strong the liquor was, that I was obliged to break off abruptly. O God! lay not this sin to my charge!

THE DIARY OF THE REV. GILES MOORE
(Rector of Horstead Keynes from 1655–79)

THE KING'S HEALTH

From Berkshire (in May 1650) that five Drunkards agreed to drink the King's health in their blood, and that each of them should cut off a piece of his buttock, and fry it upon the gridiron, which was done by four of them, of whom one did bleed so exceedingly, that they were fain to send for a Chirurgeon, and so were discovered. The Wife of one of them hearing that her husband was amongst them, came to the room, and taking up a pair of tongs laid about her, and so saved the cutting of her husband's flesh.

MEMORIALS OF ENGLISH AFFAIRS
Bulstrode Whitelocke, 1682

THE JOLLY TOPER; OF THE ECCENTRICITIES OF INTOXICATION

An Irregular Oration

'WINE does wonders'—So it does! For it transforms a rational creature into an ass; a valiant man into a bully; and a man of property into a beggar. Wine, indeed, when taken in moderation, has often very salutary effects on the human constitution, and therefore should not be rejected

27

A Jolly Toper

by the wise and prudent. More water-drinkers meet premature death, than jolly fellows who can carry off an honest gallon under their girdle. When a wine-bibber engages with Charon for a passage over the Styx, he takes his eventful journey without despair or fear; but a water-bibber, almost on his arrival at a far-distant coast, is sometimes rowed back again to his native land, by the intercession of the Humane Society. But, why do I rave about Humane Societies and water-drinkers—Bring me another flaggon, and let it be of the best vintage—pure and unadulterated!— Moderation is a sneaking vice, and what my greatest enemies cannot alledge against me!

THE CARLTON-HOUSE MAGAZINE, 1795

ILLICIT DISTILLING

As smuggling died out local and illicit distillation began, to grew up, and became quite a trade among us. The leading men were well known. They belonged chiefly to the labouring class, brokendown smugglers, and others of lazy habits, men who would chance detection for the large profit of the traffic and avoidance of regular work. There was here and there a wise man among them; that is, wise enough to take care of his money. One especially I knew, who told me that the first £100 he saw he had earned and put by from illicit distilling, and he became in after-life a successful and an honourable man. The country carriers were deeply compromised in the trade—carrying in their carts the liquor to the various towns in the neighbourhood, where the publicans and the merchants became ready purchasers.

For some years the Excise officers made but few captures. But, as usual, boldness grew with success; then followed detection, conviction, heavy fines, and imprisonment without limit. So the traffic collapsed and died out.

The spirit was a vile liquid, easily detected by taste or smell. It had a slang name—'Dicker Flint'. Why, I never could learn. The detection and capture, at times, of a party at full work has been somewhat exciting, and the various places chosen to put the 'still' odd and romantic. It might be in the hollow of a wood, near some running stream; sometimes in a cottage or an out-house, close to the roadside; and one place of all others the most droll and daring was an old-fashioned wayside inn. The publican having more rooms in his house than his legitimate trade required, let two off for two such opposite purposes that the thought almost makes one laugh. The parish, which is large and scattered, has the church quite at the eastern end, so that the north and west were considered to be suffering from want of spiritual teaching and influence. There being no other accommodation to be had but at the inn, the good clergyman, making the best he could of the situation, hired of the publican a front room on the ground floor for weekly evening service, and here those who felt inclined met and worshipped, and the minister experienced great satisfaction in being able to administer to the spiritual wants of the people, and the landlord had the double gratification of pocketing the rent and supplying a local need. But the publican had another tenant just through the wall and on the same floor. There was the distiller at full work, and while one was offering spiritual advice and a prospect of heaven, without money and without price, the other, all silent and alone, was watching the drops trickling from the worm of the 'still' that was making him the money—the publican taking rent from both parties, and all concerned working on together in perfect harmony; the clergyman, of course, in utter ignorance of his neighbour, the distiller. I have heard the publican and the distiller laugh over the affair, and tell with great glee how nicely they had managed to dish the parson and the Exciseman.

HOME-MADE WINE

Oliver Mills was the jester and rhymester of the Workhouse. In his young days he had been drafted for the Militia. When at drill, putting the muzzle of the musket to his shoulder, Oliver said in his own rhyme—

> He cut such a figure,
> A-pulling the trigger,

that the drill-sergeant sent him home again. He was too bad even for the awkward squad. At Christmas, for many years, he was our chief caroller. On Boxing Day evening we children, as well as fathers and mothers, expected to hear him tune-up at the street door. Poor old fellow! There was sure to be a good deal of aheming-ing and haw-ing, as he was certain to have a bad cold; but, husky as he might be, his hoarseness soon melted away under the genial influence of a little mulled home-made port—the ever famous elderberry.

The housewives of those days prided themselves on the quality of their home-made wines. The process of making, the age, the quantities, and sorts—from grape-cuttings to parsnips—were the points which over a friendly glass these good women delighted to discuss and dwell upon, and if you only praised their beverage, it was enough to establish you in good favour ever after. There was, too, in this, as in many other matters, a dash of rivalry and commendable pride. If you could compare favourably with their neighbour's make, you further enhance your position as a person of discrimination among good liquors; and who could refuse the quiet, kind invitation of the mistress of the house, when she put forth her sparkling gooseberry or blushing two-year-old currant, which had cost her so much time and skill? She had fortified it, too, with a little brandy, and would demonstrate its strength by throwing a few drops on the fire. Who, I ask, after all this, could refuse? I have suffered the just penalty, over and over again, of thus partaking and praising when I knew I should suffer in sickness and headache; and though I detested the liquor, it was years before I could muster courage to say the word 'No'.

It was not so with our friend Oliver. A little good liquor could do him no harm. It appeared to tighten his relaxed muscles, to brace his nerves, to brighten his dull eye, to loosen his tongue, clear his throat, mellow his voice, and to re-make the man altogether. The wine lit up his flagging confidence, and it was then he sang from a full heart and with the greatest vigour. His songs were those of the festive season, and all of the olden time—'While shepherds watched', 'Christians awake', and 'God rest you, merry gentlemen', made up his programme; and when he had sung these and pocketed his fee—for which he had always a ready eye and hand—Oliver thought it time to seek other patrons. He had his special houses, where for years he received a hearty welcome. To tell the truth, the poor old man was but a sorry singer; but he had no rival. He was our only solo serenader, and this post of honour drew many a penny into honest Harry's pocket from old acquaintances whom he chanced to meet. I saw him borne to his narrow home in the churchyard on the tottering shoulders of four old men, fellow-inmates of the Workhouse—a pauper's funeral! There were no mourners, and but one attendant—an old woman in her barb of blue, the pauper's livery. The bell tolled its most melancholy note, and the coffin sank into the grave without a tear to follow it. Oliver's relations had all gone before him. It was then the earth became his best friend, and received him. The surface of the grave is now level with the sward. No one knows the spot, and in a few years his name will be forgotten.

OUR SUSSEX PARISH
Thomas Geering, 1884

ANOTHER LITTLE DRINK

The Man in the Moon, if an old song is to be believed, drinks claret, but other legendary figures stuck to mead out of mazers. Their wassailing, while evidently jolly, fast and furious, has, hitherto, been rather obscure, because scarcely anyone has known quite what mead was or—if the truth must out—what was a mazer. A first hazy notion of alcoholic honey in a wooden bowl is dispelled by the Worshipful Company of Meadmakers who, loyally claiming their ancient tipple to be as good as wine, bring forward an agreeable sounding list of its varieties and give their ruling on the traditional vessels from which it was drunk. Mead and sack mead, metheglin (with the accent on the 'eg'), cyser and pyment or clarre, and melomel will, it is said, keep glasses appropriately charged from beginning to end of the most festive dinner.

Glasses must, alas! be put up with, for such trophies as silver and maple wood mazers are only to be found in All Souls and other favoured places, but a ritual may still be followed. Mead is described as like a strong hock or moselle, sack mead as an Imperial Tokay or White Hymetus, cyser (which has apple-juice mixed with the honey) as a sherry, pyment as a light, red wine, something like madeira, and melomel as a rose mead, suitable for mixing with gin. An evening that began with a few rounds of sack metheglin—the mead variant of vermouth—and closed with a bottle

31

or so of pyment should revive forgotten glories of old England. 'Have it in tumblers', exclaimed one of his fellow workers, when Kipps celebrated his good fortune by standing champagne all round at 3s. 6d. a bottle. 'It isn't a wine like you have in glasses. It cheers you up, but you don't get drunk. It isn't hardly stronger than lemonade'. That was a gallant, but ill-founded judgment, and, up to now, few if any connoisseurs would have been more knowing about mead than Kipps was with his champagne.

Those who have the privilege of tasting mead, when it has had judicious icing (for it should be served below room temperature) will, in spite of the encouragement given by the Worshipful Company, be embarking into the unknown. Memory recalls one kindly host who produced on particular nights some very ancient beer brewed on a historic occasion, and he was ready to bet his guests that they could not tell what it was. After various polite guesses of sherry, madeira, and so forth, one of them remarked, 'I seem to have tasted something like this out of a physic bottle'. Then, with true knightly courtesy, he asked for a second glass. Something of this mystery will cling for the time being to mead, but it will be a pleasant expectation of being introduced to a new enjoyment. The only dash of poison in the mazer cup is, alas! that so much of these honeyed drinks must go down the wide throat of the export trade.

THE TIMES
17 March, 1949

THE OLD MASTERS

In smoky inns whose loft is reached by ladders,
    And with a grimy ceiling splashed by shocks
Of hanging hams, black-puddings, onions, bladders,
    Rosaries of stuffed game, capons, geese, and cocks,
Around a groaning table sit the gluttons
    Before the bleeding viands stuck with forks,
Already loosening their waistcoat buttons,
    With wet mouths when from flagons leap the corks—
Teniers, and Brackenburgh, and Brauwer, shaken
    With listening to Jan Steen's uproarious wit,
Holding their bellies dithering with bacon,
    Wiping their chins, watching the hissing spit.
Their heavy-bodied Hebes, with their curving
    Bosoms in linen white without a stain,
Are going round, and in long jets are serving
    Wine that a sunbeam filters through the pane,

32

Before it sets on fire the kettles' paunches
  The Queens of Tippling are these women, whom
Their swearing lovers, greedy of their haunches,
  Belabour as befits their youth in bloom,
With sweating temples, blazing eyes, and lolling
  Tongue that keeps singing songs obscenely gay,
With brandished fists, bodies together rolling,
  Blows fit to bruise their carcases, while they,
With mouth for songs aye ready, throat for bumpers,
  And blood for ever level with their skins,
Dance fit to split the floor, they are such jumpers,
  And butt their dancer as around he spins,
And lick his face in kisses endless seeming,
  Then fall with ransacked corsage, wet with heat.
A smell of bacon fat is richly steaming
  From the huge platters charged with juicy meat;
The roasts are passed around, in gravy swimming,
  Under the noses of the guests, and passed
Around again, with fresh relays of trimming.
  And in the kitchen drudges wash up fast
The platters to be sent back to the table;
  The dressers bulge, crowded with crockery;
The cellars hold as much as they are able;
  And round the estrade where this agape
In glowing red, from pegs hang baskets, ladles,
  Strainers, and saucepans, candlesticks, and flasks.
Two monkeys in a corner show their navels,
  Throning, with glass in hand, on two twin casks;
A mellow light on every angle glimmers,
  Shines on the door-knob, through the great keyhole,
Clings to a pestle, filters through the skimmers,
  Is jewelled on the monster gala bowl,
And slanting on the heated hearthstone sickens,
  Where, o'er the embers, turns to brown the flesh
Of rosy sucking-pigs and fat cock-chickens,
  That whet the edge of appetite afresh.
From dawn to eve, from eve to dawn, and after,
  The masters with their women revel hold—
Women who play a farce of opulent laughter:
  Farce cynical, obscene, with sleeves uprolled,

In corsage ript a flowering gorge not hiding,
  Belly that shakes with jollity, bright eyes.
Noises of orgy and of rut are gliding,
  Rumbling, and hissing, till they end in cries;
A noise of jammed iron and of vessels banging;
  Brauwer and Steen tilt baskets on their crowns;
Brackenburgh is two lids together clanging;
  Others with pokers fiddle gridirons, clowns
Are all of them, eager to show their mettle;
  They dance round those who lie with feet in air;
They scrape the frying-pan, they scrape the kettle;
  And the eldest are the steadiest gluttons there,
Keenest in kisses, and the last to tumble;
  With greasy nose they lick the casseroles;
One of them makes a rusty fiddle grumble,
  Whose bow exhausts itself in cabrioles;
Some are in corners vomiting, and others
  Are snoring with their arms hung round their seats;
Babies are bawling for their sweating mothers
  To stuff their little mouths with monster teats.
Men, women, children, all stuffed full to bursting;
  Appetites ravening, and instincts rife,
Furies of stomach, and of throats athirsting,
  Debauchery, explosion of rich life,
In which these master gluttons, never sated,
  Too genuine for insipidites,
Pitching their easels lustily, created
  Between two drinking-bouts a masterpiece.

EMILE VERHAEREN (1855–1916)
Translated by Jethro Bithell

DRINKS OF ALL NATIONS
To the Right Honourable the Lord Cliff

My Lord,

  Since among other passages of entertainment we had lately at the
Italian ordinary (where your Lordship was pleas'd to honour us with
your presence) their happen'd a large discourse of *wines*, and other *drinks*
that wer us'd by severall Nations of the earth, and that your Lordship
desir'd me to deliver what I observ'd therein abroad, I am bold now to

34

confirm and amplifie in this letter what I then let drop *extempore* from me, having made a recollection of myself for that purpose.

It is without controversie that in the nonage of the world, men and beasts had but one buttery which was the fountaine and river, nor do we read of any vines or wines till two hundred years after the flood, but now I do not know or hear of any nation that hath *water* only for their drink except the *Japonois*, and they drink it hot too; but we may say that what beverage soever we make either by brewing, by distillation, decoction, percolation or pressing, it is but *water* at first, nay *wine* it self is but water sublim'd, being nothing else but that moysture and sap which is caus'd either by rain or other kind of irrigations about the roots of the vine and drawn up to the branches and berries by the virtuall attractive heat of the Sun, the bowells of the earth serving as a limbec to that end, which made the Italian vineyard-man (after a long drouth, and an extream hot summer, which had parch'd up all his grapes,) to complain that *per mancamento d'acqua, bevo del' acqua, se io havessi acqua, beverei el vino,* for want of water, I am forc'd to drink water, if I had water I would drink wine; it may be also applied to the Miller when he hath no water to drive his mills.

The vine doth so abhor cold, that it cannot grow beyond the 49 degree to any purpose; Therefore God and nature hath furnish'd the Northwest Nations with other inventions of beverage. In this Island the old drink was *Ale*, noble *Ale*, than which, as I heard a great forren Doctor affirm, ther is no liquor that more encreaseth the radicall moisture, and preserves the naturall heat, which are the two pillers that support the life of man; but since *Beer* hath *hopp'd* in among us, *Ale* is thought to be much adulterated, and nothing so good as Sir *John Old Castle* and *Smug* the Smith was us'd to drink; Besides Ale and Beer, the naturall drink of part of this Isle may be said to be *Metheglin, Braggot, and Mead,* which differ in strength according to the three degrees of comparison. The first of the three, which is strong in the superlatif, if taken immoderately, doth stupifie more than any other liquor, and keeps a *humming* in the brain, which made one say. that he lov'd not *Metheglin* because he was us'd to speak too much of the *house* he came from, meaning the hive: *Sider and Perry* are also the naturall drinks of part of this Isle; But I have read in som old Authors of a famous drink the ancient Nation of the *Picts*, who lived 'twixt *Trent* and *Tweed* and were utterly extinguished by the over-powring of the *Scot*, wer used to make of decoction of flowers, the receipt wherof they kept as a secret and a thing sacred to themselves, so it perish'd with them: These are all the common drinks of this Isle, and of *Ireland* also, where they are more

35

given to milk and strong waters of all colours, the Prime is *Usquebagh* which cannot be made any where in that perfection, and wheras we drink it heer in *aqua vitæ* measures, it goes down there by beer glassfulls, being more naturall to the nation.

In the seventeen Provinces hard by, and all low *Germany*, *beer* is the common naturall drink, and nothing else, so is it in *Westfalia*, and all the lower circuit of *Saxony*, in *Denmark*, *Swethland*, and *Norway;* the Prusse hath a beer as thick as hony, in the Duke of Saxes Country, ther is beer as yellow as gold made of wheat, and it inebriates as soon as Sack. In som parts of *Germany* they use to spice their beer, which will keep many years, so that at som weddings ther will be a but of beer drunk out as old as the Bride. *Poland* also is a beer Country, but in *Russia*, *Muscovie*, and *Tartary* they use *mead*, which is the naturallest drink of the Country, being made of the decoction of water, and hony, this is that which the Ancients call'd *Hydromel;* Mares milk is a great drink with the Tartar, which may be a cause why they are bigger than ordinary, for the Physicians hold, *that milk enlargeth the bones, Beer strengtheneth the nerves, and wine breeds bloud sooner than any other liquor.* The *Turke* when he hath his tripe full of pelaw, or of Muton and Rice, will go to natures cellar, either to the next Well or River to drinke water, which is his naturall common drink, for *Mahomet* taught them, that ther was a devill in evry berry of the grape, and so made a strict inhibition to all his sect from drinking of wine as a thing prophane; he had also a reach of policy therin, because they should not be incumbred with luggage when they went to war as other Nations do, who are so troubled with the carriage of their wine and beverages: yet hath the *Turk* peculiar drinks to himself besides, as *Sherbet* made of juice of lemon, sugar, amber and other ingredients; he hath also a drink call'd *Cauphe*, which is made of a brown berry, and it may be call'd their clubbing drink between meales, which though it be not very gustfull to the palate, yet it is very comfortable to the stomack, and good for the sight; but notwithstanding their prophets Anathema, thousands of them will venture to drink wine, and they will make a precedent prayer to their soules to depart from their bodies in the interim, for fear she partake of the same pollution: nay, the last *Turk* died of excess of wine, for he had at one time swallow'd three and thirty okes, which is a measure near upon the bignes of our quart, and that which brought him to this, was the company of a *Persian* Lord that had given him his daughter for a present, and came with him from *Bagdat*; besides one accident that happened to him was, that he had an Eunuch who was used to be drunk, and whom he had commanded twice upon pain of life to restrain, swearing by *Mahomet* that he would cause him to be strangled if he found him the third time so, yet the Eunuch still continued in his drunkenes, heerupon the *Turk* conceiving with himself that ther must needs be som extraordinary delight in drunkenes because this man preferred it before his life, fell to it himself, and so drunk himself to death.

In *Asia* ther is no *beer* drunk at all, but Water, Wine, and an incredible variety of other drinks made of Dates, dried Raisons, Rice, divers sorts of Nutts, fruits and roots: In the Orientall Countries as *Cambaia*, *Calicut*, *Narsingha*, ther is a drink call'd *Banque*, which is rare and precious, and 'tis the height of entertainment they give their guests before they go to sleep, like that *Nepenthe* which the Poets speak so much of, for it provokes pleasing dreames, and delightfull phantasies, it will accommode it self to the humor of the sleeper, as if he be a souldier he will dream of victories and taking of towns, if he be in love he will think to enjoy his mistress, if he be covetous he will dream of mountaines of Gold, etc. In the *Moluccas* and *Philippines* ther is a curious drink call'd *Tampoy* made of a kind of Gilliflowers, and another drink call'd *Otraqua* that comes from a Nut, and is the more generall drink. In *China* they have a holy kind of liquor made of such sort of flowers for ratifying and binding of bargaines, and having drunk therof, they hold it no less than perjury to break what they promise, as they write of a River in *Bythinia*, whose water hath a peculiar vertue to discover a perjurer, for if he drink therof, it will presently boyl in his stomack, and put him to visible tortures; this makes me think of the River *Styx* among the Poets which the Gods were used to swear by, and it was the greatest oath for performance of any thing.

Nubila promisse Styx mibi testis trit.

It puts me in mind also of that which som write of the River of *Rhine* for trying the legitimation of a child being thrown in, if he be a basterd he will sink, if otherwise he will not.

In *China* they speak of a tree call *Maguais*, which affords not only good drink being pierced, but all things else that belong to the subsistence of man; they bore the trunk with a nawger, and ther issueth out sweet potable liquor; 'twixt the rinde and the tree ther is a cotton or hempie kind of moss which they wear for their cloathing; it beares huge nuts which have excellent food in them; it shoots out hard prickles above a fathom long, and those arme them, with the bark they make Tents, and the dotard trees serve for firing.

Afric also hath a great diversity of drinks, as having more need of them being a hotter Countrey far: In *Guiney* or the lower *Ethiopia* ther is a famous drink call'd *Mingol*, which issueth out of a tree much like the Palm, being bored; But in the upper *Ethiopia* or the *Habassers* countrey, they drink *Mead* decocted in a different manner, ther is also much wine there; the common drink of *Barbary* after water, is that which is made of Dates; But in *Egypt* in times passed ther was beer drunk, call'd *Zitbus* in latin, which was no other than a decoction of Barly and water, they had also a famous composition (and they use it to this day) called *Chiffi*, made of divers cordialls and provocative ingredients, which they throw into water to make it gustfull, they use it also for fumigations, But now the generall drink of *Egypt* is *Nile* water, which of all waters may be said to be the best. It doth not only fertilize, and extremely fatten the soil which it covers, but it helps to impregnat barren women, for ther is no place on earth wher peeple encrease and multiply faster; 'tis yellowish and thick, but if one cast a few Almonds into a potfull of it, it will becom as clear as rock water, it is also in a degree of luke-warmes as *Martialls* boy.

Tolle pues calices tepidique *toreumata Nili*

In the new world they have a world of drinks, for ther is no root, flower, fruit or pulse but is reducible to a potable liquor, as in the *Barbado* Island the common drink among the *English*, is *Mobbi* made of Potato roots: In *Mexico*, and *Peru* which is the great continent of *America*, with other parts, it is prohibited to make Wines under great penalties for fear of starving of trade, so that all the Wines they have are sent from *Spain*.

Now for the pure Wine Countries, *Greece* with all her Islands, *Italy*, *Spain*, *France*, one part of foure of *Germany*, *Hungary*, with divers countries therabouts, all the Islands in the mediterranean and *Atlantic* sea, are Wine Countries.

The most generous wines of *Spain*, grow in the mid-land parts of the continent, and Saint *Martin* beares the bell which is near the Court; Now as in Spain so in all other wine Countries one cannot pass a daies journey but he will find a differing race of wine, those kinds that our Merchants carry over are those only that grow upon the sea-side, as *Malagas*, *Sheries*, *Tents*, and *Aligants;* of this last ther's little comes over right, therfore, the Vinteners make *Tent* (which is a name for all Wines in *Spain* except white) to supply the place of it; Ther is a gentile kind of white wine growes among the mountains of *Galicia*, but not of body enough to bear the sea, called *Ribadavia*; *Portugall* affords no wines worth the transporting; they have an od stone we call *Yef* which they use to throw into their Wines, which clarifieth it, and makes it more lasting. Ther's also a drink in *Spain* called Alosha, which they drink between meales in hot weather, and 'tis a *Hydromel* made of water and hony, much of the tast of our *Mead*. In the Court of *Spain* ther's a German or two that brews beer; but for that ancient drink of *Spain* which *Pliny* speaks of, compos'd of flowers, the receit therof is utterly lost.

In *Greece* ther are no wines that have bodies enough to bear the sea for long voyages, som few Muscadells, and Malmsies are brought over in small Casks; nor is ther in *Italy* any wine transported to *England* but in bottles as *Verdé* and others, for the length of the voyage makes them subject to *pricking* and to lose colour, by reason of their delicacy.

France participating of the clymes of all the Countries about her affords wines of quality accordingly, as towards the Alpes and *Italy* she hath a luscious rich wine call'd *Frontiniac*; In the Country of *Province* toward the *Pyrenies* in *Languedoc* ther are wines congustable with those of *Spain;* one of the prime sort of white wines is that of *Beaume*, and of Clarets that of *Orleans*, though it be interdicted to wine the Kings Cellar with it in regard of the corrosiveness it carries with it; As in *France* so in all other wine Countries the white is called the *female*, and the Claret or red wine is called the *male*, because commonly it hath more sulpher, body and heat in't: The wines that our Merchants bring over upon the River of *Garond* near *Bourdeaux* in *Gascogny* which is the greatest Mart for wines in all *France*; The *Scot* because he hath alwaies bin an usefull confederate to *France* against *England* hath (among other privileges) right of preemption or first choice of wines in Bourdeaux; he is also permitted to carry his Ordnance to the very walls of the Town, whereas the *English* are forc'd to leave them at *Blay* a good way distant down the river: Ther is a hard green wine that grows about *Rochell* and the Islands therabouts, which the cunning *Hollander* somtime used to fetch, and he hath a trick to put a bag of herbs, or som other infusions into it (as he doth brimstone in *Rhenish*) to give it a whiter tincture, and more sweetnes, then they reimbark it for *England*, where it passeth for good *Bachrag*, and this is called *stooming* of wines; In *Normandy* there's little or no wine at all grows, therfore the common drink of that Countrey is cyder, specially in low *Normandy*; Ther are also many beer houses in *Paris* and elsewhere, but though their barley and water be better than ours, or that of *Germany*, and though they have *English* and *Dutch* brewers amongst them, yet they cannot make beer in that perfection.

The prime wines of *Germany* grow about the Rhine specially in the Psalts or lower Palatinat about *Backrag*, which hath its Etimologie from *Bacchi ara*, for in ancient times ther was an Altar erected there to the honour of *Bacchus*, in regard of the richnes of the wines. Here and all France

39

over 'tis held a great part of incivility for maidens to drink wine untill they are married, as it is in *Spain* for them to wear high shooes or to paint till then; The Germain mothers, to make their sons fall into hatred of wine, do use when they are little to put som owles eggs into a cup of Rhenish, and somtimes a little living eel which twingling in the wine while the child is drinking so scares him that many com to abhor and have an antipathy to wine all their lives after. From *Backrag* the first stocks of vines which grow now in the grand Canary Island were brought, which with the heat of the Sun and the Soyle, is grown now to that height of perfection, that the wine which they afford are accounted the richest, the most firm, the best bodied and lastingst wine, and the most desecated from all earthly grossenes of any other whatsoever, it hath little or no sulphur at all in't, and leaves less dreggs behind, though one drink it to excess; French wines may be said but to pickle meat in the stomack, but this is the wine that digests, and doth not only breed good bloud, but it nutrifieth also, being a glutinous substantiall liquour; of this wine, if of any other, may be verified that merry induction, That good wine makes good bloud, good bloud causeth good humors, good humors cause good thoughts, good thoughts bring forth good works, good works carry a man to heaven, *ergo* good wine carrieth a man to heaven; if this be true surely more English go to heaven this way than any other, for I think ther's more Canary brought into *England* than to all the world besides, I think also ther is a hundred times more *drunk* under the name of Canary wine than ther is *brought* in, for *Sherries* and *Malagas* well mingled pass for Canaries in most Taverns more often than Canary it self, els I do not see how 'twere possible for the Vinter to save by it; or to live by his calling unless he were permitted somtimes to be a Brewer. When Sacks and Canaries were brought in first among us, they were us'd to be drunk in *Aquavita* measures, and 'twas held fit only for those to drink of them who us'd to carry their *leggs in their hands, their eyes upon their noses,* and an *Almanack in their bones;* but now they go down every ones throat both young and old like milk.

The Countries that are freest from exces of drinking are *Spain* and *Italy;* If a Woman can prove her Husband to have been thrice drunk, by the ancient laws of *Spain* she may plead for a divorce from him: Nor indeed can the *Spaniard* being hot braind bear much drink, yet I have heard that *Gondamar* was once too hard for the King of *Denmark* when he was here in *England;* But the Spanish Souldiers that have bin in the Wars of *Flanders* will take their cups freely, and the Italians also; when I liv'd to'ther side the Alpes, a Gentleman told me a merry tale of a Ligurian

Souldier who had got drunk in *Genoa* and Prince *Doria* going a horseback to walk the round one night, the Souldier took his horse by the bridle, and ask'd what the price of him was for he wanted a horse, the Prince seeing in what humor he was, caus'd him to be taken into a house and put to sleep: In the morning he sent for him and ask'd him what he would give for his horse, Sir, said the recovered Souldier, *the Merchant that would have bought him yesternight of your Highnesse, went away betimes in the morning.* The boonest compagnions for drinking are the *Greeks* and *Germains;* But the Greek is the merrier of the two, for he will sing and dance and kiss his next compagnion; but the other will drink as deep as he; if the Greek will drink as many glasses as ther be letters in his Mistresses name, the other will drink the number of his yeers, and though he be not apt to break out into *singing,* being not of so airy a constitution, yet he will drink often musically a health to every one of these 6 notes, *Ut, Re, Mi, Fa, Sol, La;* which, with his reason, are all comprehended in this Exameter.

Ut Relevet Miserum Fatum Solitosque Labores.

The fewest draughts he drinks are three, the first to quench the thirst pass'd, the second to quench the present thirst, the third to prevent the future: I heard of a company of low Dutchmen that had drunk so deep, that beginning to stagger and their heads turning round they thought verily they were at Sea, and that the upper chamber, wher they were, was a ship, insomuch that it being foul windy weather they fel to throw the stools, and other things out of the window to lighten the vessell for fear of suffering shipwrack.

Thus, have I sent your Lordship a *dry* discourse upon a *fluent* subject, yet I hope your Lordship will please to take all in good part, because it proceeds from

Your most humble and ready

Servitor, J.H.

Westmin. 17 *Octo.*
1634.

A NEW VOLUME OF FAMILIAR LETTERS
James Howell, Second Edition, 1650

DRINKING CUPS

Of *drinking cups* divers and sundry sorts we have; some of elme, some of box, some of maple, some of holly, etc., mazers, broad-mouth'd dishes, noggins, whiskins, piggins, crinzes, ale-bowles, wassell-bowles, court-dishes, tankards, kannes, from a bottle to a pint, from a pint to a gill. Other bottles we have of leather, but they most used amongst the shepheards and harvest-people of the country; small jacks wee have in many ale-houses, of the citie and suburbs, tip't with silver, besides the great black jacks and bombards at the court, which when the Frenchmen first saw, they reported, at their returne into their country, that the Englishmen used to drinke out of their bootes: we have besides, cups made of hornes of beasts, of cocker-nuts, of goords, of the eggs of estriches, others made of the shells of divers fishes brought from the Indies and other places, and shining like mother of pearle. Come to plate, every taverne can afford you flat bowles, French bowles, prounet cups, beare bowles, beakers; and private householders in the citie, when they make a feast to entertaine their friends, can furnish their cupboards with flagons, tankards, beere-cups, wine-bowles, some white, some percell guilt,[1] some guilt all over, some with covers, others without, of sundry shapes and qualities.

PHILOCOTHONISTA, OR THE DRUNKARD OPENED, DISSECTED, AND ANATOMIZED
Thomas Heywood, 1635

[1] (That is, partly gilded.)

PLEDGING

Truely I thinke hereupon comes the name of *good* fellow, quasi *goad* fellow, because he forceth and goads his fellowes forward to be drunke with his persuasive termes, as I dranke to you, *pray pledge me*, you dis-honour me, you disgrace mee, and with such like words doth urge his consorts forward to be drunke, as oxen being prickt with goads are compel'd and forced to draw the waine.

ENGLAND'S BANE, OR THE DESCRIPTION OF DRUNKENNESS
Thomas Young, 1617

He that beginneth the health hath his prescribed orders: first uncovering his head, hee takes a full cup in his hand, and settling his countenance with a grave aspect, hee craves for audience: silence being once obtained, hee begins to breath out the name, peradventure of some honourable personage, that is worthy of a better regard than to have his name polluted amongst a company of drunkards: but his health is drunke to, and *hee that pledgeth, must likewise off with his cap*, kisse his fingers, and bowing himself in signe of a reverent acceptance. When the leader sees his follower thus prepared, he soups up his broath, turnes the bottom of the cup upward, and in ostentation of his dexteritie, gives the cup a phillip, to make it cry *Twango*. And thus the first scene is acted. The cup being newly replenished to the breadth of an haire, he that is *the pledger* must now beginne his part, and thus it goes round throughout the whole company, privided alwaies by a cannon set downe by the founder, there must be three at the least still uncovered, till the health hath had the full passage: which is no sooner ended, but another begins againe.

THE IRISH HUBBUB, OR THE ENGLISH HUE AND CRIE
Barnabe Rich, 1617

REELING HOME

Of reeling home, when you have got your load;
Of Noise and Quarrels all along the Road;
Of Household Jars before you go to Rest;
Of Deeds to the next Day adapted best:

All Things, as one cou'd wish, b'ing order'd so,
With more than double Noise prepare to go.
Bid none Farwel; no Speech of Thanks compile,
To tire 'em with a Period of a Mile:
By this my Host would your departure smoke,
And thus the Neck of your Design is broke.

With horrid Clamour ev'ry Street annoy!
Such nightly Pleasures our drunken Guests enjoy!
Each drowsy Neighbour at the Sound awakes,
Of pleasing Sleep the soft Enchantment breaks.

Provoke this Man with Words, and that with Blows,
If in thy Breast one Spark of Courage glows:
Old Feuds revive, old Grievances repeat;
You're drunk, and shou'd abuse whoe'er you meet.

If at your Challenge they prepare for Fight,
We'd have you soon betake yourself to Flight;
For, shou'd they chance to cut an Artery,
You thence would in apparent Danger be;
From the wide Wound a purple River flows,
And Life departs in strong convulsive Throws.

Nor shall our Verse those warlike Scow'rers blame,
Who Stones and Brickbats at the Windows aim:
Thou (courteous Reader) shouldst sometimes do this,

Drunkards, we know, can never act amiss;
Each from the Bowl his Inspiration draws,
And soars above the low Restraint of Laws.

TAKING HOME

If to the Compter now you march in State,
Attended by the Watch, you're truly great;
Secure from Foes when in the Compter laid,
You cannot then suspect an Ambuscade;
No Drifts of Snow nor Rain you've cause to fear,
Nor scorching Sun-beams ever enter here.

If you're so happy not to be pursu'd,
Nor barr'd from acting as it seemeth good;
When you have ravag'd all the Streets throughout,
With Ruin upon Ruin, Rout on Rout;
Go Home . . . your Mischief, being fully done,
Will make you sleep as well as Laudanum.

Now learn what Tumults at your Door to raise,
And greet your Wife, with pretty, winning Ways.

Strike, loud as Thunder, in a dreadful Squall,
Rattling along the dark aerial Hall:
With frequent Blows the stubborn Door provoke,
Till, with repeated Blows, the stubborn Door is broke.

If your sweet Spouse, a kind indulgent She,
Officiously gets up, and turns the Key,
If with soft Looks, and many an easy Word,
She strives to sooth her topsy-turvy Lord;
Let on her Head your double Fist descend,
Nor suffer Innocence to stand her Friend,
But every stroke with keen Reproaches blend.
Make her to know your Meaning by a Nod,
Rule her your Vassal, with an iron Rod.

A Wife, an Ass, a Walnut-tree ('tis thought)
Except they're thrashed, are never good for aught;
Then strike your Wife, for fear the Jade be dull,
And write your Memorandums on her scull.

Sleep not yourself, till at your Coming rise
The Family, who scarce had clos'd their Eyes;
Then prove how well the one can bear Reproof,
And if another's Bones are Cudgel-proof.
Now, to each Individual, number o'er
Their Faults committed all this Year and more;
Fear to whom Fear by this they learn to pay,
And tremble, tho' but half a Word you say.

Your household Rules so very well dispenc'd;
Climb up to Bed, to let your Eyes be drench'd;
Lie snoaring there, what length of Time you please,
And on the Coverlet your Stomach ease:

The greasy Quilt next Morn the Damsels rub,
While the Soap lathers o'er the foaming Tub.
Shou'dst thou not oft such sweet Employs procure,
Thy Place would dwindle to a Sine-cure.

When you from warm and downy Pallet rise,
And *Sol* has travers'd over half the skies,
When you've concocted what you drank at Night,
And find your Body tolerably tight,
Your Brethren of Iniquity and Wine
We'd have you meet, while they prepare to dine;
With them, till Dinner on the Table smokes,
On divers Subjects utter divers Jokes:
Charm their sick Stomachs, their Affections woo,
And with your little Wit make much ado.
Repeat what Yesternight was done or said,
When frantick *Bacchus* did the Brain invade.
Say who behav'd obscenely o'er his Pot,
Tho' all the rest his Errors have forgot:
Each Deed you view'd in Order as it rose,
And now each Deed to all the World disclose;
Many at this will smile, but more will swear,
So various human Dispositions are.

With Brags your Conversation interweave,
How much was guzzl'd down from Morn to Eve;
That when at Night you stagger'd Home to Bed,
Your feet could scarce support your heavy Head:
But yet you drank till Knights and Squires were drown'd
None went off Scot-free from the fatal Ground;
So thou shalt stand enroll'd the Prince of Sots,
Great is the Praise of emptying many Pots.

As soon as e'er you rise, 'tis Time you think
Of fit Materials to eat and drink:
Mull'd Claret with a Toast we first prescribe,
The noblest Anodyne of all the Tribe!
Thus having drank and eat, we hold it best

While Dinner's getting, to renew your Rest:
Your careful Consort, whom it most behoves,
Prepares the sav'ry Meat your Soul approves;
This done, go dine; and never fail to keep
Your constant Rounds of Gluttony and Sleep.

When Dinner's brought (you know the Women's Way)
She'll cry, God bless ye! how d'ye do To-day?
Last Night my Love was desperately bad,
His Looks disorder'd, Words and Actions mad:
Of oaths, Ill-names, and many ugly Tricks,
She now relates a Story too prolix;
How this, how that came broke, she dares complain,
And preaches in a Presbyterian Strain.

As these unseasonable Truths are told,
You'll soon be tir'd and bid her cease to scold;
If she obeys, 'tis well; if, more perverse,
Your Deeds she'll (not withstanding this) rehearse,
Snatch up whate'er will give a goodly Bruise,
Rage finds you Arms, and teaches how to use;
Those, brandish'd at her Head, enjoin her Peace,
Thenceforth the conjugal Petard shall cease.

We cou'd be long in Precepts, but we fear
That many Precepts wou'd offend your Ear;
Besides a Genius we suppose in thee,
Self-taught that Genius many Things may see:
We only figure out a gen'ral Plan,
Nor wou'd we bolt the Matter to the Bran;
Add thou the rest, to make thy Rudeness known,
Which Brutes themselves would hardly blush to own.

GROBIANUS; OR, THE COMPLEAT GENTLEMAN
An Ironical Poem. Done into *English*, from the original *Latin* of Friderick
Dedekindus, by Roger Bull, Esq.; Second Edition, 1739

Tippling

A DRINKING MATCH

I have seene a company amongst the very woods and forests drinking for a *muggle*. Sixe determined to trie their strengths who could drinke most glasses for the muggle. The first drinkes a glasse of a pint, the second two, the next three, and so every one multiplieth till the last taketh sixe. Then the first beginneth againe and taketh seven, and in this manner they drinke thrice a peece round, every man taking a glasse more than his fellow, so that he that dranke least, which was the first, drank one and twentie pints, and the sixth man thirty-six.

ENGLAND'S BANE OR THE DESCRIPTION OF DRUNKENNESS
Thomas Young, 1617

MANCHESTER HOSPITALITY

. . . . I must tell,
How men of Manchester did use me well.
Their loves they on the tender-hooks did rack,
Roast, boiled, baked, too—too—much, white, claret, sack,
Nothing they thought too heavy or too hot,
Can followed can, and pot succeeded pot;
That what they could do, all they thought too little,
Striving in love the traveller to whittle.
We went into the house of one John Pinners,
A man that lives amongst a crew of sinners,
And there eight several sorts of ale we had,
All able to make one stark drunk or mad.
But I with courage bravely flinched not,
And gave the town leave to discharge the shot.
We had at one time set upon the table,
Good ale of hyssop, 'twas no Æ sop-fable:
Then had we ale of sage, and ale of malt,

And ale of wormwood, that could make one halt,
With ale of rosemary, and betony,
And two ales more, or else I needs must lie.
But to conclude this drinking aley-tale,
We had a sort of ale, called scurvy ale.
Thus all these men, at their own charge and cost,
Did strive whose love should be expressed most,
And father to declare their boundless loves,
They saw I wanted, and they gave me gloves;
In deed, and very deed, their loves were such,
That in their praise I cannot write too much.
They merit more than I have here compiled,
I lodged at the Eagle and the Child,
Whereas my hostess, a good ancient woman,
Did entertain me with respect, not common.
She caused my linen, shirts, and bands be washed,
And on my way she caused me be refreshed;
She gave me twelve silk points, she gave me bacon,
Which by me much refused, at last was taken.
In troth she proved a mother unto me,
For which, I evermore will thankful be;

A FEAST AT HUNTINGTON

From Stamford the next day we rode to Huntington, where we lodged at the Postmaster's house, at the sign of the Crown; his name is Riggs. He was informed who I was, and wherefore I undertook this my penniless progress; wherefore he came up to our chamber, and supped with us, and very bountifully called for three quarts of wine and sugar, and four jugs of beer. He did drink and begin healths like a horse-leech and swallowed down his cups without feeling, as if he had had the dropsy, or nine pound of sponge in his maw. In a word, as he is a post, he drank post, striving and calling by all means to make the reckoning great, or to make us men a great reckoning. But in his payment he was tired like a jade, leaving the gentleman that was with me to discharge the terrible shot, or else one of my horses must have lain in pawn for his superfluous calling, and unmannerly intrusion.

THE PENNILESS PILGRIMAGE
John Taylor, 1618

A LETTER TO A GENTLEMAN WHEREIN IS DESCRIB'D THE HUMOURS OF A DRUNKEN RENCOUNTER

Dear Jack!

Tho' at this present juncture, I am in no very good condition to write Letters, because my Head akes, and with last Night's drinking my Hand trembles, yet I cannot forbear, to send you an Account of our meeting at the *Sun*, and what happen'd upon it, but I'll endeavour to be as brief as I can, for I hate Prolixity and all its Works. You must know then, that a parcel of young Fellows of us, met at the *Sun* to drink some Token sent out of the Country. At first we were exceedingly chearful and merry, the Glasses troll'd about like lightning, we drank Prosperity to old *England*, nor was the best in Christendom forgot. So far then every thing went well, but you know the old saying, Pleasure has a Sting in its Tail, People seldom know when to give off, for mark what follow'd, we had the Devil and all to do before we parted, nothing but Bloodshed and Desolation, and a Woman occasion'd it all. One in the Company it seems was deeply in Love so he began his Mistresses Health in a Bumper, swearing she was an Angel, a Goddess, and I know not what, but his next Neighbour, like a Fool, refus'd to Pledge him. Upon which Rogue and Rascal strait ensued, one ill Word begot another, after which Bottles and Candlesticks flew like Hail, and some undermining Moles in the Company, that no Body cou'd tell what to make of, blew up the Coals to make more Mischief, 'till at last all of us were hooked into the Quarrel. 'Twas to no purpose to preach up Peace and Moderation, for the Wine was in, and the Wit was out. One with his Mazzard demolished, fell down on the Floor, and lay as flat as a Flounder; t'other with his Nose dismounted, fell a swearing like a Dragon, and flung the Monteith at his opposite. A third had his Eyes clos'd up. A fourth his Lac'd Cravat and Perriwig torn to pieces. In short, the Distraction was universal, it reign'd from *Dan* to *Beersheba*, for by this time all of us were at pell-mell; but such a Noise, and such a Confusion, good Lord! I warrant you there was work enough for the Chirurgions, but it is an ill Wind, you'll say, that blows no Body good. At last the Man of the House appear'd, with a Constable and a Mob of Watchmen at his Heels, commanding us in the King's Name to keep the Peace, and not to fight like Beasts or *Dutchmen* over our Drink: What, says he, do ye think there are no Magistrates in the Neighbourhood? Or do ye know my Lord-Mayor and the City no better? Come pack up your Awls and be gone, or I shall send you all to the Counter. Upon this the Mutiny was soon squash'd, and to conclude, this was the issue of

THIEVES' KITCHEN

this Tragical Night; but who the Plague could have foreseen it. However, I shall have more Wit for the future, so begging your Pardon for this tedious Letter, I promise you, *Ne quid nimis*, shall hereafter be the Word, with

Your most humble

L.I.

AMUSEMENTS SERIOUS AND COMICAL, CALCULATED FOR THE MERIDIAN OF LONDON.
Thomas Brown, 1700

DRUNKEN SCHOOLMASTERS

We lived in a country that had but little preaching at all. In the village where I was born there was four readers successively in six years time, ignorant men, and two of them immoral in their lives, who were all my schoolmasters. In the village where my father lived there was a

51

reader of about eighty years of age that never preached, and had two churches about twenty miles distant. His eyesight failing him, he said Common Prayer without a book; but for the reading of the psalms and chapters he got a common thresher and day-labourer one year, and a tailor another year (for the clerk could not read well); and at last he had a kinsman of his own (the excellentest stage-player in all the country, and a good gamester and good fellow) that got Orders and supplied one of his places. After him another younger kinsman, that could write and read, got Orders. And at the same time another neighbour's son that had been a while at school turned minister, one who would needs go further than the rest, and ventured to preach (and after got a living in Staffordshire), and when he had been a preacher about twelve or sixteen years he was fain to give over, it being discovered that his Orders were forged by the first ingenious stage-player. After him another neighbour's son took Orders, when he had been a while an attorney's clerk, and a common drunkard, and tippled himself into so great poverty that he had no other way to live. It was feared that he and the more of them came by their Orders the same way with the forementioned person. These were the schoolmasters of my youth (except two of them) who read Common Prayer on Sundays and Holy-Days, and taught school and tippled on the week-days, and whipped the boys, when they were drunk, so that we changed them very oft. Within a few miles about us were near a dozen more ministers that were near eighty years old apiece, and never preached; poor ignorant readers, and most of them of scandalous lives. Only three or four constant competent preachers lived near us, and those (though comfortable all save one) were the common marks of the people's obloquy and reproach, and any that had but gone to hear them, when he had no preaching at home, was made the derision of the vulgar rabble under the odious name of Puritan.

THE AUTO-BIOGRAPHY OF RICHARD BAXTER, 1696

THE QUAKERS' TAVERN

Being now well tired with the day's fatigue, our thirsty veins and drooping spirits called for the assistance of a cordial flask. In order to gratify our craving appetites with this refreshment, we stood a while debating what tavern we should choose. My friend recollected a little sanctified Aminadab in Finch Lane, whose purple nectar had acquired a singular reputation among the staggering zealots of the sober fraternity.

When we had entered our land of promise, which overflowed with riches more healthful than either milk or honey, we found all things were as silent as the mourning attendance at a rich man's funeral; no ringing of bar-bell, bawling of drawers, or rattling of pot-lids, but a general hush ordered to be kept through the whole family.

In the entry we met two or three blushing Saints, who had been holding forth so long over the glass, that had it not been for their flapping umbrellas, puritanical coats, and diminutive cravats, shaped like the rose of a parson's hat-band, I should have taken them by their scarlet faces to be good Christians. They passed by us as upright and as stiff as so many figures in a raree-show; as if a touch of the hat had been committing a sacrilege, or ceremonious nod a rank idolatry.

A drunken-looking drawer showed us the kitchen, which we told him we were desirous of being in for the sake of warmth. Several slouching disciples sat hovering over their half-pints, like so many coy gossips over their quarterns of brandy, as if they were afraid anybody should see 'em. They cast as many forward looks upon us, who were wearing swords, as so many misers would be apt to do upon a couple of sponging acquaintances, staring as if they took us for some of the wild Irish, that should have cut their throats in the beginning of the Revolution.

However, we bid ourselves welcome into their company, and like true Protestant topers, scorning the hypocrisy of tippling by half-pints, as if we drank rather to wash away our sins than our sorrows, appeared barefaced and calling for a quart at once, soon discovered our religion by our drinking; whilst they, like true Puritans, were unwilling to be caught over more than half a pint, though they'll drink twenty of these at a sitting.

We had not sat long, observing the humours of the drowsy saints about us, but several amongst them began to look as cheerful, as if they had drowned the terrible apprehensions of futurity and thought no more of damnation. The drawer was now constantly employed in replenishing their scanty measures; for once warmed they began to drink so fast that 'twas the business of one servant to keep them going.

By this time the subtle spirits of the noble juice had given a fresh motion to the wheels of life, insomuch that my friend must needs be so frolicsome as to tune his pipes, and entertain us with a song. And because the words happened to be in some measure applicable to that present juncture, I have thought it not amiss to insert 'em.

53

SONG

Why should Christians be restrained
 From the brisk enliv'ning Juice,
Heaven only has ordained
 (Thro' love to men) for human use?
Should not claret be deny'd
 To the Turks, they'd wiser grow;
Lay their Alcoran aside
 And soon believe as Christians do.

CHORUS

For wine and religion, like music and wine
As they're good in themselves, do to goodness incline,
And make both the spirit and flesh so divine
That our faces and graces both equally shine.
Then still let the bumper round Christendom pass,
For Paradise lost may be found in a glass.

Just as my friend had ended his sonnet, in came the little lord of the tippling tenement, about the height of a ninepin, with his head in a hat of such capacious demensions that his body was as much drowned under the disproportioned brims of this unconscionable castor, as a pigmy under the umbrage of a gian't bongrace. He was buttoned in a plain vestment that touched no part of his body but his shoulders, his coat being so large and his carcase so little that they hung about him like a scarecrow upon a cross-stick in a country pease-field, his arms dangling like a mob's Taffy mounted upon a red-herring on St David's Day, and his legs so slender that they would bid defiance to any parish stocks.

He waited a little while for the motion of the Spirit, and when he had composed his countenance, and put himself in a fit posture for reproof, he breaks into this following oration. 'Pray, friend, forbear this profane halloing and hooting in my house! The wicked noise thou makest among my sober friends is neither pleasing to them nor me, and since I find this wine too powerful for thy inward man, I must needs tell thee I will draw thee no more of it. I therefore desire thee to pay for what thou hast had, and depart my house, for I do not like thy ways, nor does anybody here approve of thy ranting doings.'

We were not surprised at this piece of fanatical civility, it being no more than what we expected; but the manner of his delivery rendered his words so very diverting that we could not forbear laughing him into such a passion, that the looks of the little Saint revealed as great a devil

54

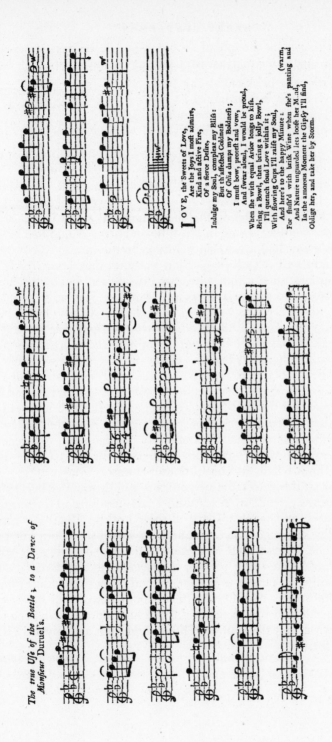

The true Use of the Bottle; to a Dance of Monsieur Duruel's.

LOVE, the Sweets of Love,
    Are the Joys I most admire,
    Kind and active Fire,
Indulge my Soul, compleat my Bliss:
    But th'affected Coldness
    Of Celia damps my Boldness;
    I must bow, protest and vow,
    And swear aloud, I would be proud,
When she with equal Ardor longs to kiss.
Bring a Bowl, then bring a jolly Bowl,
    I'll quench foul Love within it ;
With flowing Cups I'll raise my Soul,
    And here's to the happy Minute :
For flush'd with brisk Wine when she's panting and   (warm,
    And Nature unguarded lets loose her M nd,
    In the amorous Moment the Gipsy I'll find,
Oblige her, and take her by Storm.

A SONG FROM *THE MERRY MUSICIAN OR A CURE FOR THE SPLEEN*, 1730 in his heart as a pious disciple of his bigness could be well possessed with. Then, according to his request, we paid our reckoning, and left him in a great ferment.

THE LONDON SPY
Ned Ward, 1703

CANDIDATE FOR PARLIAMENT

I have been plagued, pestered, teized to death, and hurried out of my wits, ever since I have been in this odious country. O my dear, how I long to be in town again! *Pope* and the poets may talk what they will, of their purling streams, shady groves, and flowery meads: but I had rather live all my days among the cheese-mongers shops in *Thames-Street*, than pass such another spring in this filthy country. Would you believe it? I have scarce touched a card since I have been here: and then there has been such ado with us about election matters, that I am ready to die with the vapours: such a rout with their hissing and hollowing, my head is ready to split into a thousand pieces! If my Sir *John* must be in parliament, why cannot he do as your lord does, and be content with a borough where he might come in without all this trouble, and take his seat in the house, though he has never been within an hundred miles of the place.

Our house, my dear, has been a perfect inn, ever since we came down; and I have been obliged to trudge about as much as a fat landlady. Our doors are open to every dirty fellow in the county, that is worth forty shillings a year; all my best floors are spoiled by the hob nails of farmers stumping about them; every room is a pig-stye, and the *Chinese* paper in the drawing-room stinks so abominably of punch and tobacco, that it would strike you down to come into it. If you knew what I have suffered, you would think I had the consitution of a washerwoman to go through it. We never sit down to table without a dozen or more of boistrous two-legged creatures as rude as bears; and I have nothing to do but to heap up their plates, and drink to each of their healths. What is worse than all, one of the beasts got tipsy, and nothing would serve him but he must kiss me, which I was forced to submit to for fear of losing his vote and interest. Would you think it, dear *Charlotte*?—do not laugh at me—I stood godmother in person to a huge lubberly boy at a country farmer's, and they almost poisoned me with their hodge-podge they called caudle, made of four ale and brown sugar. All this and more I have been obliged to comply with, that the country fellows might not say, my lady is proud and above them.

THE CONNOISSEUR
13 June, 1754

MY WIFE'S RELATIONS

If poligamy was allowed in this country, I am sure I might maintain a seraglio of wives at less expence, than I have brought upon myself by marrying one woman. One did I say? Alas! I find it to my cost, that a wife, like a polypus, has the power of dividing and multiplying herself into as many bodies as she pleases. You must know, I took a woman of small fortune, and made her my own flesh and blood: but I never thought that all her relations would likewise fasten on me with as little ceremony as a colony of fleas. I had scarce brought her home, before I was obliged to marry her mother; then I was prevailed upon to marry her two maiden sisters; after that I married her aunts; then her cousins—In short, I am now married to the whole generation of them. I do not exaggerate matters, when I say that I am married to them all; for they claim as much right to every thing that is mine, as the person whom the world calls my wife. They eat, drink, and sleep with me: every room in the house is at their command, except my bed-chamber: they borrow money of me: and since I have the whole family quartered upon me, what signifies which of them takes upon her my name,—my wife, her sister, or her twentieth cousin?

I never sit down to table without the lamentable prospect of seeing as much victuals consumed, as would dine a whole vestry. So many mouths constantly going at my expence!—And then there is such a variety of provisions! for cousin *Biddy* likes one dish; my aunt *Rachel* is fond of another; sister *Molly* cannot abide this; and mother could never touch that:—though I find they are all of them unanimous in liking the best of every thing in season. Besides, I could entertain a set of jolly topers at a less rate, than it costs me in light wines for the women. One of them drinks nothing but *Lisbon*; with another nothing goes down but *Rhenish* and *Spa*; a third swallows me an ocean of *Bristol Milk*, with as little remorse as she would so much small beer: my eldest aunt likes a glass of dry *Mountain*; while the other thinks nothing helps digestion so well as *Madiera*. It was but last week, that my wife expressed a desire of tasting some *Claret*, when immediately all my good-natured relations had a mighty longing for it: but with much ado I at last prevailed on them to compound with me for a chest of Florence.

THE CONNOISSEUR
7 August, 1755

A SUSSEX TRADESMAN

If I am home, or in company abroad, I will never drink more than four glasses of strong beer: one to toast the King's health, the second to the Royal Family, the third to all friends, and the fourth to the pleasure of the company. If there is either wine or punch, never upon any terms of perswasion to drink more than eight glasses, each glass to hold no more than half a quarter of a pint.

Sunday. Feb. 8. 1754.

This day being my birthday, I treated my scholars with about five quarts of strong beer, and had an issue cut in my leg.

June 20th. 1755.

I went down to Jones, where we drank one bowl of punch and two muggs of bumboo; and I came home again in liquor. Oh! with what horrors does it fill my heart, to think I should be guilty of doing so, and on a Sunday too! Let me once more endeavour never, no never, to be guilty of the same again.

Sunday, 28th. 1756.

We went down to Whyly, and staid and supped there; we came home between twelve and one o'clock—I may say, quite sober, considering the house we was at, though undoubtedly the worst for drinking, having, I believe, contracted a slight impediment in my speech, occasioned by the fumes of the liquor operating too furiously on my brain.

Jan. 26. 1757.

We supped at Mr Fuller's, and spent the evening with a great deal of mirth, till between one and two. Tho. Fuller brought my wife home upon his back. I cannot say I came home sober, though I was far from being bad company. I think we spent the evening with a great deal of pleasure.

Feb. 2. 1757.

About four P.M. I walked down to Whyly. We played at bragg the first part of the even. After ten we went to supper, on four boiled chicken, four boiled ducks, minced veal, sausages, cold roast goose, chicken pasty, and ham. Our Company, Mr and Mrs Porter, Mr and Mrs Coates, Mrs Atkins, Mrs Hicks, Mr Piper and wife, Joseph Fuller and wife, Tho. Fuller and wife, Dame Durrant, myself and wife, and Mr French's family. After supper our behaviour was far from that of serious, harmless mirth; it was downright obstreperous, mixed with a great deal of folly and stupidity. Our diversion was dancing or jumping about, without a violin or any musick, singing of foolish healths, and drinking all the time as fast as it could be well poured down; and the parson of the parish was one among the mixed multitude. If conscience dictates right from wrong, as doubtless it sometimes does, mine is one that I may say is soon offended; for, I must say, I am always very uneasy at such behaviour, thinking it not like the behaviour of the primitive Christians, which I imagine was most in conformity to our Saviour's gosple. Nor would I be thought to be either a cynick or a stoick, but let social improving discourse pass round the company. About three o'clock finding myself to have as much liquor as would do me good, I slipt away unobserved, leaving my wife to make my excuse. Though I was very far from sober, I came home, thank GOD, very safe and well, without even tumbling; and Mr French's servant brought my wife home, at ten minutes past five. (probably upon his back).

Wednesday. Feb. 22nd. 1757.

This morning about six o'clock, just as my wife was got to bed, we was awakened by Mrs Porter, who pretended she wanted some cream of tartar; but as soon as my wife got out of bed, she vowed she should come down. She found Mr Porter, Mr Fuller and his wife, with a lighted candle, and part of a bottle of wine and a glass. The next thing was to have me down stairs, which being apprized of, I fastened my door. Up stairs they came, and threatened to break it open; so I ordered the boys to open it, when they poured into my room; and, as modesty forbid me to get out of bed, so I refrained; but their immodesty permitted them to draw me out of bed, as the common phrase is, topsy-turvey; but, however, at the intercession of Mr Porter, they permitted me to put on my ———, and, instead of my upper cloaths, they gave me time to put on my wife's petticoats; and in this manner they made me dance, without shoes and stockings, untill they had emptied the bottle of wine, and also a bottle of my beer. . . . About three o'clock in the afternoon, they found their way to their respective homes, beginning to be a little serious, and, in my opinion, ashamed of their stupid enterprise and drunken preambulation. Now, let any one call in reason to his assistance, and seriously reflect on what I have before recited, and they will join with me in thinking that the precepts delivered from the pulpit on Sunday, tho' delivered with the greatest ardour, must lose a great deal of their efficacy by such examples.

Thursday. Feb. 25. 1757.

On Tuesday, March 7, the same party, with the addition of Mr Calverley and Mrs Atkins, met at supper Mr Joseph Fuller's:—

We continued drinking like horses, as the vulgar phrase is, and singing till many of us were very drunk, and then we went to dancing and pulling of wigs, caps, and hats; and thus we continued in this frantic manner, behaving more like mad people than they that profess the name of Christians. Whether this is consistent to the wise saying of Solomon, let any one judge: 'Wine is a mocker, strong drink is raging, and he that is deceived thereby is not wise'.

Tuesday. Mar. 7. 1757.

In the morn, my brother and self set out for Eastbourne. We dined on a shoulder of lamb, roasted, with onion sauce—my family at home dining on a sheep's head, lights, etc., boiled. We came home about ten P.M., but not sober. I may say, by the providence of GOD, my life was preserved, for, being very drunk, my horse took the wrong way, and ran into a travase with me, and beat me off; but, thanks be to GOD, I received no damage. . . . Oh, let me reflect how often, when I have been in liquor, I have been protected by the providence of Almighty GOD, and rescued from the jaws of death, and received no hurt; and how many instancies do we almost daily see of people's receiving hurt when in liquor; nay, even death itself has often, too, too often, been their unhappy lot!

Sept. 27. 1757.

Mr ——, the curate of Laughton, came to the shop in the forenoon, and he having bought some things of me (and I could wish he had paid for them), dined with me, and also staid in the afternoon till he got in liquor, and being so complaisant as to keep him company, I was quite drunk. How do I detest myself for being so foolish!

Nov. 25. 1763.

THE DIARY OF THOMAS TURNER OF EAST HOATHLY

THE PARSONS' CORKSCREWS

I was in a company where there were ten parsons, and I made a wager privately—and won it, that among them there was not one prayer-book. I then offered to make another wager that, among the ten parsons there were half a score of corkscrews—it was accepted, the butler received his instructions, pretended to break his corkscrew, and requested any gentleman to lend him one, when each priest pulled a corkscrew from his pocket.

Lord Mansfield (1705–93)

ELECTION EXPENSES
Wootton Bassett in 1774

(For food and drink at the inns.)	£	s.	d.
Star	52	4	7
King of Prussia	90	10	0
Shoulder of Mutton	56	10	0
Horse and Jockey	107	4	0
Wm. Henley's	35	0	0
Waggon and Horses	78	11	0
Oak	336	0	0
Three Tuns	54	0	0
Three Goats' Herds	47	0	0
Cross Keys	90	0	0
Hay and Corn	3	16	0
King's Head	76	17	1
For Cockades	77	13	0
First Canvass	152	0	0
Money paid for various expenses	11	11	0
Total of votes, then computed at 135, 30 guineas each .	4,252	10	0
Money to men deserted or dead	441	1	1
	£5,962	7	9
Item	11	0	0
	£5,973	7	9

THIEVES

Since I came home I have been disturbed with a strange, foolish woman,
that lives at the great corner house yonder; she is an attorney's wife, and
much given to the bottle. By the time she has finished that and day-light,
she grows afraid of thieves, and makes the servants fire minute guns out of
garret windows. I remember persuading Mrs Kerwood that there was a
great smell of thieves, and this drunken dame seems literally to smell it.
The divine Asheton, whom I suppose you will have seen when you receive
this, will give you an account of the astonishment we were in last night
at hearing guns; I began to think that the duke had brought some of his
defeats from Flanders.

Strawberry Hill, Sept. 3, 1748.

THE GOUT

Mr Chute tells me that you have taken a new house in Squireland, and have given yourself up for two years more to port and parsons. I am very angry, and resign you to the works of the devil or the church, I don't care which. You will get the gout, turn methodist, and expect to ride to heaven upon your own great toe.

Strawberry Hill, April 15, 1768.

THE ENGLISH

Indeed, all the way I came home, I could but gaze at the felicity of my countrymen. The road was one string of stage-coaches loaded within and without with noisy jolly folks, and chaises and gigs that had been pleasuring in clouds of dust; every door and every window of every house was open, lights in every shop, every door with women sitting in the street, every inn crowded with jaded horses, and every ale-house full of drunken topers; for you know the English always announce their sense of heat or cold by drinking.

Strawberry Hill, July 17, 1793.

LETTERS OF HORACE WALPOLE

THE WOMEN OF EDINBURGH

A few evenings ago I had the pleasure of being asked to one of these entertainments by a lady. At that time I was not acquainted with this scene of 'high life below stairs'; and therefore, when she mentioned the word 'oyster-cellar', (I imagined I must have mistaken the place of invitation: she repeated it, however, and I found it was not my business to make objections; so agreed immediately. I waited with great impatience till the hour arrived, and when the clock struck away I went, and inquired if the lady was there.) 'O yes' cried the woman, 'she has been here an hour, or more.' The door opened, and I had the pleasure of being ushered in, not to one lady, as I expected, but to a large and brilliant company of both sexes, most of whom I had the honour of being acquainted with. The large table, round which they were seated, was covered with dishes full of oysters and pots of porter. For a long time I could not suppose that this was the only entertainment we were to have, and I sat waiting in expectation of a repast that was never to make its appearance. The table was cleared, and glasses introduced. The ladies were now asked whether they would choose brandy or rum punch? I thought this question an odd one, but I was soon informed by the gentleman who sat next me, that no wine was sold here, but that punch was quite 'the thing'; and a large bowl was immediately introduced. The conversation hitherto had been insipid, and at intervals: it now became general and lively. The women, who, to do them justice, are much more entertaining than their neighbours in England, discovered a great deal of vivacity and fondness for repartee. A thousand things were hazarded, and met with applause; to which the oddity of the scene gave propriety, and which could have been produced in no other place. The general ease with which they conducted themselves, the innocent freedom of their manners, and their unaffected good-nature, all conspired to make us forget that we were regaling in a cellar, and was a convincing proof that, let local customs operate as they may, a truly polite woman is every where the same. When the company were tired of conversation they began to dance reels, their favourite dance, which they performed with great agility and perseverance. One of the gentlemen, however, fell down in the most active part of it, and lamed himself; so the dance was at an end for that evening. On looking at their watches, the ladies now found it time to retire; the coaches were therefore called, and away they went, and with them all our mirth. The company were now reduced to a party of gentlemen; pipes and politics were introduced: I took my hat and wished them good night. The bill for entertaining half a dozen very fashionable women, amounted only to two shillings apiece. If you will not allow the entertainment an elegant one, you must at least confess that it was cheap.

LETTERS FROM EDINBURGH, 1774–5
Captain Edward Topham, 1776

THE CLERICAL DISPUTE

I introduce you into Oxford, by one of the finest, the longest, and most beautiful streets, not only in this city, but in England, and I may safely add, in all Europe.

The beauty and the magnificence of the street I could not distinguish; but of its length I was perfectly sensible by my fatigue; for we still went on, and still through the longest, the finest, and most beautiful street in Europe, which seemed to have no end; nor had I any assurance that I should be able to find a bed for myself in all this famous street. At length my companion stopped to take leave of me, and said, he should now go to his college.

And I, said I, will seat myself for the night on this stone-bench, and await the morning, as it will be in vain for me, I imagine, to look for shelter in an house at this time of night.

Seat yourself on a stone, said my companion, and shook his head: No! no! come along with me to a neighbouring ale-house, where, it is possible, they mayn't be gone to bed, and we may yet find company. We went on, a few houses further, and then knocked at a door. It was then nearly twelve. They readily let us in; but how great was my astonishment, when, on our being shown into a room on the left, I saw a great number of clergy-men, all with their gowns and bands on, sitting round a large table, each with his pot of beer before him. My travelling companion introduced me to them, as a German clergyman, whom he could not sufficiently praise, for my correct pronunciation of the Latin, my orthodoxy, and my good walking.

I now saw myself, in a moment as it were, all at once transported into the midst of a company, all apparently, very respectable men, but all strangers to me. And it appeared to me extraordinary, that I should, thus at midnight, be in Oxford, in a large company of Oxonian clergy, without well knowing how I had got there. Meanwhile, however, I took all the pains in my power to recommend myself to my company, and, in the course of conversation, I gave them as good an account as I could of our German Universities, neither denying, nor concealing, that, now and then, we had riots and disturbances. 'O we are very unruly here too', said one of the clergymen, as he took a hearty draught out of his pot of beer, and knocked on the table with his hand. The conversation now became louder, more general, and a little confused: they enquired after Mr Bruns, at present Professor at Helmstadt, and who was known by many of them.

Among these gentlemen, there was one of the name of *Clerk*, who seemed ambitious to pass for a great wit, which he attempted, by starting sundry objections to the Bible. I should have liked him better if he had confined himself to punning and playing on his own name, by telling us, again and again, that he should still be, at least, a *Clerk*, even though he should never become a *clergyman*. Upon the whole, however, he was, in his way, a man of some humour, and an agreeable companion.

Among other objections, to the Scriptures, he started this one to my travelling companion, whose name I now learnt was *Maud*, that it was said, in the Bible, that God was a *wine-bibber*, and a *drunkard*. On this Mr Maud fell into a violent passion, and maintained that it was utterly impossible that any such passage should be found in the Bible. Another

Divine, a *Mr Caern*, referred us to his absent brother, who had already been forty years in the church, and must certainly know something of such a passage, if it were in the Bible, but he would venture to lay any wager his brother knew nothing of it.

Waiter! fetch a Bible! called out Mr Clerk, and a great family Bible was immediately brought in, and opened on the table, among all the beer jugs.

Mr Clerk turned over a few leaves, and in the Book of Judges, 9th chapter, verse xiii, he read, 'Should I leave my wine, which cheareth God and man?'

Mr Maud and Mr Caern, who had before been most violent, now sat as if struck dumb. A silence of some minutes prevailed, when, all at once, the spirit of revelation seemed to come on me, and I said, 'Why, gentlemen! you must be sensible, that is but an allegorical expression: and I added how often, in the Bible, are Kings called Gods!'

'Why, yes, to be sure', said Mr Maud and Mr Caern, 'it is an allegorical expression; nothing can be more clear; it is a metaphor, and therefore it is absurd to understand it in a literal sense'. And now they, in their turn, triumphed over poor *Clerk*, and drank large draughts to my health. Mr *Clerk*, however, had not yet exhausted his quiver; and so he desired them to explain to him a passage in the Prophecy of Isaiah, where it is said, in express terms, that *God is a barber*. Mr Maud was so enraged at this, that he called *Clerk* an impudent fellow; and Mr *Caern* again still more earnestly referred us to his brother, who had been forty years in the church; and who, therefore, he doubted not, would also consider Mr Clerk as an impudent fellow, if he maintained any such abominable notions. Mr Clerk, all this while, sat perfectly composed, without either a smile or a frown; but turning to a passage in Isaiah, chapter vii, v. 20, he read these words:—'In the same day, the Lord shall shave with a razor— the head, and the hair of the feet; and it shall also consume the beard'. If Mr Maud and Mr Caern were before stunned and confounded, they were much more so now; and even Mr Caern's brother, who had been forty years in the church, seemed to have left them in the lurch! for he was no longer referred to. I broke silence a second time and said: 'Why, gentlemen, this also is clearly metaphorical, and it is equally just, strong, and beautiful'. 'Aye, to be sure it is', rejoined Mr Maud and Mr Caern, both in a breath; at the same time, rapping the table with their knuckles. I went on, and said; you know it was the custom for those who were captives to have their beards shorn; the plain import, then, of this remarkable expression is nothing more, than that God would deliver the rebellious

Jews to be prisoners to a foreign people, who would shave their beards!'
'Ay to be sure it is; any body may see it is; why it is as clear as the day!
so it is', rejoined Mr Caern; and my brother, who has been forty years in
the church, explains it just as this gentleman does.

We had now gained a second victory over Mr Clerk; who, being,
perhaps, ashamed either of himself, or of us, now remained quiet; and
made no further objections to the Bible. My health, however, was again
encored, and drank in strong ale; which as my company seemed to like
so much, I was sorry I could not like. It either intoxicated, or stupified me;
and I do think it overpowers one much sooner than so much wine would.
The conversation now turned on many other different subjects. At last
when morning drew near, Mr Maud suddenly exclaimed, d — n me,
I must read prayers this morning at All-Soul's! *D — n me* is an abbrevia-
tion of G — d d — n me; which, in England does not seem to mean
more mischief, or harm, than any of our, or their common expletives in
conversation, such as *O gemini! or the Duce take me!*

DEALER IN FOREIGN SPIRITUOUS LIQUORS

It is here not at all uncommon to see on doors in one continued succession,
'children educated here'; *'Shoes mended here'*; *'Foreign spirituous liquors sold
here'*; and *'Funerals furnished here'*. Of all these inscriptions, I am sorry to
observe, that *'Dealer in foreign spirituous liquors'* is by far the most frequent.
And indeed it is allowed by the English themselves, that the propensity of
the common people to the drinking of brandy or gin, is carried to a great
excess: and I own it struck me as a peculiar phraseology, when, to tell
you, that a person is intoxicated or drunk, you hear them say, as they
generally do, that *he is in liquor*. In the late riots, which even yet, are
hardly quite subsided, and which are still the general topic of conversation,
more people have been found dead near empty brandy-casks in the streets,
than were killed by the musket balls of regiments, that were called in.

TRAVELS OF CARL PHILIPP MORITZ IN ENGLAND IN 1782

BISHOPS IN TAVERNS

Johnson's profound reverence for the Hierarchy made him expect from
Bishops the highest degree of decorum; he was offended even at their
going to taverns; 'A bishop (said he) has nothing to do at a tippling-
house. It is not indeed immoral in him to go to a tavern; neither would

it be immoral in him to whip a top in Grosvenor-square: but, if he did, I hope the boys would fall upon him, and apply the whip to *him*. There are gradations in conduct; there is morality,—decency,—propriety. None of these should be violated by a bishop. A bishop should not go to a house where he may meet a young fellow leading out a wench.' BOSWELL. 'But, Sir, every tavern does not admit women.' JOHNSON. 'Depend upon it, Sir, any tavern will admit a well-drest man and a well-drest woman; they will not perhaps admit a woman whom they see every night walking by their door, in the street. But a well-drest man may lead in a well-drest woman to any tavern in London. Taverns sell meat and drink, and will sell them to any body who can eat and can drink. You may as well say, that a mercer will not sell silks to a woman of the town.'

THE LIFE OF SAMUEL JOHNSON, LL.D.
by James Boswell, Esq., 1791

GLUTTONY

A young man, about nineteen, an apprentice to Mr Turner, watchmaker, in Aldersgate-street, eat a leg of pork of six pounds weight, and a pease-pudding weighing in proportion, at a public-house in Islington, for a trifling wager, in less than three-quarters of an hour; after which, he drank a pint of brandy off, at two draughts, and went away, seemingly in perfect health.

ANNUAL REGISTER, 1766

Walter Willey, a brewer's servant, devoured at a public-house in Aldersgate-street, a roasted goose that weighed six pounds, and a quartern loaf, and drank three quarts of porter, in an hour and eight minutes, for a wager of two guineas. He was allowed an hour and a half.

ANNUAL REGISTER, 1765

On Monday the 22d of April last, a young man, sixteen years of age of the name of Mr H–d–n eat one pound of cheese, three penny loaves, a quart of ale to his drinking; after which he undertook for a trifling wager, to eat two pound of funeral biscuits in five minutes, which he performed with ease and alacrity in four minutes and a quarter, to the astonishment of all the beholders.

THE WONDERFUL MAGAZINE, 1793

A PUBLIC HOUSE TRICK

Last night one Bradford, a journeyman plasterer, drinking at a public house in Oxford-road, got so much intoxicated, that he offered to lick a

red-hot poker for a tankard of beer, which somebody present was in-
human enough to offer him; upon which, disdaining to be worse than his
word, he proceeded immediately to perform his part of the agreement,
but burned his tongue and lips in so dreadful a manner, that his recovery
is looked upon as very dubious.

THE WONDERFUL MAGAZINE, 1793

AN IRISH WAKE

Paddy O'Conner, who was lately hanged at Tyburn for a footpad robbery,
was descended from an ancient family in the kingdom of Ireland, and
as he was a *worthy* person whilst living, his generous countrymen were
determined to pay the highest honours to the remains of the deceased.
Donnol o'Neale, who was the most particular friend of the late Paddy,
now summoned all his acquaintance upon this mournful occasion; he
very obligingly introduced them into a cellar not very far from St Giles's.
When they had descended about a dozen steps or so, they found themselves in a subteraneous region, but fortunately not uninhabited. On the
right hand sat three old bawds drinking whiskey, smoking tobacco out
of *two-inched pipes* (by which means I believe their noses were *red*), and
swearing and blasting between every puff. One of the visitors was immediately saluted by the most sober of the ladies, who kindly offered him a
glass of the enlivening Nectar, and led him up to the bed, exactly opposite
the door where Paddy was laid in state and begged him to pray for the
repose of his shoul. He answered, he never prayed, as he thought that
was the proper business of the parsons, and they were paid for it. His
dulcinea, however, burst out into the following exclamation: 'Arrah! by
Jesus, why did you die? It was not for the want of milk, meal, or potatoes'.

In a remote corner of the cellar were three draymen, six of his majesty's
body guards, four sailors, five haymakers, ten chairmen, and six evidence
makers, together with three bailiff's followers, who came by turns to view
the body and drink repose to Paddy's shoul; and to complete the group,
they were attended by Jack Ketch's journeyman. The company were
much entertained with an old friend Mr Edward M'Quick, who was
swearing that he could carry a fare, hear mass, knock down a Middlesex
freeholder, murder a peace officer, and afterwards receive a pension.

At the head of the bed, where the remains of Paddy was placed, was
the picture of the Virgin Mary, on one side, and that of St Patrick on
the other; and at his feet was depicted, the devil and some of his angels,
with the blood running down their backs, occasioned by the flaggellations

68

The Humours of an IRISH-WAKE, *as Celebrated at* Sᵗ GILES's, LONDON.—

Pub.ᵈ by C. Lebojon

which they had received from the disciple of Kentigern. One was swearing, a second counting his beads, a third drinking whisky, a fourth evacuating that load with which he had already overcharged himself; and whilst the priest was making an assignation with Catherine O'Reily, Jemmy Gahagan picked his pocket of his watch and a green purse, containing a lock of St Patrick's whiskers, esteemed an effectual remedy for the tooth-ache. I could not help taking notice of the priest, that whilst he was engaged with his doxey, he often turned to the deceased, and repeated the words, *Requiscat in pace*.

This was an entertainment too agreeable to last long; about three in the morning, Mr M'Quick, who had retired to rest in the garret, being either disturbed in his sleep, by dreaming of Brentford and the Old Bailey, or something else, he started up, crying, Fire! Fire! It is impossible to describe the confusion that ensued; the priest and his mistress took to their heels; the sailors who had got into the street first, with the gallon pots in their hands, filled them in the kennel and poured the contents on the chairmen, who, in endeavouring to escape, had wedged themselves in the stairs, and I know not whether they might not have been suffocated, had not a press gang arrived and conducted the tars to a rendezvous: At that instant, a constable with a dozen watchmen conducted as many as they could lay hold on to the Round-house, whilst some who hid themselves under the bed, as soon as they were gone, escaped into the street, and left Paddy to repose there 'till next day, when he was to be carried to Pancrass.

THE NEW WONDERFUL MAGAZINE, 1795

THE TAVERN CAROUSE

Once a week, generally some singular evening that, being alone, I go to bed at the hour I ought always to be a-bed; just close to my bed-room window is the club-room of a public-house, where a set of singers, I take them to be chorus singers of the two theatres, (it must be *both of them*,) begin their orgies. They are a set of fellows (as I conceive) who, being limited by their talents to the burthen of the song at the play-houses, in revenge have got the common popular airs by Bishop, or some cheap composer, arranged for choruses; that is, to be sung all in chorus. At least I never can catch any of the text of the plain song, nothing but the Babylonish choral howl at the tail on't. 'That fury being quenched' —the howl I mean—a burden succeeds of shouts and clapping, and knocking of the table. At length overtasked nature drops under it, and escapes for a few hours into the society of the sweet silent creatures of dreams, which go away with mocks and mows at cockcrow.

LETTER OF CHARLES LAMB TO MRS WORDSWORTH. 18 February, 1818

LORD NEWTON

DRUNKEN EDINBURGH LAWYERS

The late Lord Newton was one of the ablest lawyers, and profoundest drinkers, of his day. He had a body of immense breadth, width, and depth, which could hold (without affecting in the least degree the broad, wide, and deep head attached to it) six bottles of port. He was never so able to

71

do business as after drinking that enormous quantity of liquor. Upon one occasion, after having dined with two friends, and, to use his own phrase, drunk them both under the table, he dictated to his clerk a law-paper of sixty pages, which that gentleman has since declared to be one of the ablest and clearest he had ever known his lordship produce.—Lord Newton often spent the night in all manner of convivial indulgences, in a tavern somewhere in the High Street; at seven in the morning he drove home; slept two hours, and, mounting the bench at the proper time, showed himself as well qualified to perform his duty as if his fancy had been on this side, instead of beyond the Pole.

Simond, the French traveller, tells in his book (1811), that he was quite surprised, on stepping one morning into the Parliament house, to find in the dignified capacity, and exhibiting all the dignified bearing of a judge, the very gentleman with whom he had just spent a night of de-bauch, and from whom he had only parted an hour before, when both were excessively intoxicated. . . . It is related of a certain Lord of Sessions who died within the last twelve years (preceding 1823) that, going home after one of his *Saturday-nights'* debauches, he stumbled among the sooty-man's bags at the end of the Old Town-guard-house in the High Street, and, being there overtaken by sleep, did not come to his senses till next forenoon, when the sound of the Tron Kirk bell, rung at ten o'clock to denote the church-going hour, roused him from his dirty lair in the full view of persons passing along the street.

The debaucheries of the great lawyers were imitated by their depend-dents, and possibly while lords of Sessions and advocates of high practice were bousing over stoups of French claret, or playing at 'High Jinks', in Mrs ——'s best room, the very next apartment contained their equally joyous clerks who transacted the same buffooneries, drank the same liquor, swore the same oaths, and retailed the yesterday's jokes of their masters. A thousand pictures might be drawn, and ten thousand anecdotes related, of these inferior practitioners in the courts of wit and drinking. Jamie M—— was one of those singularly accomplished clerks, who, whether drunk or sober, could pen a paper equally well. His haunt was Luckie *Middlemass's* in the Cowgate, where he had a room, with a chair by the fire in winter and one by the window in summer, between which were his only migrations. At late hours, and when far gone, he was often sent for by his master, and, with a sad heart, had to leave his jovial companions and snug parlour, in order to sit down at the dry desk and write some tedious law-paper, which would keep him at work the whole night. On one of these dreary occasions, when apparently both blind and insensible,

72

he found himself at a table in his master's bed-room, required to write a very long paper, which was wanted to be sent to press early next morning. The advocate, being in bad health, lay in bed, with the curtain drawn, and, though his clerk seemed worse than usual, did not entertain the slightest doubt as to his capability of performing the duties of an amanuensis, which he had often done faithfully and well when in a similar condition. Jamie, perfectly confident in his own powers, began in the usual way, by folding in the usual marginal allowance of foolscap, and the bed-fast advocate opened up his flow of dictation, implicitly believing that not one of his precious words would be suffered to escape by his infallible dependent. He continued to sentence forth his long-winded paragraphs for several hours, and then drawing aside the curtain in order to rise he was thunder-struck, on observing that his clerk—for once faithless—was profoundly sleeping in his chair, with the paper before him unconscious of ink, and the whole business just as it was before he began to dictate.

TRADITIONS OF EDINBURGH
Robert Chambers, 1823

BROOKS'S CLUB

The Duke of York, Colonel St Leger, Tom Stepney, and two others, one morning, about three o'clock, came reeling along Pall-Mall, highly charged with the juice of the grape, and ripe for a row. Meeting with nothing worthy of their attention, they entered St James's-street, and soon arrived at Brooks's, where they kicked and knocked most loudly for admission, but in vain; for, nine-tenths of the members were then out of town, and of course the family and servants had for hours been wrapped in the mantle of Somnus. Our heroes, however, were resolved on effecting an entrance, and would soon have made one for themselves, if some of the inmates, roused by the dreadful noise, and apprehensive of fire, had not run downstairs and opened the outer door.

Whilst all possible haste was exerted to effect this on the inside, it was proposed by one of the gentry outside, to rush in pell-mell, and knock down the waiters and every thing else that should impede their progress. No sooner said than done: when they arrived in the inner hall, they commenced the destruction of chairs, tables, and chandeliers, and kicked up such a horrible din as might have awakened the dead. Every male and female servant in the establishment now came running towards the hall from all quarters, in a state of demi-nudity, anxious to assist in protecting the house, or to escape from the supposed house-breakers. During this *mêlée* there was no light; and the uproar made by the maid-servants, who,

73

in the confusion, rushed into the arms of our heroes, and expected nothing short of immediate violence and murder, was most tremendous.

At length, one of the waiters ran for a loaded blunderbuss, which having cocked, and rested on an angle of the banisters, he would have discharged amongst the intruders. From doing this, however, he was most providentially deterred by the housekeeper, who, with no other covering than her chemise and flannel-petticoat, was fast approaching with a light, which no sooner flashed upon the faces of these midnight disturbers, than she exclaimed, 'For Heaven's sake, Tom, don't fire! it is only the Duke of York!'—The terror of the servants having vanished by this timely address, the intruding party soon became more peaceable, and were sent home in sedan-chairs to their respective places of residence.

A MARINE

It has been remarked, since the death of the Duke of York, that he could never be accused of saying one good thing—that is, uttering one *bon mot*; this is certainly true.

At a dinner at Chelsea Hospital, the bottle had passed round pretty freely. The Duke, who was in high spirits, having just emptied a bottle, said to one of the attendants, 'Here, away with this *marine*'.

Upon which, a general of that body, piqued for the honour of the corps, whom he considered to be insulted by such an observation, said, 'I don't understand what your Royal Highness means by likening an empty bottle to a marine'. The Duke immediately replied, 'My dear general, I mean a good fellow that has done his duty, and who is ready to do it again'.

THE KNIGHTHOOD

'The jovial administration of the Duke of Rutland will be remembered in Dublin for many a long day; it was marked by that festivity and splendour which ensured the good-will of all ranks. The viceroy was, moreover, very fond of mixing and conversing with the lower orders, and many a laughable tale could be told of the eccentric adventures of himself and his jolly companions.

'One evening, his Grace, Colonel St Leger, and one or two others, having entered into a public-house in the *Liberty*, they found the landlord to be so comical a blade, that they invited him to sit down to supper with them. Darby Monaghan, who knew his Grace by sight, took good care that the entertainment should be such as to give every satisfaction to his guests, and he contrived to season it with such an abundant flow of native wit and drollery, that they were quite delighted with him. His wine and whiskey-punch were so good, that by two in the morning they were all quite jolly, and ready to sally out into the street in quest of adventures. This, however, was prevented by the politic Darby, who contrived, by the humour of his songs, and the waggery of his jests, to fascinate them to the spot, until, one after another, they fell drunk under the table.

'During their libations, and after Darby had said several good things in succession, the Duke, in a fit of good-humour, and by way of a joke, turned round to him and said, "D— me! landlord, you are a glorious fellow, and an honour to your country; what can I do for you, my boy? (hiccup.) I'll *knight you*, by G–d! so (hiccup again) down upon your marrow-bones this instant!" "Your Grace's high commands shall be obeyed", said Darby, kneeling. The Duke drew his sword, and although Colonel St Leger endeavoured to prevent his carrying the joke too far, he struck him over the shoulder, and uttered the ominous words, "Rise up, Sir Darby Monaghan!" Darby having humbly thanked his Grace, and sworn fealty to the King of England in a bumper, an immense bowl of punch was ordered in; this was filled and re-filled, until at length the whole party became blind-drunk, as before stated.

'The weather being warm, and the great quantity of punch which they had drunk, prevented the topers from feeling any inconvenience from the hardness of their couch, and they slept as soundly as they would have done on a down bed, either at the Castle or at the Lodge. Darby, who from long seasoning was soon enabled to overcome the effects of the whiskey, rose betimes, and having bustled about, soon prepared a comfortable breakfast of tea, coffee, and chocolate for the sleeping partners of his debauch.

'When all was ready, not liking to rouse them by shaking or otherwise, he stepped into the room upon tiptoe, and gently opened the window-shutters. The sun shining in full upon them, they soon awoke from their slumbers, wondering where they were. The landlord, who was listening at the door, speedily put an end to their suspense, by thrusting in his black head and nodding to his Grace, assuring him, "That they were safe and sound, and not a bone broke, in Darby Monaghan's own comfortable and fashionable *hotel*; also, that if his Honour's Grace and the other jontlemen would just shake themselves a bit, and *sluish* their faces with a little nice cowld spring water, they might fall to without any more delay; for there was a breakfast, fit for a lord, laid out for them in the next room."

75

'This intelligence was received with much pleasure by the party, who having put themselves in decent trim, adjourned to the breakfast-room, where they found everything of the best laid out in homely style: but what pleased them the most, was Darby's attention in bringing in a bottle of whiskey under one arm, and one of brandy under the other. Pouring out several glasses, he presented them to each, according to their choice; taking "the blessed Vargin to witness that a glass of good sperits was the best maid'cine iver envinted for waekness of the stomach, after straitching it with punch the over-night."

'Darby's courtesy was taken in good part; and after he had retired, the conversation turned upon his extraordinary humour. At length, Colonel St Leger, seeming to recollect himself, said, "I am afraid, my Lord Duke, your Excellency made a bit of a blunder last night: you conferred the honour of knighthood on this same landlord".—"Did I, by heavens!" exclaimed his Grace. "That you did", replied the Colonel. "D—n it! how unfortunate!—why didn't you prevent me?"—"I endeavoured to do so with all my might, but your Excellency's arm was too potent; and I preferred seeing your weapon fall upon *his* shoulder, rather than have it thrust into me."—"What an unfortunate affair!" exclaimed the Duke, rising; "but I suppose the fellow doesn't recollect the circumstances more than myself: let us call him in. I wouldn't have such a thing reported at St James's for the world. I should be recalled, and be the laughing stock of every one at the Court. B——d and 'hounds! to knight the landlord of a common punch-house!—the thing is surely impossible!"

' "Both possible and true", said the Colonel; "but let us ring for him, and hear what he himself knows about the matter".—Darby, who was in attendance on the outside of the door, heard all that passed, and resolved to resist every attempt at depriving him of his newly acquired honours. On his entering the room, the following dialogue took place:

'*Duke of Rutland.* I say, landlord, we were all quite jolly last night?

'*Darby Monaghan.* Your Honour's noble Grace may say that same: we drank thirteen whacking bowls of punch amongst five of us.

'*Duke.* Ah! so we did, I believe,—thirteen to the dozen,—and you supped with us?

'*Darby.* Many thanks to your Grace's Excellency, Darby Monaghan did himself that same honour.

'*Duke.* No honour at all, my good fellow. But I say, Darby, do you recollect any thing particular that I did,—in the way of joke, you know; some foolish thing, when we were all as drunk as fiddlers?

'*Darby.* By J——s! yer Dukeship may say that, any how. I dare say the

Colonel well remimbers your filling up the last bowl from the whiskey jug, instade of from that containing the hot water. By the powers! I could not stand that; it set me off, whizzing like a top; and I doesn't recollect one single thing after we emptied it.

'*Duke.* (*laughing.*) Oh, then you don't remember my drawing my sword, and threatening to run you through the body?

'*Darby.* The Lord above for iver presarve yer Dukeship's Highness from cru'l murder and sudden death, all the days of yer life! I don't remimber any such thing; but I remimber well the whack yer Excellency's Royl Highness gave me with that same sword over my shoulder, when ye bid me "rise up, Sir Darby Monaghan."

'*Duke.* You do? eh! But that was all in jest, you know, Darby; and so we must think no more about it.

'*Darby.* Long life to your Highness! but I took it in right arnest; more by token that my shouldher aches at this moment with the blow: but I mustn't mind that, for it was given upon an honourable occasion, and resaived with good will: so, thanks to yer Excellency for all favours, now and hereafter.

'*Duke.* But you don't presume to suppose, my good fellow, that I actually conferred upon you the honour of knighthood?

'*Darby.* By the powers! yer Highness, but I do. Sure, I wouldn't be after doing yer Highness such discredit as to think ye meant to break yer royl word to man or mortal.

'*Duke.* Oh, the devil! (*whispering.*) I say, Colonel, what is to be done?

'*Colonel.* (*whispering.*) Give him some birth, and make him promise to say nothing about the frolic.

'*Duke.* Well, Darby, I don't mean to act scurvily towards you; I can give you a tide-waiter's place, or something in the excise, that will bring you in about one hundred and fifty pounds a-year, and make you independent for life.

'*Darby.* (*kneeling, and kissing the Duke's hand.*) Let me go on my marrey-bones once again, to thank yer Royl Highness for being so good and marcifull to poor Darby Monaghan! He'll niver forgit to remimber to pray for yer Excellency to the blessed Saints, on Sunday or holyday.

'*Duke.* Well, then, Darby, it is settled that you give up the title, and that nothing shall ever be said about last night's adventure?

'*Darby.* Give up the title! yer Grace? and not be called Sur! after all?—I thought the hundred and fifty pounds a-year was to keep up my style as a true and loyal knight.

'*Duke.* No, faith! you sha'n't have place and title too: so choose without delay.

'*Darby.* (*pausing.*) Well, yer Grace, if yer Excellency plaises, I'd rather keep the title: for, d'ye see, it'll be such a wonderment for a punch-house to be kept by Sir Darby Monaghan, that I'll soon have all the custom of Dublin city; and that'll be better than a tide-waither's place, any how.

'*Duke.* (*laughing.*) Well, then, without more argument about the matter, you shall have a place of two hundred and fifty pounds a-year, and you must give up your knighthood this instant.

'*Darby.* (*going out.*) Plase yer Excellency, then, I'll just step upstairs and ax her *Ladyship's* advice; and, I dare say, she'd rather have the money. So, I'll inform your Honour's Grace in a twinkling.

'Her *Ladyship* was accordingly consulted on this important question; and she wisely, and without hesitation, voted for the income of two hundred and fifty pounds, which they enjoyed for many years. The *title*, too, stuck by them till the last; for, after the Duke's departure from his Viceroyalty, the affair was bruited abroad, to the great amusement of the middle and lower orders in Dublin, who never failed to address the fortunate couple by the appellations of "Sir Darby and Lady Monaghan".'

THE SIXTY-SIXTH REGIMENT OF FOOT

The Sixty-sixth Regiment of Foot, commanded by General Gabbet, was quartered, some years ago, at Nenagh, in Ireland, a populous and fashionable neighbourhood, where the officers had received great civility and attention. To return this, in some sort, the general invited all the gentry round about to a ball and supper, the evening before their departure for other quarters.

However reluctant the writer may be to mention this fact, truth demands the avowal; that, though the general was a most magnificent fellow, it was very difficult to extract payment of the debts which he was in the habit of contracting, from the untoward circumstance of his expenditure vastly exceeding his means. Whatever debts he did pay, however, were usually discharged by his *Aide-de-camp*, Major Vowell, a gentleman of as much tact in the settlement of a bill, as his commanding officer was in contracting the same: the major was quite *au fait* at lopping off extra charges; or, if need were, in genteelly evading payment altogether.

On the day appointed, Nenagh, and its vicinity, were all in motion. The company being arrived at the principal inn, or hotel, which was kept by one Forrester,—tea, coffee, and excellent punch were served—card-tables were displayed—the dance commenced—dozens upon dozens of the best claret and champaigne were decanted, and quaffed; all was hilarity; and, at length, a most splendid supper was set before the guests. During the whole of this time, the gallant general, with his grand chamberlain and secretary, the major, did the honours of the assembly, in a manner which did great *honour* to the regiment. They were to be seen every where, in polite attendance on the guests—the male portion of whom, loudly and repeatedly expressed their satisfaction, by toasts and healths 'to the Sixty-sixth!' whilst the ladies sighed at the prospect of being to be so soon bereaved of the society of so noble a corps!

The repast being at an end, the ball recommenced; and now was the time judged most fit by Forrester to present his bill. For this purpose, he sought for the general throughout all the apartments, but in vain, for the latter was nowhere, to be found: he and Major Vowell had slipped off, and taken their departure, just in the nick of time when poor Forrester's appearance was suspected.

At length the poor fellow thus addressed Captain Breviter:—'Blood and thunder! captain, where is the general?'

Breviter, perfectly understanding the drift of the question, replied,— 'O, damn it, Forrester, our general is great at a retreat.'

The landlord, who was greatly chagrined by this intelligence, exclaimed: 'By Jasus, then, has he walked off with himself entirely?—If so, by the holy poker! I'm clane done out of house and home. But, captain, sure enough his honour has left Vowell to settle the score?'

Breviter, laughing heartily, replied: 'O, yes, by G–d! he has left you three Vowells—I-O-U'.

THE CLUBS OF LONDON, 1828

A *T.B.*

Another kind and social soul was Whitfield; not the conventicler, but the comedian; as polite and well-behaved a man as ever met in festive circle; with only one weakness,—and that was his unbounded attachment to the initial letters *T.B.*, so well translated in the theatrical language, by the words 'T'other bottle'.

THE JUDGE PRONOUNCES

The next time I saw Lord Mansfield was on the trial of Mrs Rudd, an enchantress whose charms, so fatal to the unfortunate Perreaus, seemed

Engraved by W. Holl

LORD MANSFIELD

to inspire his Lordship with fresh eloquence, and the liveliest zeal in her behalf. She was, indeed, the very head of that fascinating and dangerous class of women of whom it may be said,

> If to her share some female errors fall,
> Look in her face, and you forget them all.

Lord Mansfield was very desirous of long life, and, whenever he had old men to examine, he generally asked them what their habits of living had been. To this interrogatory an aged person replied, that he had never been drunk in his life. 'See, gentlemen,' said his Lordship, turning to the younger barristers, 'what temperance will do'. The next, of equally venerable appearance, gave a very different account of himself, he had not gone to bed sober one night for fifty years. 'See, my Lord,' said the young barristers, 'what a cheerful glass will do'. 'Well, gentlemen,' replied his Lordship, 'it only proves, that some sorts of timber keep better when they are wet, and others when they are dry.'

MEMOIR OF JOSEPH BRASBRIDGE
Second Edition. 1824

THE TEA DRINKERS

My grandmother's name was West. She had a good fortune, and resided in a large house, facing Montpellier Row, Twickenham. She was a most good-humoured and excellent old lady; a very devotee in all the pursuits of genteel senility. Her house was a perfect curiosity shop; Indian bronzes, Chinese josses, shells, scraps of virtu, squalling parrots in smart lackered cages, tame cats, and mumming monkeys. Add to this description that, excessive neatness and care were universally conspicuous, from the extra polish on the stoves, to that, on the face of the shining lap-dog: that, piping shepherds, dancing shepherdesses, attitudinizing Cupids, and similar nicknackeries in china ware, together with gold fish in huge globuled basins, and various other frangible ornaments and disfigurements, stood on brackets, or lined the chimney-pieces; and that, the arrangement of the whole *derangement* was so methodical, that the minutest alteration in the position of a shell, or a scent bottle, would have ensured an immediate detection—imagine, then, the importation of a rude and noisy boy into the midst of the establishment.

Elected by suffrage and courtesy, my grandmother reigned queen of all card-players in that card-playing place. To such extent was this infatuation carried, that the four old maids of Montpellier Row, her principal subjects, were chiefly known in the neighbourhood, by the names of *Manille*, *Spadille*, *Basto*, and *Punto*.

Every night, they assembled at one of their houses in succession; and on the first of every month, each took her turn to give a grand party. I arrived on the last day of December, and the next night, in honour of the new-year, a fête of more then usual splendour was to be given by my grandmother. An unlucky period for a debut like mine.

The evening at length arrived, and its principal attraction was Mrs Clive, the celebrated actress, who having retired from the stage on a handsome competency, rented a villa on the banks of the Thames, of Horace Walpole, adjacent to his own seat of Strawberry Hill, and in the immediate vicinity of Twickenham. Owing to her amazing celebrity as comic actress, and as, during her long theatrical career, calumny itself had never aimed the slightest arrow at her fame, honest Kate Clive (for so she was familiarly called) was much noticed in the neighbourhood. Yet, from her eccentric disposition, strange, uncertain temper, and frank blunt manner, Mrs Clive did not always go off with quite so much eclât in private as in public life; particularly, if she happened to be crossed by that touchstone of temper, gaming.

Were I to live a thousand years, I never should forget the stately dulness and formality of this, antiquated party. Nothing was heard, above the sipping and gurgling of tea, but whispering comparisons on their losses and gains at cards, congratulations on the others and their own, 'extreme good looks', and mutual informations on the state of the weather. Some admired the parrots, and patted the dogs, while others displayed their ignorance in learned disquisitions on the Indian bronzes, and Chinese josses.

Among the first that entered from Montpellier Row, were *Manille*, *Spadille*, *Basto*, and *Punto*. Huge caps, and little heads; rouged faces, white wigs; compressed waists, extended hips, and limping gaits, were the characteristics of this antidiluvian quartetto. At sight of them, whether from astonishment, fear, or laughter, the cup, from which I was drinking, slipt from my grasp, into the lap of a lady next me. Here was confusion! All the stately corpses immediately came to life, buzzing about the scene of disaster. The lady screamed that she was scalded; I blushed, and begged pardon, and my grandmother almost wept over the fragments of one of her choicest cups.

As soon as tranquility and formality were again restored, quadrille was proposed, and all immediately took their stations, either as players or letters. Impelled by my dramatic propensity, I stationed myself close to

Mrs Clive. Of this occupation, however, I soon began to weary, and closing my eyes, uttered a loud and protracted yawn. Then approaching *Manille and Co.*, I tweedled their chairs and their gowns, mixed their tricks by hunting for the court cards, and stole snuff from their boxes, which I continued to cram up my nose, till I had induced a fit of sneezing, violent enough to threaten the destruction of every ligament in my little frame. Then, the paroxysm finished, more wearied than ever, I began to yawn again. In course, all these various manœuvres drew on me the black looks of my grandmother; but unhappy that I was, my destiny led me to merit yet blacker, before the close of the evening.

It did not require much discrimination, or knowledge of the game, to discover the loser from the winner. I soon observed Mrs Clive's countenance alternately redden, and turn pale; whilst her antagonist vainly attempted the suppression of a satisfaction that momentarily betrayed itself, in the curling corners of her ugly mouth, and in the twinkling of her piggish eyes. At this sight, Mrs Clive's spleen seemed redoubled. At last, her Manille went, and with it, the remnants of her temper. Her face was of an universal crimson, and tears of rage seemed ready to start into her eyes. At that moment, as *Saton* would have it, her opponent, a dowager, whose hoary head and eyebrows were as white as those of an Albiness, triumphantly and briskly demanded payment for the two black aces.

'Two black aces!' answered the enraged loser, in a voice, rendered almost unintelligible by passion; 'here, take the money, though, instead, I wish I could give you *two black eyes*, you *old white cat*!'—accompanying the wish with a gesture, that threatened a possibility of its execution.

The stately, starched old lady, who in her eagerness to receive her winnings, had half risen from her chair, astonished at her reception, could not have sank back into it with more dismay, if she had really received a blow. She literally closed her eyes, and opened her mouth; and for several moments thus remained, fixed by the magnitude of her horror.

The words sounded through the room, with an awful clearness of articulation, that fixed every guest, (like the stone subjects of the King of the Black Isles,) in the action of the previous moment. One old lady's hand stuck midway between her snuff-box and her nose; while '*Basto*', who had turned the cock of a lemonade urn, stood abstractedly staring, as the fluid overflowed her glass, then the tray, and at last the floor.

At this sight, or rather combination of sights, I shall never forget my delight; it seemed to accumulate in spite of myself, until totally unable longer to retain it, I burst into a loud and continued laugh. This sound, that at any time would have been searing to ears unaccustomed, for at least half an age, to any audible expression of gratification above that of a whimpering and accordant titter, now by its strong contrast with their silly horror, was rendered terrific. Recovering herself with dignity, my grandmother advanced, and with imperial frowns, expressed her commands for an immediate silence, in vain—like an alarum, whose spring once removed, will not cease till unwound, so my visible machinery once set in motion, was only to be stopped by satiety. In fact, I remained roaring with increasing glee, till a hand was placed on my shoulder, and I was genteely turned out of the room.

The conclusion of the evening may be imagined. I was put to bed; Mrs Clive, treated with cold and averted looks, left the card-table, and shortly afterwards the house; and the polite buzzing, and gambling continued till an early hour of the morning.

THE HORSE GUARDS

Invited again by my friend Barrington Bradshaw to dine at the Horse Guards—aware of their Bacchanalian pranks, went *prepared*. Beheld, as usual, arranged round the room, 'dozens of port and claret'. After dinner, all evinced a determination to make the playwright drunk.

It would not do—saw half of them under the table—and among the first, the person next to me, a young page of the Queen. His breeches and stockings, before dinner, a brilliant white, were now discovered to be incarmardined—'one red'. Major Lemon, Mawhood, and Bradshaw, wondered how this strange circumstance could have occurred. So, did not I—mum! had got Morgan to sew a *large piece* of *sponge*, in my dark coloured pocket handkerchief, which raising to my mouth with every glass, I slyly deposited above half the contents of the latter, into this *little tank*—then obliged occasionally to squeeze it, the aforesaid contents issued over the stockings and breeches of my insensible neighbour.

Further to conceal this *ruse*, I frequently vociferated 'Bumpers no heel taps!—buz!—I see skylight!'—to the astonishment, and even to the annoyance of these established topers. Regarding me as a phenomenon, the whole mess at last confessed themselves beaten. As I handed Bradshaw down stairs he muttered out,

'I, and the Major, can carry off six bottles—but, zounds! Reynolds, if you continue at this rate, you will be shortly prosecuted, for moving off a whole dozen *without a permit*.'

Let the present race of *water drinkers* remember, this happened thirty-five years ago, when a *three bottle man*, was deemed little better than a *milksop*.

MEDENHAM ABBEY

A large house on the bank of the Thames, formerly a convent of Cistertian monks. It was hired by several well known fashionable and political characters, as a house for revels, of which strange stories have been told. On the entrance porch was written in large letters, 'Fais ici ce que tu voudras';—and, at the end of the room, was a full-sized picture of the Medicean Venus, with one of the club, habited as a monk, kneeling at her feet in an attitude of adoration. I have heard a story of two or three of the members conspiring together, and one night dropping a chimney sweeper, and a quantity of soot, (from the ceiling of the vaulted room, where they had effected a concealed aperture,) full on the banquet table, during the very summit of the orgies of their companions. Half blinded by the soot, and confounded by their intemperance, all voted their new acquaintance to be the devil; and on their knees, these valiant heroes attempted to conciliate the trembling and astonished sweep.

THE LIFE AND TIMES OF FREDERICK REYNOLDS
Written by Himself. 1826

DO I AT LAST SEE YOU SOBER!

But, to return to the Limerick road: to perform our journey, Brereton and I had a handsome post-chaise, our driver a smart, clever, intelligent youth. When we arrived at the inn at ——, our landlady coming through the passage to receive us, with curtseying formalities, our post-boy walking on before us; she looked at him, exclaiming—'Why, Tim, you devil, and do I at last see you sober!' He, with his hat in his hand, made her a low bow, and said, 'Madam, you do, and I wish I could return the compliment'. But such jokes are common among all ranks of Ireland.

SEEING LONDON

Mr Heaphy and his son, my brother-in-law, Gerald, coming to England at that time, they were accompanied by a very rich Irish gentleman, who wished to see London, in company with his friends, who could show him about, and bring him everywhere. They were dining with me one day, when I happened to praise very much some Florence wine, of which I had formerly bought a chest. This gentleman had lodgings exactly opposite to us in the court. A few days after, he sent for a chest of Florence, said he was got very deaf, put on a great red night-cap, shut himself up in his apartments, and none of us saw him for three weeks; but the servant of the

85

house reported, that he left the empty flasks as a perquisite to her. However, at his request, we brought him to Dolly's chop-house, where he was entirely affronted with all sorts of London manners, by the waiter refusing to bring us finger-glasses in the great public room, and telling us if we chose to remove into a private dinner-room up stairs, we should have them. This is all that our Irish gentleman chose to see of London.

TRINITY COLLEGE, DUBLIN

It was a custom with the students to lend their cellar-books to a friend. These books, consisting of seven leaves, were passports to the college cellar. One of them being lent to me, I brought with me two companions, and, on hearing the bell ring at nine o'clock, the notice that the cellar is open, we went. It was on the left hand of the first court, and stretched under the great dining-hall, in low arches, extending very far, and containing large butts of ale regularly arranged. Close by the entrance, on the left hand, was a little box, like a kind of pulpit, and there sat the college butler, as he was termed. I delivered to him the little book, he with a few words, quiet and proper in his manner, gave his orders to his attendants, and we were led to a large table, of which there were many in the cellar. On our table was a great iron candlestick with three legs, and in it a wax candle, as thick as my wrist, which spread a brilliant light through the vaulted gloom. A silver cup or vase, with two handles, was placed before us; this was full of the college ale, called Lemon October: the cup held about three quarts. A wicker basket was brought full of small loaves, called by them Manchets; but such ale or such bread, I never tasted before or since, except in this college cellar. The tinkling bell continued ringing until half-past nine, the signal when the cellar doors are closed. While we were enjoying this, indeed, delicious regale, we observed numbers of the servants of the collegians giving the little books to the butler up in his box, for them to receive ale, and take it to their masters in their several apartments: the butler's business was to put down in those books the quantity delivered out or drunk in the cellar. I once went to the entrance of the college kitchen, and saw five or six spits, one over another, and of great length, full of legs of mutton roasting: the notice for dinner was, a man bawling under the cupola, 'The Dean's in the hall!'

THE LAWYER'S WORD

When I was a child, I saw the famous Sir Toby Butler, a favourite lawyer of his time, his powers of oratory being great; but he always drank his bottle before he went to the courts. A client, very solicitous about the success of his cause, requested Sir Toby not to drink his accustomed bottle that morning. Sir Toby promised on his honour he would not. He went to the court, pleaded, and gained a verdict. The client met him exulting in the success of his advice; when, to his astonishment, Sir Toby assured him that if he had *not* taken his bottle, he should have lost the cause. 'But your promise, Sir Toby?'—'I kept it faithfully and honourably, I did not *drink* a drop—I poured my bottle of claret into a wheaten loaf and *ate* it. So I had my bottle, you your verdict, and I am a man of my word.'

RECOLLECTIONS OR THE LIFE OF JOHN O'KEEFFE
Written by Himself. 1826

DOCTOR AND PATIENT

Doctor Fordyce sometimes drank a good deal at dinner. He was summoned one evening to see a lady patient, when he was more than half-seas-over, and conscious that he was so. Feeling her pulse, and finding himself unable to count its beats, he muttered, 'Drunk, by God!' Next morning, recollecting the circumstance, he was greatly vexed: and just as he was thinking what explanation of his behaviour he should offer to the lady, a letter from her was put into his hand. 'She too well knew', said the letter, 'that he had discovered the unfortunate condition in which she was when he last visited her; and she entreated him to keep the matter secret in consideration of the enclosed (a hundred-pound bank-note).'

TABLE TALK
Samuel Rogers (1763–1855)

A DRINK ON STAGE

But Blanchard, like Edwin and Weston, was the comedian of private life— the originality of his ideas could only be equalled by his mode of delivering them. What amused me most, was his imperturbable complacency; there seemed to be no circumstance under heaven, serious or ludicrous, that was capable of disturbing it; whether on the stage, or in the street, in encountering a creditor, or (from some gross lapsus) the risible thunder of an audience, never would a muscle of his countenance relax, or any intelligence dwell about it, to affirm that he was conscious of his situation. Out of the abundance of proofs I received upon this point, perhaps my reader will permit me to lay one before him.

Bristol was the first engagement that brought him into notice. Previously, he had served his stage apprenticeship by strolling; and it was in

87

Engraved by Ridley from a Painting by De Wilde

MR BLANCHARD
of the Theatre Royal, Covent Garden

one of the neighbouring villages Mr Palmer first observed him. Tom was well known in Bristol; and a few of his friends were in the habit of paying him a weekly visit, to felicitate him with the novelty of a supper, and by patronising his benefit, prevent it from becoming his temporary ruin.

On one occasion, these worthies had been discomfiting the blue devils by the aid of a potent force of white spirits, and entered the boxes in a very hilarious and discriminative condition. The play was 'Macbeth', and Blanchard, by doubling Banquo, a Witch, and Macduff, was laying claim to the theatric eulogy of being a 'host in himself'. Versatility was Garrick's distinction; and presuming Tom played tragedy badly, in this play he could not be the 'first murderer'. His friends made their appearance at the moment Macduff receives the news of his wife and children's destruction;

88

every humane person here, or at least every parent, has a sympathetic thrill, and flies to snuff or pocket handkerchief to disembogue his feelings. Tom had no doubt worked himself up to throw half-a-dozen matrons and milk-maids into hysterics; but his companions, expecting to find him reveling in some broad comedy character, were incapable of excitement; they listened to his first burst of agony, (which might have been moderately well given,) in a kind of stupid surprise, but further attention was impossible. Simultaneously, they rose up in their seats, characterised the whole thing as a —— humbug; and one of them having brought a bottle of whisky in his pocket, publicly produced it—cursed Tom's wife and children, and bade him leave off 'howling there like a house-dog', and come and drink with them. Such a request, at such a moment, any one will allow, was, to say the least of it, indecorous; but, however Melpomene might frown, the actor feel, or the prompter stare, Blanchard instantly perceived that, coming from such an influential quarter, the request was not to be denied. His presence of mind, on this trying occasion, would have done honour to a life's instruction in the schools. He politely bowed to his inviter, begged the messenger and gentlemen about him to suspend their conversation for an instant, approached the box, took the bottle, drank, smacked his lips, bowed again, returned to his place, resumed his attitude, recollected his murdered wife and children, and proceeded as if nothing had happened. His friends were now no longer his foes, and Macduff triumphed alike over usurper and spectator.

THE PINT BACK STAGE

The same day (at Braintree) I was given Romeo to study, to Mrs Osborn's Juliet. This lady had that kind of originality in her style, which not merely disdained a resemblance to any other persons, but was altogether unlike any thing else in human nature. In the performance of the play, owing to the limited number of our corps, we were reduced to many shifts—the most humorous of which was Romeo's having to toll the bell, and Juliet the dead to sing her own dirge. To consummate the effects of the evening, an old gentleman in the company, by the name of Weeks, who played the Friar, (and whose body seemed to resemble a Norwegian deal, never fit for use till it had had a good soaking,) on arriving at the concluding speech, which as it contained a moral was never omitted in the country—
'From such sad feuds, what dire misfortunes flow,'
—espied a carpenter behind the scenes very cautiously, but decidedly, approaching a tankard of ale, with which he had been solacing himself

during the evening, in order, as he used to say, 'to get mellow in the character'. The tankard was placed in a convenient niche, with a good draught at its bottom; and whenever he was on, his eye would glance off, to watch over its safety. Being a little tipsied, he was somewhat stupified at the treachery of the varlet; and fixing his eyes, cat-a-mountain like, on him, momentarily forgot his audience in himself, who interpreting this as a piece of deep acting, began to applaud. The carpenter was now within a step of the tankard, and Weeks slowly articulated—

'Whate'er the cause—
(Here the fellow raised his hand)

'the sure effect is—

The knight of the hammer had clenched the pewter,—Weeks at the same instant staggered off, wrenching the jeopardised liquid from his grasp,— the friar tucked it under his arm, and popping his head on at the wing, with a significant nod, shouted the last word—'woe!'—at which the curtain fell, amidst a roar of laughter,—a termination very rarely contemplated to the 'Tragedy of Tragedies'.

LOW LIFE IN LONDON

About midnight we were reduced to a dozen persons; and then, when I expected, after passing a sociable evening, we should go soberly home, his Lordship (Lord Barrymore) gave a signal, and two members took my arm to the door, where I perceived a dozen chairs in waiting. Into one of these I was crammed willy-nilly, and then informed his Lordship was 'going his rounds'. Opposition was now useless, and I submitted to become a 'humbug' out of doors.

On this memorable night, or rather morning, we stopped at a dozen different cellars and houses, in the most secret and seductive recesses of St Gile's and Drury Lane, his Lordship acting as conductor to the fleet and manifesting, by the ease and distinctness of his directions, his familiarity with the navigation of these regions obscure. Punch and mulled claret with eggs were our potations, and his Lordship made himself at home with the various barmaids and hostesses, smoking his pipe meanwhile, and spouting 'Bobadil' with good effect—

'The cabin is convenient, Master Matthews.'

At about four in the morning, we had accomplished the circumference of this 'lower world', in a tavern at the 'Seven Dials', where we were obliged to disguise ourselves as much as possible, give false names, and pay a 'footing' of sixpence each, to be admitted members of the 'Two o'clock

LOW LIFE

Club'; a society which met at that early hour every morning, and was composed, as it appeared to me, of all the unemployed 'artists of the night', in London. Certainly, I had no correct idea of a 'Macheath's Gang', till on that occasion. Having emptied my pockets, however, I had nothing to fear, particularly as his Lordship was installed in the chair for the time he remained, with the greatest honours and acclamations. I did not learn that he was the founder of this meeting; but, by an inspection of the 'footing-book', I perceived that he was in the habit of supplying twice a-week two-thirds of its visitors.

When the signal was at length given for our departure, I, being an 'uneducated' fellow, expected it was to turn our steps homeward; but my companions kindly dispelled the mists of my ignorance, by saying, that the orthodox conclusion to every London night's ramble was the 'Finish', that being the established point where all the 'bloods' of the metropolis, after their respective courses, coagulated. I was however as vulgar as uninformed, and feared that this 'finish' to my night might prove one to my days. I accordingly made a sudden exit at the door, dispensing with the ceremony of a farewell; but his Lordship was bent on completing my experience;— a pursuit was instantly commenced, and 'Stole away, stole away!' was the cry, my companions running, yoicking and whooping, like a pack of huntsmen after an unfortunate fox. The sounds, 'stole away!' struck on the watchman's ears, who, taking me for a pickpocket, stopped me till my pursuers arrived; and then, as I was about to 'charge' the whole company, his Lordship's presence elicited from the 'guardians of the night' a shout of welcome and applause. A few words explained my situation and his intentions, and the remaining contents of his purse secured from the aged traitors the most cordial obedience. I was abandoned to my fate; and the chairs coming up, in spite of entreaties or struggles, was thrust in again, and carried off to the 'Finish'.

Upon the scene that presented itself here I am not willing to dwell; for if it were agreeable, I should require the pen of a Fielding or a Smollet to trace its lineaments with any truth. The number of the depraved and dying that lined the seats of this receptacle, the contrasts of dress and countenance, the faded finery and sunken eye of one, the inebriated madness of another, and the still, settled aspect of despair of a third, were sights I could not then, under the combined powers of punch, claret, and brandy, behold with indifference: to say nothing of the maniac medley of sounds, the laughter, crying, and imprecations of numerous beings in the most fearful state of excitement, which gave the whole perhaps the closest resemblance to our ideas of the infernal regions. Suffice it, that at about half-past six I effected my escape, leaving Lord Barrymore in all his glory, to go home for an hour's rest, and half an hour's lecture from Mrs Bernard.

RETROSPECTIONS OF THE STAGE
John Bernard. 1830

THE ARTIST'S MODEL

He (Harry Liverseege 1803–32) was continually on the look out for singular heads and curious characters to suit him for models in designs which he had made. He began a painting of 'Christopher Sly and the Landlady', from Shakespeare, but was long before he could find such a cobbler as he desired. At length he found a man he imagined would suit; and, having placed him in his studio, set down a bottle of strong gin beside him, saying, 'Drink whenever you please'. The liquor vanished in a short time, the spirit of the cobbler refused to stir, he sat as sober as a judge on the circuit; another bottle of gin was brought; it went the same way in course of time, and the son of Crispin sat steady as ever. 'Begone', cried the painter in a passion, 'it will cost me more money to make you drunk than the picture will fetch'.

THE LIVES OF THE MOST EMINENT BRITISH PAINTERS, SCULPTORS AND
ARCHITECTS
Allan Cunningham. 1833

THE ROVING IRISH

This day week a dozen poor fellows who had walked all the way from county Mayo into Bedfordshire came up to the door of the inn where we were fishing, and called for small beer. We made their hearts merry with good Ale; and they went off flourishing their sticks, hoping all things, enduring all things and singing some loose things.

LETTER OF EDWARD FITZGERALD TO W. F. POLLOCK
14 August, 1839

THE CARLYLES' SERVANT

If you *had* come last Wednesday! Verily it would have been the wonderfullest *realized ideal* that you ever assisted at in this world! Not a morsel of victual was cooked in the house that day: my Husband had to seek his dinner at a Tavern; and I—Oh, think of it!—I had to glide stealthily to the nearest cook-shop, and buy myself, all blushing, a few ounces of cold beef! And if you would know the meaning of all which questionable phenomena, it was, in plain prose, that my maid, my only Help, was throughout that whole day, and part of next, lying *dead drunk* on the kitchen floor, amid a chaos of upset chairs, broken crockery, and heaven knows what besides, '*fragmenta rerum non bene junctarum*'. In fact the sunk-story of this respectable, æsthetic house was by one of those sudden yawnings of 'the universal volcanic gulf underneath our feet', converted into a lively epitome of St Giles's, or, to speak more accurately, of a place one may not name.

Now the poor little Disgraziáta is on her legs again—for a time—I embrace the favourable moment to ship her off to Scotland, where she will at least get drunk on *genuine* whisky instead of blue ruin.[1]

LETTER OF JANE WELSH CARLYLE TO JOHN FOSTER
August 1840

[1] Helen Mitchell did not go at this time.

On Monday last we drew up at our door in Captain Sterling's carriage meaning to drive on to *his* Town house to settle some concern of a Governess for him, when I should have deposited my Husband and luggage at home. We rapped and rang a long time without being opened to; at last the door opened, and an apparition presented itself, which I shall certainly never forget as long as I live! There stood Helen; her mouth covered with blood; her brow, cheek and dark dress whitened with the chalk of the kitchen floor, like a very ill-got up stage-ghost; her hair streaming wildly from under a crushed cap; and her face wearing a smile of idiotic self-complacency! My first thought was that thieves had been murdering her (at one in the forenoon!); but the truth came fast enough: 'she is mortal drunk!' Mr C. had to *drag* her down into the kitchen; for she was very insubordinate and refused to budge from the door,—Captain Sterling and his coachman looking on! Of course I remained in my own house for the rest of the day. A woman who lives close by came to help me, and take care of the drunk creature, who, so soon as she got her legs again, rushed out for more drink! She had had *half a pint of gin* in the morning, in the afternoon *half a pint* of rum, and some ale!! That is what one would call good drinking! Between nine and ten she returned; and lay locked up all night insensible; then she had a fit of delirium tremens; then twenty-fours hours of weeping and wailing and trying to take me by compassion, as she had done so often before; but it would not do. I have never liked her ways since she returned to me. The fact has been, tho' I did not know it, that she was always partially drunk. So I felt thankful for this *decided* outbreak to put an end to my cowardly off-putting in seeking myself a new servant.

LETTER OF JANE WELSH CARLYLE TO MRS RUSSELL
22 February, 1849

THE SERVANTS' HALL

Mr Plumer (Robert Plumer Ward, novelist and politician, 1765–1846) was riding with a friend in the neighbourhood of Gilston, when they were met by a well-to-do-looking man in the garb of a butcher, who stopped and saluted 'the Squire' very respectfully, and was noticed cordially in return as follows:

'Ah, Dick—how are you? Why, I never see you at Gilston now, Dick. Why don't you come? You're always welcome there. I've a great respect for you, Dick. You're an excellent friend of mine (meaning in connection with the election). Let's see you at Gilston. The celler's always open to you.'

'Thank your honour, kindly,' said Dick, and rode away.

Meeting the Squire's companion alone the next day, Dick addressed him thus—

'Why, Mister—, Squire don't seem to know what be going on at Gilston. Why, I ha' got glorious drunk in servants' hall every night last week.

MY FRIENDS AND ACQUAINTANCE
P. G. Patmore, 1854

A SAILOR ASHORE

In 1856 a case was heard at the Tynemouth Police Court. A man named Glover, the landlord of a low public-house in Clive-Street, a crimp and sailors' lodging-house keeper, was summoned under the 235th and 236th clauses of the Merchant Shipping Act of 1854, charged with having taken into his possession the moneys and effects of James Hall, a seaman, and with having refused to return and pay the same back to Hall when requested to do so. It appears, after being engaged in the Black Sea in the transport service during the late war, Hall, who had to receive £30. 15s., took up his quarters at Glover's, and made him his 'purser'. Glover charged 14s. a-week for his lodgings, the same as the Sailors' Home, but at the end of 16 days he told him that his money was all gone, and bought the plaintiff's neckerchief of him for 1s., which he also spent in drink. The sailor, finding himself destitute, had applied to the authorities, who summoned Glover. Glover, in his defence, stated that Hall had spent his money in drink and treating, keeping a couple of bagpipers to play to him all the time he was on the spree. Glover produced the following extraordinary account against Hall:—'Dec. 9th.—20 pints of rum, £2. 6s. 6d.; 20 quarts of beer, and 15 ounces of tobacco, 15s. 10th.—8 glasses of rum, and 2s. 6d. borrowed money, 4s. 6d. 11th.—borrowed money, 2s. 6d.; 5 pints of rum, 5 gills of rum, and 15 quarts of ale, £1. 12s. 6d.; 6 ounces of tobacco, 2 glasses of gin, and 2 gills of brandy, 6s. 6d. 12th.—Cash, 2s., 15 pints of rum, and 28 gills of rum, £3; 4 quarters, half a gallon, and 22 gills of beer, £1. 3s. 9d.; 15 glasses of rum and 11

95

inted for & Sold by CARINGTON BOWLES.　　　　　No 69 St Paul's Church Yard, LON?

FLEET OF SMUGGLERS
with a Man-of-War in Tow. (1791)

glasses of beer, 9s. 3d.; pint of brandy and 16 glasses of gin, 8s.; 36 ounces of tobacco and 3½ glasses of gin, 12s. 4½d. 13th.—18 pints of rum, 15 gills of rum, and 26 quarters of beer, £3. 4s.; 26 bottles of lemonade, and 28 gills of beer, £1; 14 ounces of tobacco, 6 glasses of gin, 6s. 2d.; 12 glasses of gingerade, and cash 5s., 8s.: 1 week's board, 14s. Paid for clothes, £1. 2s. 6d.; 2 pints of rum, 10 gills of rum, and 4 glasses of beer, 16s.; 24 glasses of spirits, 9 quarts of beer, and 7 ounces of tobacco, 14s. 7d. 15th.—16 half glasses of spirits, 10 glasses and 2 gills of rum, and 1½ ounce of tobacco, and beer, 2s. 10d.; fortnight's board, £1. 8s.; cash, £2. 18s. 0d.; spirits, tobacco, and rum, 4s. 1½d.; cash 5s. 17th.—Cash, 7s.; 20 glasses of spirits, and 8 quarts of ale, 9s. 4d. 18th.—Ale, spirits, and tobacco, 16s. 4d. 19th.—35 glasses of spirits, and 20 glasses of ale, and 2 glasses of brandy, £1. 4s. 10d. 20th.—Ale, tobacco, and cash, 7s. 24th, 25th, and 26th.—Ale and spirits, 7s. 11d., and other items, making up the amount in hand. The defendant had refused to deliver up Hall's clothes on the plea that the man was in his debt.

RATCLIFFE-HIGHWAY

Up and down Ratcliffe-highway do the sailors of every country under heaven stroll—Greeks and Scythians, bond and free. Uncle Tom's numerous progeny are there—Lascars, Chinese, bold Britons, swarthy Italians, sharp Yankees, fair-haired Saxons, and adventurous Danes—men who worship a hundred gods, and men who worship none. They have ploughed the stormy main, they have known the perils of a treacherous sea and of a lee shore; but there are worse perils, and those perils await them in Ratcliffe-highway. It is night, and the glare of gas gives the street a cheerful appearance. We pass the Sailor's Home, a noble institution which deserves our cordial support and praise, and find at almost every step pitfalls for poor Jack. Every few yards we come to a beer-shop or a public-house, the doors of which stand temptingly open, and from the upper room of which may be heard the sound of the mirth-inspiring violin, and the tramp of toes neither 'light nor fantastic'. There were public-houses here—I know not if the custom prevails now—to which was attached a crew of infamous women; these bring Jack into the house to treat them, but while Jack drinks gin the landlord gives them from another tap water, and then against their sober villany poor Jack has no chance. I fear many respectable people in this neighbourhood have made fortunes. Jack is prone to grog and dancing, and here they meet him at every turn. Women, wild-eyed, boisterous, with cheeks red with rouge and flabby with intemperance, decked out with dresses and ribbons of the gayest hue, are met with by hundreds—all alike equally coarse, and insolent, and unlovely in manners and appearance, but all equally resolved on victimising poor Jack. They dance with him in the beer-shop—they drink with him in the bar—they walk with him in the streets—they go with him to such places as Wilton's Music Hall, where each Jack Tar may be seen sitting with his pipe and his pot, witnessing dramatic performances not very artistic, but really, on the score of morality, not so objectionable as what I have seen applauded by an Adelphi audience, or patronised by the upper classes at her Majesty's Theatre. And thus the evening passes away; the publicans grow rich, the keepers of infamous houses fatten on their dishonest gains—obese Jews and Jewesses become more so. The grog gets into Jack's head—the unruly tongue of woman is loosened—there are quarells, and blows, and blood drawn, and heads broken, and cries of police, and victims in abundance for the station-house, or the hospital, or the union-house, or the lunatic asylum, save when some forlorn one (and not seldom either is this the case), reft of hope or maddened by drink and shame, plunges in the muddy waters of some neighbouring dock, to find the oblivion she found not in the dancing and drinking houses of Ratcliffe-highway.

THE NIGHT SIDE OF LONDON
J. Ewing Ritchie. Second Edition. 1858

THE TAP OF TEMPERANCE

Sir! Hoy! Mr Drummond! You, Sir, member for West Surrey. Here is an advertisement to which your attention is requested. It has appeared in a provincial paper:—

> George Newbutt, of the Three Gimlets Inn, Charminster, begs to inform the Public in general, that he has always for SALE, a First Class FAMILY ALE, at 1s. per Gallon.
> Also, some splendid XXXX, at 2s. per Gallon.
> N.B. Any Person Drinking more than Four glasses of the latter Potent Beverage at one sitting, can be carefully sent home gratis in a Wheelbarrow, if required.

There may be no landlord at Charminster named Newbutt, and the inn kept there by a gentleman of a very similar name may not exactly be called the Three Gimlets: therefore, let not the foregoing announcement, in connection with the following remarks, be taken as an acknowledgment of that gratuitous ride which it concludes by promising. It is recommended to the notice of Mr Drummond, by reason of the memorable observation which that honourable gentleman made not long ago in the House of Commons—one of the truest things ever said there—to the effect, that no really good strong beer, such as what used to be brewed of old, is now anywhere to be met with. Mr Newbutt's XXXX appears to be an exception to this generally too unquestionable rule. Four glasses of the beer which Mr Drummond meant were about as much as any man could take without requiring to be carried home. When this necessity now occurs, which is frequently the case in the agricultural districts, it is almost always the result of gross intemperance,—the effect of some gallons,—the consequence of excess; or the state which constitutes the necessity is not a state of beer, but a state of *Cocculus Indicus*, or a state of the stuff which is called 'bitter ale'. We should like to have Mr Drummond's opinion about Mr Newbutt's ale. There is something like it at the Bull's Head, Barnes, of which, to judge from the operation of two glasses,—the utmost of our experience,—the effect, in a quantity exceeding four, would probably require a wheelbarrow. Ordinarily, one glass of this beverage will be found sufficient and satisfactory; and, as moral purpose is our aim in making these remarks, we will conclude with the reflection, how much better it is to brew, honestly, good beer, the strength of which naturally tends to compel moderation, than to concoct a villanous liquor which is not malt, which is unworthy of the name of swipes, and which is the fruitful parent of intoxication and its consequent evils.

16 April, 1859

TOM ARCHER FROM DRURY LANE

I took the Worthing Theatre for six weeks for Henry Spicer, and engaged a good company, Archer of Drury Lane being the leading man. Unfortunately he drank too much. He sent his wife and children on in advance to 'pickle' themselves (such was his expression), a week before he came. Archer's pockets were ever scantily filled with coin; when he reached Brighton, per rail, the supplies were exhausted, and the poor player had to trudge on to Worthing under a burning hot sun and along dusty roads; add to this a large brown-paper parcel, containing his 'props' (wigs, collars, boots etc.). He had lost his wife's address, and to crown his troubles, all the public-houses were closed. His first misadventure was at a turnpike, two or three miles from Worthing. Hearing a loud knocking and bawling, the pike-man, rushing out, asked him what he wanted.

99

'My wife, kids, and a drink.'

The indignant and irate gate-keeper slammed the door in his face, muttering 'Fool!' as he did so. To make matters worse, down went his 'props', bursting their paper covering. Swearing, stuffing his wigs, tights, etc., in his pockets, our unfortunate actor resumed his way. It was church-time, and everything was quiet; not a soul was to be seen in the streets. Tom found himself in an open space, under a large lamp, mounted on steps, just opposite a church. He sat down grumbling, deploring his lost family, and by degrees dropped into a doze. With his 'props' peeping out of their hiding-places, he represented a somewhat startling figure. Service over, the square was filled with worshippers returning homewards. The noise awoke Archer. Up he sprang, and addressed the astonished people as follows:

'Romans, countrymen, and lovers, don't stare; I'm Tom Archer, from Drury Lane, come here to astonish you. See me act hump-backed Dick. Where's my wife, partner of all my joys? Let me catch her, lewd minx. Lend me a horse, I'll ride to——'

A crowd surrounded the madman, a constable was sent for, and Archer shut up with his 'props' in the lock-up, protesting by Magna Charta, and all the Acts of Parliament, that he would ruin Worthing for this. Thornton, the local magistrate, liberated him with a caution to mind hereafter what he was about; and Mrs Archer led him home pacified, his 'props' included.

JACK ON THE STAGE

Liverpool Amphitheatre, forty-five years ago.—Playing a popular drama, entitled 'El Hyder, Chief of the Gaunt Mountains', a famous old Cobourg favourite, written by W. Barrymore; my *rôle* a British tar, one of the old school, who only had to look at a Frenchman on the stage to frighten him into fits. Turks or niggers collapsed at the very sound of his 'Shiver my timbers!' 'Britons never will be slaves!' or 'Come on, you lubbers!' Tom encounters a party of the enemy in a rocky defile; nothing daunted, at them he goes; a desperate combat of eight—seven to one; awful struggle! yet, strange to relate, no one appeared killed or wounded. During the *mêlée*, a real sailor, half-seas-over, slid down the gallery and box pillars, jumped into the circus, climbing over double-basses, fiddlers, French horns, and reached the scene of action on the stage, placing himself by my side, threw down his jacket, calling out, 'Messmate, I'll stand by you; seven to one ain't fair noways. Pour a broadside into the blackamoor lubbers. Hurrah!' he knocked two down, the others wisely taking to their heels. Cheered by the house, Jack Tar No. 1. left the boards with Jack Tar No. 2, glad to get rid of him.

THE STICK OF WHISKEY

Macdonald, one of our actors in Bass's troupe, Dundee, always carried a large-sized bamboo cane, at all times his companion. We were crossing the river Tay in a ferry-boat from Dundee, careworn, hungry, and tired; no money, salaries unpaid; yet Jemmy Macdonald seemed little to feel it. There came no repinings from him; this was a riddle to us starvelings. Aboard the boat he whispered to me: 'Laddie, come abaft.' *Sotto voce*, 'Not a word, laddie,' unscrewing his bamboo, the top a cup, the stick a whiskey bottle. 'Tak' a drink, laddie—real Glenlivat; nae excise-man ever took gauge of this whiskey.' This I believe; it was I don't know what above proof. In the stick lay 'Jemmy's' hilarity. Doubtless many of us find comfort in the stick at times.

OLD DRURY LANE. FIFTY YEARS' RECOLLECTIONS OF AUTHOR, ACTOR AND MANAGER. Edward Stirling. 1881

THE COUNTRY DOCTOR

In economies Dr Long had no method: he could never make the two ends of expenditure and income meet. The former always overlapped the latter. Both in his house and stable the inmates felt the pinch. On the other hand, he adored the sex, and was lavish. Upon one occasion, when asked by his creditors to account for his insolvency, he exclaimed, 'The ladies, the ladies, and the juice of the grape!' He was not afraid of port; the liquor of the ruby fruit inspired him. 'Twas then you'd see him. He would sing, give a toast, or improvise a speech at call. He was patriotic and despised the French. Dibdin was his poet, and 'The sweet little cherub that sits up aloft', together with 'Poor Jack', were his constant and un-failing themes. In his revels, when others thought of going, he thought of staying. Then he would say, 'Shall I give you another of Charley Dibdin's?' When he thus volunteered, things had become serious, and his com-panions knew well what they had to expect. The doctor meant, 'We won't go home till morning'; and he would keep his word, too. Though the guests had all departed, and the host had retired to bed, the man of science kept singing. Company or no company, it was all one to him, till sleep overtook him, and next morning he was found upon the floor. Our hero was soon himself again. He had great recuperative powers, and though he had spent the night 'down among the dead men', he would early next day be bustling about visiting his patients and friends, feeling the pulse, bleeding and sending out his medicines.

OUR SUSSEX PARISH
Thomas Geering, 1884

RELIGIOUS CEREMONIES

Some twenty-five years ago I knew another, a fine scholar, an old bachelor, living in a very large rectory. He was a man of good presence, courteous, old-world manners, and something of old-world infirmities. His sense of his religious responsibilities in the parish was different in quality to that affected now-a-days.

He was very old when I knew him, and was often laid up with gout. One day, hearing that he was thus crippled, I paid him a visit, and encountered a party of women descending the staircase from his room. When I entered he said to me, 'I suppose you met little Mary So-and-so and Janie What's-her-name going out? I've been churching them up here in my bed-room, as I can't go to church.'

When a labourer desired to have his child privately baptized, he provided a bottle of rum, a pack of cards, a lemon, and a basin of pure water, then sent for the parson and the farmer for whom he worked. The religious rite over, the basin was removed, the table cleared, cards and rum produced, and sat down to. On such occasions the rector did not return home till late, and the housekeeper left the library window unhasped for the master, but locked the house doors. Under the library window was a violet bed, and it was commonly reported that the rector had on more than one occasion slept in that bed after a christening. Unable to heave up his big body to the sill of the window, he had fallen back among the violets, and there slept off the exertion.

THE VILLAGE SONGSTER

James Parsons, a very infirm man, over seventy, asthmatic and failing, has been a labourer all his life, and for the greater part of it on one farm. His father was famed through the whole countryside as 'The Singing Machine'. He was considered to be inexhaustible. Alas! he is no more, and his old son shakes his head and professes to have but half the ability, memory, and musical faculty that were possessed by his father. He can neither read nor write. . . . At one time his master sent him to Lydford on the edge of Dartmoor, to look after a farm he had bought. Whilst there, Parsons went every pay-day to a little moorland tavern, where the

COUNTRY REVELS

Rowlandson

Pub.ᵈ April.1.1806. at R. Ackermann's.101 Strand.

miners .met to drink, and he invariably got his 'entertainment' for his singing. 'I'd been zinging there', said he, 'one evening till I got a bit fresh, and I thought 'twere time for me to be off. So I stood up to go, and then one chap, he said to me, "Got to the end o' your zongs, old man?" "Not I," said I, "not by a long ways; but I reckon it be time for me to be going." "Looky here, Jim," said he. "I'll give you a quart of ale for every fresh song youn sing us to-night." Well, your honour, I sat down again, and I zinged on—I zinged sixteen fresh songs, and that chap had to pay for sixteen quarts.'

'Pints, surely', I said.

'No, zur!' bridling up. 'No, zur—not pints, good English quarts. And then—I hadn't come to the end o' my zongs, only I were that fuddled, I couldn't remember no more.'

'Sixteen quarts between feeling fresh and getting fuddled!'

'Sixteen. Ask Voysey; he paid for'n.'

Now this Voysey is a man working for me, so I did ask him. He laughed and said, 'Sure enough, I had to pay for sixteen quarts that evening.'

OLD COUNTRY LIFE
S. Baring Gould, 1890

BARNES!

In connection with one of the more notorious of these haunts, in Panton-street, an amusing incident once occurred. A rising young *littérateur*, who had been dining too well at some swell gathering, dropped in at the establishment in question, where he was very well known, in a fuddled and helpless condition during the small hours of the morning. The proprietor, seeing the state he was in, charitably conducted him to a cab, and told cabby to drive Brompton way, where it was understood our young friend lived. The cab started off, but had not gone many yards before its obfuscated occupant, leaning out of the window, hiccuped, 'Barnes!' then subsided into the cab again, and dropped off to sleep. Cabby believed, or affected to believe that Barnes, and not Brompton, was his fare's place of residence, and foreseeing a ten shilling job, whipped up his horse and was soon coursing through Kensington Gore.

His inebriate fare, however, simply wished to be driven a few dozen yards—to a neighbouring Haymarket tavern, kept by one Barnes, and notorious for its late hours and mixed company. The motion of the cab only conduced to the soundness of the fare's slumbers, and by the time Hammersmith-bridge was crossed, and Barnes was reached, he was in that comatose state that no information whatever as to where he desired to alight could be extracted from him. Cabby thereupon drew him gently from his vehicle, and stood him against a neighbouring lamp-post, when the breeze from the river so far freshened him up that by means of much arguing and coaxing he was prevailed on to pay the somewhat exorbitant demand made upon him, and the cab rumbled back to town.

It was then near 6 a.m., and it chanced that the man-servant of a well-known London architect, who had lately leased a neighbouring river-side villa and was superintending its repair, caught sight of an individual of melancholy mien, and in full evening dress, walking slowly and unsteadily along the river bank. His first thoughts were of an intending suicide, and he rushed back to the house to communicate his supicions to his master, who hurried with him, in the hope of dissuading the stranger from his rash purpose. In the meanwhile, the latter had quietly seated himself on the damp grass, and was peering intently into the swiftly flowing stream, as though hesitating whether he should take a sudden 'header' or slide gently down the slippery bank, and so shuffle off this burdensome mortal coil. The architect on nearing him, at once recognised in him an intimate friend, and with his servant's assistance raised him up and led him to his new villa, where, observing his utterly helpless condition, he had him instantly put to bed. Here, the good-natured architect used to say, his young literary friend slept four and twenty hours off the reel, and as soon as he was awake clamoured for devilled kidneys and bottled stout.

JUMPING OUT OF BED

I remember a practical joke played off prior to the war upon a couple of planters, intimate friends, who, on their way to some slave auction at a considerable distance from their own homes, had to seek accommodation in the house of another planter for the night. Here several guests chanced to be already staying, and during the evening gambling went on for heavy stakes, and old Bourbon whiskey was freely consumed. As the day had been sultry and the two planters had liquored up frequently on their journey, they found themselves effectually overcome about midnight, and were conducted in an unconscious state by a couple of negro servants to their sleeping quarters—a large apartment, formerly the state bedroom of the old-fashioned mansion, which dated back prior to the War of Independence. In it was a cumbersome, antiquainted four-post bedstead, a family heirloom, which, being too heavy to be moved whenever the room

Plate 82.

A Promenade to a Rout on a fair Evening

Woodward del

London Published by Allen & Co. 15, Paternoster Row March 25 1797.

Cruikshanks f.

Plate 83

Returning from a Rout on a Rainy Night

Woodward del

London Published by Allen & Co. 15, Paternoster Row March 25, 1797

Cruikshanks f.

underwent its periodic cleaning, had been provided in the old days with an apparatus of ropes and pulleys, enabling it to be hoisted up to the lofty ceiling well out of the way.

One or two mischievous young fellows among the guests, who knew of this bedstead and its ropes and pulleys arrangement, thought it would be capital fun to play off a practical joke upon the pair of obfuscated planters; and, entering the apartment, where they were snoring loudly, on tiptoe, they moved the few articles of furniture into a corner, drew up the bedstead seven feet or so from the ground, and closed the shutters so as to leave the room in perfect darkness. They then retired and left events to take their course.

By and by one of the planters woke up with a burning thirst, with 'hot coppers' as he expressively phrased it in his throat, and sprung out of bed for the water-jug. To his astonishment, instead of alighting at once upon his feet, he tumbled into space, and eventually plumped down on his hands and knees on the bare boards, falling, as it seemed to him, some twelve to fifteen feet. After seeking such relief as a few southern oaths and sundry loud groans afforded him, he shouted to his friend in order to wake him up, but only succeeded in extracting from him a few incoherent grunts. By steady perseverance, however, he at last aroused him sufficiently for him to hiccup out an enquiry as to what was up now, although he firmly believed that his friend was far too intoxicated to give him a coherent reply.

'Fell through some darned trap!' the latter piteously rejoined. 'For heaven's sake jump up and light a candle, but don't get out on my side of the bed!'

'All right!' exclaimed the other, dimly comprehending that some accident had happened; and he agilely stepped out of bed on his own side, when, after turning an involuntary somersault, he alighted on one of the hardest planks in the flooring on the small of his back. His heavy fall caused the room to shake, and as soon as the mixed moans and maledictions in which he indulged had ceased, his friend asked him whereabout they were, and if he could recollect how it was they came there. But neither of them could remember anything beyond playing at cards for big stakes and backing their ill luck with libations of Bourbon whiskey. They both groped about cautiously on their hands and knees in the dark, vainly hoping to discover some elucidation of the mystery, and eventually finished their night's rest on the hard and uncomfortable couch, on to which they had unwittingly tumbled.

When morning broke, a few gleams of light penetrating through the chinks of the shutters disclosed to them the bedstead floating, as it were, in the air. Being rather of a superstitious turn, they ascribed this to some supernatural agency, and looked upon the mishap that had befallen them in the light of a chastening for their many shortcomings. Both thereupon mentally vowed to amend their ways, and especially to moderate their consumption of Bourbon spirit in the future. But when the day had fairly dawned, and they had flung back the shutters and discovered the ropes and pulleys by means of which the bedstead had been hoisted up, and realised the practical joke that had been played upon them, all their good resolutions went by the board, and they were troubled almost nightly with 'hot coppers' in their throats.

BLOWING OUT THE CANDLE

Another good story was of some tippling Mike or Larry, and a disciple of Father Matthew's who, when other means of reformation failed, sought to frighten the incorrigible toper with the fearful fate which he pretended had befallen another whiskey-drinking sot, whose breath, he said, caught fire while he was blowing out the candle just before stumbling, as he intending doing, into bed; when the typical torch-light procession passed in reality down his throat and set him in a blaze. In Mike's eyes, however, the story pointed an entirely different moral to what his well-meaning upbraider had intended. 'Begor!' exclaimed he, 'that's a rale warning to me; and I promise yer honour, be all the saints, I'll niver blow out another blessed candle agin as long as I live'.

GLANCES BACK THROUGH SEVENTY YEARS
Henry Vizetelly, 1893

THE BENEVOLENT CLERGYMAN

The Rev Oliver Rose had a brother-in-law, Mr Edward Waddon of Stanbury; and the cronies used to meet and dine alternatively at each other's house. As they grew merry over their port, the old gentlemen uproariously applauded any novel joke or story by rattling their glasses on the table. Having laughed at each other's venerable anecdotes for the last twenty years, the introduction of a new tale or witticism was hailed with the utmost enthusiasm. This enthusiasm reached such a pitch, that, in their applause of each other's sallies, they occasionally broke their wine-glasses.

The vicar of Morwenstow, when Mr Waddon snapped off the foot of his glass, would put the foot and a fragment in his pocket, and treasure it;

for each wine-glass broken was to him a testimony to the brilliancy of his jokes, and also a reminder to him of them for future use.

In time he had accumulated a considerable number of broken wine-glasses, and he had them fitted together to form an enormous lantern; and thenceforth, when he went to dine at Stanbury, this testimony to his triumphs was borne lighted before him.

The lantern fell into the hands of Mr Hawker, and he presented it to the lineal descendant of Mr E. Waddon, as a family relic. It is still in existence, and duly honoured. It is of oak, with the fragments of wine-glasses let in with great ingenuity in the patterns of keys, hearts, etc., about the roof, the sides being composed of the circular feet of the glasses. . . .

The generosity of the vicar to the poor knew no bounds. It was not always discreet, but his compassionate heart could not listen to a tale of suffering unaffected; nay, more, the very idea that others were in want impelled him to seek them out at all times, to relieve their need.

On cold winter nights, if he felt the frost to be very keen, the idea would enter his head that such and such persons had not above one blanket on their beds, or that they had gone, without anything to warm their vitals, to the chill damp attics where they slept. Then he would stamp about the house, collecting warm clothing and blankets, bottles of wine, and any food he could find in the larder, and laden with them, attended by a servant, go forth on his rambles, and knock up the cottagers, that he might put extra blankets on their beds, or cheer them with port wine and cold pie.

The following graphic description of one of these night missions is given in the words of an old workman named Vinson.

It was a very cold night in the winter of 1874–75, about half-past nine: he called me into the house, and said: 'The poor folk up at Shop will all perish this very night of cold. John Ode is ill, and cannot go: can you get there alive?

'If you please, sir, I will, if you'll allow me', I said.

'Take them these four bottles of brandy', he says; and he brought up four bottles with never so much as the corks drawed. 'Now', says he, 'what will you have yourself?' And I says, 'Gin, if you plase, sir', I says. And he poured me out gin and water; and then he gi'ed me a lemonade bottle of gin for me to put in my side-pocket. 'That'll keep you alive', he says, 'before you come back'. So he fulled me up before I started and sent me off to Shop, to four old people's houses, with a bottle of brandy for each. And then he says: 'There's two shillings for yourself; and you keep pulling at that bottle, and you'll keep yourself alive afore you come back'.

So I went there, and delivered the bottles; and I'd had enough before I started to bring me home again, so I didn't uncork my bottle of gin.

And it isn't once, it's scores o' times he's looked out o' window, after I've going home at night, and shouted to me: 'Here, stay! come back; Vinson', and he's gone into the larder, and cut off great pieces of meat, and sent me with them, and p'raps brandy or wine, to some poor soul; and he always gi'ed me a shilling, either then or next day, for myself, besides meat and drink.

'They are crushed down, my poor people', he would say with energy, stamping about his room—'ground down with poverty, with a wretched wage, the hateful truck system, till they are degraded in mind and body'. It was a common saying of his, 'If I eat and drink, and see my poor hunger and thirst, I am not a minister of Christ, but a lion that lurketh in his den to ravish the poor'. . . .

One day Mr Hawker ordered his carriage to drive to Bideford, some twenty miles distant. The weather was raw and cold. He was likely to be absent all day, as he was going on to Barnstaple by train to consult his doctor. His compassion was roused by the thought of Stanlake having forty miles of drive in the cold, and a day of lounging about in the raw December air; and just as he stepped into the carriage he produced a bottle of whisky, and gave it to Stanlake.

Mr Hawker was himself a most abstemious man: he drank only water, and never touched wine, spirits, or beer.

On the way to Bideford, at Hoops, thinking the coachman looked blue with cold, the vicar ordered him a glass of hot brandy and water. When he reached Bideford Station he said: 'Now, Stanlake, I shall be back by the half-past four train: mind you meet me with the carriage'.

'All right, sir.'

But Mr Hawker did not arrive by the half-past four train.

Up till that hour Stanlake had kept sober, he had not touched his bottle of whisky; but finding that his master did not arrive, and that time hung heavily on his hands, he retired to the stable, uncorked the bottle, and drank it off.

At six o'clock Mr Hawker arrived at Bideford. There was no carriage at the station to meet him. He hurried to the inn where he put up, and ordered his conveyance. He was told that his man was incapable.

'Send him to me, send him here', he thundered, pacing the coffee-room in great excitement.

'Please, sir, he is under a heap of straw and hay in a loose box in the stable dead drunk.'

'Make him come.'

After some delay the information was brought him, that, when Mr Stanlake after great efforts had been reared upon his legs he had fallen over again.

'Put the horses to. I can drive as well as Stanlake. I will drive myself; and do you shove that drunken boor head and crop into the carriage.'

The phaeton was brought to the door; the vicar mounted the box, the drunken servant was tumbled inside, the door shut on him, and off they started for a long night drive with no moon in the sky, and frosty stars looking down on the wintry earth.

Half-way between Bideford and Morwenstow, in descending a hill the pole-strap broke; the carriage ran forward to the horses' heels; they plunged, and the pole drove into the hedge; with a jerk one of the carriage springs gave way.

Mr Hawker, afraid to get off the box without some one being at hand to hold the horses' heads, shouted lustily for help. No one came.

'Stanlake, wake up! Get Out!'

A snore from inside was the only answer. Mr Hawker knocked the glasses with his whip handle, and shouted yet louder: 'You drunken scoundrel, get out and hold the horses!'

'We won't go home till morning, till daylight doth appear', chanted the tipsy man in bad tune from within.

After some time a labourer, seeing from a distance the stationary carriage lamps, and wondering what they were, arrived on the scene. By his assistance the carriage was brought sideways to the hill, the horses were taken out, a piece of rope procured to mend the harness and tie up the broken spring; and Mr Hawker remounting the box, drove forward, and reached Morwenstow vicarage about one o'clock at night.

In the morning Stanlake appeared in the library, very downcast.

'Go away', said the vicar in a voice of thunder, 'I dismiss you forthwith. Here are your wages. I will not even look at you. Let me never see your face again. You brought me into a pretty predicament last night.'

Two days after he met the man again. In the meantime his wrath had abated, and he began to think that he had acted harshly with his servant. 'Forgive us our trespasses as we forgive them that trespass against us', ran in his head.

'Stanlake', said he, 'you played me a hateful trick the other night. I hope you are sorry for it.'

'I'se very sorry, your honour, but you gave me the whisky.'

'You think you won't do it again?'

'I'se very sure I won't, if you give me no more.'

'Then, Stanlake, I will overlook it. You may remain in my service.'

Not many weeks after, the vicar sent Stanlake to Boscastle, and, thinking he would be cold, gave him again a bottle of whisky. Of course, once more the man got drunk. This time the vicar did not overlook it; but which of of the two was really to blame?

THE VICAR OF MORWENSTOW

S. Baring Gould. Seventh Edition, 1919

A MAN ABOUT TOWN

It happened that we lived in a first floor in the Regent's Quadrant, and, at the time of which I speak, the *entresol* beneath was occupied by Mr Charles L——, who was, perhaps the wildest young dog about town of that fiercely wild epoch. He was supremely handsome—handsome even for a period when Count Alfred d'Orsay was the model of male comeliness in London. His apparel was gorgeous even for a time when gentlemen wore two or three coloured and white under-waistcoats and an over-vest of velvet or rich brocade, with a long gold chain meandering over it, and above it a high satin stock adorned by two jewelled breastpins united by a thin chain of gold—a time when young Mr Benjamin Disraeli moved in patrician circles in black velvet pantaloons and with ruffles at his wrists. Mr Charles L—— had run through a couple of fortunes, one of which at least had been squandered over French hazard at Crockford's. He was very well educated, very urbane, nay, almost fascinating in his manner; and he usually came home about four o'clock in the morning either boisterously, lyrically, pugilistically, or maniacally drunk. When he did not return to the *entresol* his manservant used to opine that his master had reached the incapable stage of intoxication, and that he had been conveyed on a stretcher to St James's Watchhouse, just round the corner; and he would philosophically proceed to wait upon him there with a change of linen and a small silver flask full of brandy. After a few seasons spent in the manner at which I have hinted, Mr Charles L—— married an Anglo-Indian widow of immense wealth.

A CITY CHOP HOUSE

I can only recall with distinctness one chop house east of St Paul's. It was somewhere near the Mansion House end of Cornhill, if I remember aright, and was one of the regular orthodox Old London luncheon houses.

THE SURPRISE

Men worth their hundred thousand pounds, bankers and merchants and stock-brokers, at the time of the railway mania, were not ashamed to lunch at this establishment, under the following primitive and unostentatious circumstances. The first thing your hundred thousand pound man did was to proceed to Bannister's, the butcher, somewhere near Threadneedle Street, and purchase his chop or steak, which was handed to him neatly wrapped up in a fresh cabbage-leaf; then, if he preferred biscuit to bread, he would repair to the shop of a baker named Moxhay, a shrewd Scotchman, who made, I think, a very large fortune, and built a huge edifice called the Hall of Commerce, which has long since been converted into a bank or insurance office, or something of that kind. With their raw meat wrapped up in a cabbage-leaf in one hand, and their bag of biscuits in the other, the City Crœsuses would placidly enter their favourite chop house, where a bald-headed waiter would take charge of

H

the viands, deliver them to the cook, and in due time bring them piping hot to the guests. Potatoes were always in readiness, together with the proper condiments and good store of Stilton and Cheddar cheese. Still, looking at the circumstance that the majority of the customers brought their own meat with them, you might ask where the chop house keeper's profits came in. The remunerative part of the business was the very large consumption of brown stout, sound sherry and Madeira, and old port, both dry and fruity. In those remote times gentlemen saw nothing derogatory in comfortably cracking a bottle of port at a chop house, after disposing with equal cheerfulness of a quart of stout, and then going back to business. There were giants in the land in those days.

THINGS I HAVE SEEN AND PEOPLE I HAVE KNOWN
George Augustus Sala. Second Edition, 1894

RATCATCHER JOE

Squire Akerman was son to Moses the farmer. His birth was marked by a mighty brew of ale at the farmhouse, and casks containing a couple of hogsheads were stored up to remain till his coming of age. When he came to be twenty-one the people on the farms were feasted and the strong ale was served out at the rate of a pint for each individual. When a third of the strong beer had been consumed other ale was poured in, and so the cask was replenished.

The Squire, according to the account of 'Crazy Dick', was 'as tall as a Yankee herrin',' and 'not worth a cold fourpence.' This description may not be entirely reliable, however, since it was the squire who put Dick's grandfather, 'Ratcatcher Joe', in the stocks and kept him there all one Sabbath till the folks went to church in the evening. Squire Akerman was both magistrate and constable at the time, and 'Ratcatcher Joe' was overfond of the liquor, and was moreover very disorderly when he had imbibed too much. Whether it was the fact of Joe's having recently come into some property or that he had secured an extraordinary haul of rats in the farmyard is uncertain, but without doubt he was very drunk or the squire would not have taken the trouble to confine him. But Joseph proved to be a greater nuisance in the stocks than as if he had been at liberty, for he did nothing but sing and shout and speak rudely to all who passed that way. In the evening, when the people were going to church, and the squire's wife and daughters were passing, he made more noises than before and shocked them with his rude irreverent expressions. Then the squire, for very shame, set him free, and no one was afterwards put in the stocks there.

This is one of 'Ratcatcher Joe's' feats. First he drank a pint of shoe-oil. Next he ate one pound of tallow candles, two pounds of boiled fat bacon, hot, and a large cow cabbage cooked with it that when cut would not go into a peck measure. Then he swallowed the greasy pot liquor, and afterwards drank a quart of beer, completing the whole within an hour.

Joe's property was of the kind described as keyhold—that is, he was master of it who happened to be holding the key. Joseph took possession of the cottage by the singular rite of striking an axe into the trunk of a large plum tree standing in front of the house. The tree, though it had never previously borne fruit, was scarcely known to fail afterwards. 'Ratcatcher Joe' did not long remain in possession of the property, for a lawyer found means to make him drunk and then induced him to sign away his rights for a song.

In sharp, cold weather Joe used to wrap the newly caught rats around his body, next the skin, in order to keep himself warm.

ROUND ABOUT THE UPPER THAMES
Alfred Williams, 1922

THE PARISH CLERK

An old parishioner of the famous Rev R. S. Hawker once told him of a very successful run of a cargo of kegs, which the obliging parish clerk allowed the smugglers to place underneath the benches and in the tower stairs of the church. The old man told the story thus:

'We bribed Tom Hockaday, the sexton, and we had the goods safe in the seats by Saturday night. The parson did wonder at the large congregation, for divers of them were not regular churchgoers at other times; and if he had known what was going on, he could not have preached a more suitable discourse, for it was, "Be not drunk with wine, wherein is excess". It was one of his best sermons; but, there, it did not touch us, you see; for we never tasted anything but brandy and gin. . . .'

I knew a very respectable man, W.K., a tailor by trade, a well-conducted man, but who felt the importance of his office to an extent that made him nervous, or (what is as bad) made him fancy he was nervous. The church was capacious, and the population over two thousand.

A large three-decker, though the pulpit was at a right angle with the huge prayer-desk and the clerk's citadel below, well stained and varnished, formed an important portion of the furniture of the church, the whole structure, as we were reminded by large letters above the chancel arch, having been 'Adorn'd and beautified 1814', the names of the churchwardens being also recorded. This clerk was observed frequently, during the service, to stoop down within his little 'pew' as if to imbibe something. He was inquired of as to his strange proceeding, when he frankly stated that he felt the trials of his duties to be so great, that he always fortified himself with a little bottle containing some gin and some water, to which bottle he made frequent appeals during the often rather lengthy services. He had to proclaim the notices of vestry meetings of all kinds, as well as to give out the hymns; but what astonishes me is that he baptized many infants at their homes instead of the most excellent vicar, when circumstances made it difficult for the really good vicar to attend. . . .

Mr Wise, of Weekley, the author of several works on Kettering and the neighbourhood, tells me of an extraordinary incident which happened in a Sussex parish church when he was a boy about seventy years ago. The clerk was a decayed farmer who had a fine voice, but who was noted for his intemperate habits. He went up as usual to the singers' gallery just before the sermon and gave out the metrical Psalm. The Psalm was sung, the sermon commenced, when suddenly from the gallery rose the words of a popular song, given by a splendid tenor voice:

> 'Oh, give me back my Arab steed,
> My Prince defends his right,
> And I will . . .'

'Some one, please, remove that drunken man from the gallery', the clergyman quietly said. It was afterwards found that some mischievous persons had promised the clerk a gallon of ale if he would sing a song during the sermon. . . .

Hawker tells a story of the parish clerk of Morwenstow whose wife used to wash the parson's surplices. He came home one night from a prolonged visit at the village inn, the 'Bush', and finding his wife's scolding not to his mind and depressing, he said, 'Look yere, my dear, if you doan't stop, I'll go straight back again.' She did not stop, so he left the house; but the wife donned one of the surplices and making a short cut stood in front of her approaching husband. He was terrified; but at last he remembered his official position, and the thought gave him courage.

'Avide, Satan!' he said, in a thick, slow voice.

The figure made no answer.

'Avide, Satan!' he shouted again. 'Doan't 'e knaw I be clerk of the parish, bass-viol player, and taicher of the singers?'

116

When the apparition failed to be impressed the clerk turned tail and fled. The ghost returned by a short cut, and the clerk found his wife calmly ironing the parson's surplice. He did not return to the 'Bush' that night . . .

At Barkham Church the clerk used to sleep sometimes during the sermon, and it was not unknown that on occasions he patronised the village inn, which was kept by a parish worthy, Mrs Collyer. One Sunday the clerk slept and dreamed. He imagined himself the centre of an admiring company at the inn. Hence, when the sermon was ended, and he was expected to utter a loud and sonorous 'Amen', he startled the congregation by shouting: 'Fill 'em again, Mrs Collyer; fill 'em again . . .'

The Rev S. E. Perry, the late vicar of St Andrews, Old Chesterton, near Cambridge, was surprised, after his first Matins on Sunday, to hear the bell solemnly tolled for some minutes. He promptly walked down to the belfry and enquired what it meant. The old clerk said: 'I ring it for the pubs. How will the publicans know when to open unless I ring this bell? . . .

The Bishop also tells of a crony of his, an old fellow of ninety-five, 'who was very proud when I arrived, because he alone had known four rectors well; and he expressed it in this way to me: "Well, I have known four rectors: There's you, and before that there was Mr Biggwither, and before him Mr Erle—but he was different, he was a gentleman—and then Mr White." I asked him what he meant by being a gentleman, and his definition was: "He used to ride about the place and swear at you, and then give you half-a-crown, or a bottle of port, to make up for it".'

THE PARISH CLERK
P. H. Ditchfield, 1907

WAS I HERE?

As I have little else to tell of these early days at the Adelphi Theatre, it may be amusing to relate something of a then well-known member of the company—Robert (always known as 'Bob') Romer. He belonged to a good family and was a connection of Lord Justice Romer. Although not an important actor, he was such an oddity that everybody had an affection for him. The management rarely entrusted him with more than a few lines, and when a new play was about to be produced, some friend would delight in asking him what his part would be in it. His reply was always the same: 'A—what have I got to do? Oh—a—nothing—a—at all—in the first and second acts—and—a—next to nothing—in the last.' He spoke in quaint, rapid jerks, and, after a slight pause, his words would seem to try to get one before the other. I remember meeting him one morning when he had just left the theatre after rehearsing in a new piece. As I saw his portly figure, I could not resist asking the well-worn question. 'What have you got to do in the new play, Mr Romer?' 'A—a—what—have I—got to do? Oh—a—the old story—a few—idiotic lines—and exit. In the last—piece but one—I—a—was—a magistrate—nothing to do but—wear a wig—and—a—take it off again. In the next—I was—a—a—rustic—nothing to do—but—to drink the health of the Squire—in an empty jug—shout out "Hurray"—laugh "Ha! Ha!" and go off—with a noisy crowd. A—in this piece—I play—an Alligator.' 'A what, Mr Romer?' 'An Alligator—curious—line of business. I'm discovered—a—at the beginning in a tank. All I have to say is "Tan—ter—ran—tan—tan!" I don't appear again till the last scene, when I say, "Whack—fal-la!" It won't—a—tax the brain much!'

I remember an amusing scene occurring one morning as I arrived at the stage-door to attend a rehearsal, when I heard Mr Romer questioning the hall-porter with a mysterious and puzzled expression on his face. I must first explain that on the previous day a little dinner had been given to him by a few friends which was kept up until ten o'clock, for Bob had not to appear on the stage before eleven, just to act one of his celebrated 'next to nothing' parts. He had partaken rather freely of the wine, and was somewhat unsteady. When he awoke on the following morning, he had a vague recollection of the dinner, but, for the life of him, could not remember anything that happened afterwards. As I arrived at the stage-door, a conversation to this effect was going on between the old actor and the hall-porter: 'A—good house—last night, Richardson?' 'Yes, sir, *very* good house.' 'A—nothing—went wrong at all?' 'Nothing, sir.' 'A—how did the farce go?' 'Not so well as usual, I was told, sir.' 'Not so well, how's that?' 'I did hear, sir, that it were 'issed.' 'Bless my soul!—a—Webster in the theatre?' 'He had gone 'home, sir.' 'Is he here this morning?' 'Yes, sir, just arrived.' 'A—did he—ask for me?' 'No, sir.' 'About last night,—a—*was I here?*'

THE STOCK SPEECH

At Plymouth I also met an amusing creature who might have sat to Dickens for his portrait of Mr Lenville. His festive temperament made him a little unreliable in the text of the dramas which were a feature on

Saturday nights, although very often, I dare say, his words were as good as the author's. Sometimes, however, he could remember none, and then, with amazing effrontery, he would take refuge in a stock speech, which he delivered with great solemnity to whoever might be on the stage with him at the time, no matter what the circumstances, the period or the costume of the play. Whether prince or peasant, virtuous or vicious, whether clad in sumptuous raiment or shivering in rags, it was all the same to him, and at the end of his harangue, he stalked off the stage, leaving his unhappy comrades to get out of the difficulty as best they could. These were the never-changing words: 'Go to; thou weariest me. Take this well-filled purse, furnish thyself with richer habiliments, and join me at my mansion straight!'

FATHER AND CHILDREN

He has several children, who take after their parent; but as the parent generally finishes his glass, it is needless to say that they take very little after him.

THE BANCROFTS. RECOLLECTIONS OF SIXTY YEARS
Squire Bancroft, 1909

THE CABBY

Or there were private theatricals at the Laboucheres; or wildly-foolish garden-parties at Toole's, where tomatoes grew on all the rose-bushes, and the vines drooped with bunches of turnips and carrots—the host had expended hours on turning his garden into a bower of nonsense. When Toole heard a new arrival engaged in a point of difference with his cabby, he rushed out and dragged in both guest and Jehu. He conducted the bewildered cabman round the garden, loaded him with cucumbers off the gooseberry bushes and onions off the cherry-trees, and toasted him in champagne. The guests hilariously followed suit. The cabby was given a glass of fizz and a fistful of silver; then Johnny led him away amid howls of laughter. 'Don't take any notice of 'em', whispered Toole 'they're none of 'em in their right minds! To tell you the truth, this is a lunatic asylum!'

'That's all right, Mr Toole', said the grinning cabby, and drove off, leaving his host gibbering at the gate.

THE HOME COMING

'Have you seen anything of Mr Farjeon, Fanny?'
'No, ma'am.'

'He hasn't been home all night.'

'Why', exclaims Fanny, 'there's the Master now!'

They run to the door. A cab has pulled up at the gate, and *what* a cab to see of a summer morning! The roof is heaped with masses of red roses; the cab door is swinging open, Ben is tumbling out, among more masses of roses; red roses spill in the gutter, his arms overflow with them, he stays on the kerb presenting bouquets of red roses to the grinning cabby, then staggers up the path to the front-door, strewing red roses round him as he comes. On reaching Maggie, he flings the rest of his armful all over her, and gaily cries, 'I'm-coming-with-you-to-Margate!'

THE SERVANT PROBLEM

Inside the house, fusses with maid-servants punctuated the days. A scandalous dinner sent Papa flying to the basement.

'You're no gentleman!' hiccoughed one offender.

'You're no cook!' retorted Papa, and left the field triumphant.

The triumph took a little tarnish when, after the departure of the delinquent, discoveries were made. Papa kept a small, but perfect, cellar, but that cook's palate wasn't for the dry; two or three dozen opened bottles of various vintages had been tried and poured away, and those part-full had been improved with sugar.

What I prayed for, on such occasions, was that Papa might not swear.

A NURSERY IN THE NINETIES
Eleanor Farjeon, 1935

THE TEETOTALLER'S HOUSE

One of our earliest friends was George Jealous—Bohemian, member of the Savage Club, and founder and editor of the *Hampstead and Highgate Express*, which still flourishes under his nephew Walter. . . . A friend of his, an official in a Government office, was one morning informed by his chief that he must obtain certain instructions from an eminent politician. He was to arrive at the great man's country house in time for dinner and spend the night there. 'You had better have a stiff peg first', added his chief, 'for you won't get anything you can call drink there. You know, he and his household are rigid teetotallers'.

At the station the official, mindful of his chief's warning, hastily swallowed a whisky-and-soda. The journey was cold and uncomfortable, and on getting out of the train, thinking it would be his last chance, he had another. When he reached the house a pleasant-mannered young secretary drew him aside and murmured in his ear, 'You know the rules here, I suppose? Nothing at dinner, you know. But just come up to my room.'

After a drink or two and a chat before a pleasant fire he was on his way to change, when, half-way up the stairs, a feminine voice whispered 'Please come with me', and he was led into a schoolroom. The owner of the voice proved to be the politician's daughter, who apologized for her unconventional behaviour, adding, 'Of course it's against the rules, and I should get into an awful row if it came out, but I couldn't bear to think of you having nothing but water, so I got my maid to fetch a little brandy from the inn and I want you to drink it now. No, *all*, please.'

Could he refuse? Impossible. He was safe during dinner, but as the coffee was served, a husky voice rumbled in his ear, 'There's a drop of Martell's in your coffee, sir—Miss Margaret's orders.' The meal and a little conventional talk in the study ended, the politician's wife said she would now leave them to their business and say good night. After the door had closed the politician leant forward and said, 'My wife is a very strict teetotaller, Mr ——, and in deference to her wishes, and because I certainly think it good for the younger members of my family, I make it a rule that nobody here should touch alcohol. But', unlocking a secret drawer of his desk, 'I always keep some whisky for my guests, though I will ask you to say nothing of this to my wife. It would distress her'.

The result of the evening in a teetotal household was that Mr Jealous's friend, always a man of moderation, had to be helped to bed.

UP TO NOW
Martin Shaw, 1929

THE LUCKY CHIMNEY SWEEP

I could take you to another cottage where lived George Lewin, a Methodist chimney-sweep, who, when at length he forced his sooty head out of the top of a chimney, would pause for breath awhile and then break out into singing.

The opening heavens around me shine.

Not far away is the chimney-stack against which the compassionate Dr Oswald Foster used to set his ladder whenever such boys began on their hazardous job. Rung by rung he would climb, with some difficulty carrying a glass in one hand and a decanter in the other, so that the

moment the chimney-sweep's head appeared from the suffocating darkness he could restore him with a bumper of his very best brown sherry.

THE STORY OF HITCHIN TOWN
Reginald L. Hine, 1939

PEASANTS

But kermesse is for them a festival,
Even for the dirtiest, the stingiest,
There go the lads to keep the wenches warm.
A huge meal, greased with bacon and hot sauces,
Makes their throats salty and enflames their thirst.
They roll in the inns, with rounded guts, and hearts
Aflame, and break the jaws and necks of those
Come from the neighbouring town, who try, by God!
To lick the village girls too greedily,
And gorge a plate of beef that is not theirs.

Savings are squandered—for the girls must dance,
And every chap must treat his mate, until
The bottles strew the floor in ugly heaps.
The proudest of their strength drain huge beer-mugs,
Their faces fire-plated, darting fright,
Horrid with bloodshot eyes and clammy mouth,
In the dark rumbling revels kindle suns.
The orgy grows. A stinking urine foams
In a white froth along the causey chinks.
Like slaughtered beasts are reeling topers floored.
Some are with short steps steadying their gait;
While others solo bawl a song's refrain,
Hindered by hiccoughing and vomiting.

In brawling groups they ramble through the town,
Calling the wenches, catching hold of them,
Hugging them, shoving at them,
Letting them go, and pulling them back in rut,
Throwing them down with flying skirts and legs.
In the taverns—where the smoke curls like grey fog
And climbs to the ceiling, where the gluing sweat
Of heated, unwashed bodies, and their smells

Dull window-panes and pewter-pots with steam—
To see battalions of couples crowd
In growing numbers round the painted tables,
It looks as if their crush would smash the walls.
More furiously still they go on swilling,
Stamping and blustering and raging through
The cries of the heavy piston and shrill flute.
Yokels in blue smocks, old hags in white bonnets,
And livid urchins smoking pipes picked up,
All of them jostle, jump, and grunt like pigs.
And sometimes sudden wedges of new-comers
Crush in a corner the quadrille that looks,
So unrestrained it is, like a mixed fight.
Then try they who can bawl the loudest, who
Can push the tidal wave back to the wall,
Though with a knife's thrust he should stab his man.
But the band now redoubles its loud din,
Covers the quarrelling voices of the lads,
And mingles all in leaping lunancy.
They calm down, joke, touch glasses, drunk as lords.
The women in their turn get hot and drunk,
Lust's carnal acid in their blood corrodes,
And in these billowing bodies, surging backs,
Freed instinct grows to such a heat of rut,
That to see lads and lasses wriggling and writhing,
With jostling bodies, screams, and blows of fists,
Crushing embraces, biting kisses, to see them
Rolling dead drunk into the corners, wallowing
Upon the floor, knocking themselves against
The panels, sweating, and frothing at the lips,
Their two hands, their ten fingers ransacking
And emptying torn corsages, it seems—
Lust is being lit at the black fire of rape.
Before the sun burns with red flames, before
The white mists fall in swaths, the reeking inns
Turn the unsteady revellers out of doors.
The kermesse in exhaustion ends, the crowd
Wend their way homewards to their sleeping farms,
Screaming their oaths of parting as they go.
The agèd farmers too, with hanging arms,

Their faces daubed with dregs of wine and beer,
Stagger with zigzag feet towards their farms
Islanded in the billowing seas of wheat.

EMILE VERHAEREN (1855–1916)
Translated by Jethro Bithell

CONVERSATION PIECE

Mother, Daddy, Sheila are assembled in the sitting-room in the early
evening.

S. Do you write many letters, Daddy?

D. As few as I can help.

S. Then why are you always nipping down to the post?

D. There are many things to do at a Post Office, like buying stamps, dog
licences, wireless licences, telephoning and—

S. Do they sell beer at Post Offices?

D. No, of course not.

S. Where do they sell beer, Daddy?

D. At pubs.

S. What exactly is a pub?

D. A pub, Sheila, is a British institution, unique to these islands and the
envy of the civilised world. It is a social centre and club where men
gather to enjoy their national beverage, good food and conversation.
It is a place for games, light-hearted banter and wit. It offers the
acme of good companionship, an escape from the miseries, worries and
frustrations of this world and warms the cockles of a man's heart.

S. We learnt how to spell 'pompous' at school to-day, Daddy.

D. Did you?

S. Yes! What is a cockle?

D. An edible shell-fish sold by ——

S. Have you got edible shell-fish in your heart?

D. I hope not, though the gnawing at this moment suggests it.

S. Then how can you warm them?

D. It was a metaphor.

S. Is a metaphor a drink?

D. No, not even when it's mixed. Ha, ha!

S. Was that funny, Daddy?

D. Yes, very.

S. Oh! Do the pubs sell a lot of beer?

D. (*guardedly*). It depends on the weather.

S. Could they fill a swimming bath with beer?

D. Yes: a wonderful thought.

S. Why don't they?

D. The bathers would spoil the beer.

S. Would they swim better in beer?

D. Very much better—for the first few lengths.

S. Why?

D. Because beer, which contains alcohol, has a greater specific gravity than water.

S. What is alcohol?

D. It is a great invigorator; it stimulates wit, brings out the sunshine in life and banishes dull care.

S. Is that why they say beer has gravity?

D. I don't know. What time is it?

S. Twenty to six. Do ladies go to pubs?

D. Yes.

S. Do they have pubs all of their own where their husbands can't go?

D. No.

S. Then how do they escape from their worries?

M. Drat! I've dropped a stitch.

S. Do you have to wash up your own glasses in a pub?

D. Good Heavens, no!

S. Who washes them?

D. The publican.

S. Is he a civil servant?

D. God forbid, though some people would like to make him one.

S. Would you let them?

D. Across my dead body.

S. If a publican poured some brandy into your dead body, would you recover?

M. Yes.

S. Are you fussy about your beer, Daddy?

D. Very.

S. Would you still be fussy in a thunderstorm?

D. Certainly! Why?

S. Well, people take any port in a storm.

D. (*Groans heavily.*)

S. Is beer expensive, Daddy?

D. No, but taxes make it so.

S. How much do you spend on beer?

D. Not much.

S. How much?

D. Not as much as I used to.

M. The tax has gone down.

S. When you say you're going to a debate, meeting, darts, poetry reading, to see a man, for a noggin or to the post, are you really going to a pub, Daddy?

M. You've been a very good girl to-night, Sheila, but you'd better run up to Nanny for your supper now; I can see that your Father is thirsting to go out for the evening paper.

THE PENNANT. July, 1949.
P. L. J. Millen.

THE LAST GO.

There's no place like home.

Old Song

Notable Drinkers

WILLIAM BUTLER, PHYSICIAN (1535–1608)

He kept an old mayd whose name was Nell. Dr Butler would many times goe to the taverne, but drinke by himselfe. About 9 or 10 at night old Nell comes for him with a candle and lanthorne, and says 'Come you home, you drunken beast'. By and by Nell would stumble; then her master calls her a 'drunken beast'; and so they did *drunken beast* one another all the way till they came home.

RALPH KETTLE, D.D. (1563–1643)

To make you merry, I'll tell you a story that Dr Henry Birket told us t'other day at his cosen Mariet's, *scilicet* that about 1638 or 1640, when he was of Trinity College, Dr Kettel, preaching as he was wont to doe on Trinity Sunday, told 'em that they should keepe their bodies chast and holy; but, said he, you fellows of the College here eate good comons, and drinke good double Beer, and breede Seede, and that will gatt-out. How would the good old Dr have raunted and beat-up his kettle-drum, if he should have seen such Luxury in the college as there is now! *Tempora mutantur.*

FRANCIS BACON (1561–1626)

His Lordship would often drinke a good draught of strong Beer (March beer) to-bedwards, to lay his working fancy asleep, which otherwise would keep him from sleeping a great part of the night.

THOMAS HOBBES (1588–1679)

I have heard him say that he did believe he had been in excess in his life, a hundred times; which, considering his great age, did not amount to above once a yeare. When he did drinke, he would drinke to excesse to have the benefit of vomiting, which he did easily; by which benefit neither his witt was disturbt longer than he was spuing nor his stomach oppressed; but he never was, nor could not endure to be habitually a good fellow, i.e. to drinke every day wine with company, which, though not to drunkennesse, spoiles the brain.

HENRY MARTIN (1602–80)

Sir Edward Baynton was wont to say that his company was incomparable, but that he would be drunke too soone.

SIR JOHN DENHAM (1615–68)

He was generally temperate as to drinking; but one time when he was a student of Lincolne's-Inne, having been merry at the taverne with his comrades, late at night, a frolick came into his head, to gett a playsterer's brush and a pott of inke, and blott out all the signs betwen Temple-barre and Charing-crosse, which made a strange confusion the next day, and 'twas Terme time. But it happened that they were discovered, and it cost him and them some moneys. This I had from R. Estcott, esq., that carried the inke-pott.

ANDREW MARVELL (1621–78)

He was of a middling stature, pretty strong sett, roundish faced, cherry cheek't, hazell eie, browne haire. He was in his conversation very modest, and of very few words: and though he loved wine he would never drinke hard in Company, and was wont to say that, *he would not play the good-fellow in any man's company in whose hands he would not trust his life.*

  He kept bottles of wine at his lodgeing, and many times he would drinke liberally by himselfe to refresh his spirits and exalt his muse.

AUBREY'S BRIEF LIVES (1669–96)

LOUIS FRANÇOIS ROUBILIAC (1695–1762)

His establishment was never splendid—he ate the annual buck of Sir Edward Walpole with a few chosen friends—but his chief haunt was the tavern, then more the resort of the elegant and the learned than now, where he enjoyed his bottle of wine and his favourite game of whist. On one occasion it is related that he had dined out—was merry with wine—and having invited a companion, who had sat too late for admission to his own chamber, to accompany him home, took the office of servant

LEWIS FRANCIS ROUBILIAC

upon himself, showed his friend to a bedroom, and wished him good-night. No sooner had they parted, than the guest stripped off his clothes and was about to make a plunge into bed, when he found it most unpleasantly occupied by a corpse. 'Roubiliac!' he shouted, till the whole house echoed— 'Roubiliac, come here!' The sculptor burst into the chamber, exclaiming, 'Mon Dieu! what is de matter?' 'The matter!' said his friend—'look there!' 'Oh dear, oh dear!' said the artist; affected, it is said, to tears— 'It is poor negro Mary, my housemaid. She died yesterday, and they have laid her out here. Poor Mary! oh dear me!—Come, I shall find you another bed'.

THE LIVES OF THE MOST EMINENT BRITISH PAINTERS, SCULPTORS, AND
ARCHITECTS. Allan Cunningham, 1830

JOSEPH NOLLEKENS (1737–1823)

One rainy morning, Nollekens, after confession, invited his holy father to stay till the weather cleared up. The wet, however, continued till dinner was ready, and Nollekens felt obliged to ask the Priest to partake of a bird, one of the last of a present from his Grace the Duke of Newcastle. Down they sat; the reverend man helped his host to a wing, and then carved for himself, assuring Nollekens that he never indulged in much food; though he soon picked the rest of the bones. 'I have no pudding', said Nollekens, 'but won't you have a glass of wine? Oh, you have got some ale'. However, Bronze brought in a bottle of wine; and on the remove, Nollekens, after taking a glass, went, as usual, to sleep. The priest, after enjoying himself, was desired by Nollekens, while removing the handkerchief from his head, to take another glass. 'Tank you, Sare, I have a finish de bottel.' 'The devil you have!' muttered Nollekens, 'Now, Sare', continued his Reverence, 'ass de rain be ovare, I vil take my leaf.'— 'Well, do so', said Nollekens, who was not only determined to let him go without his coffee, but gave strict orders to Bronze not to let the old rascal in again. 'Why, do you know', continued he, 'that he ate up all that large bird, for he only gave me one wing; and he swallowed all the ale; and out of a whole bottle of wine, I only had one glass!'

NOLLEKENS AND HIS TIMES
John Thomas Smith, 1829

JAMES BOSWELL (1740–95)

That very evening I gave a supper to two or three of my acquaintance, having before I left Scotland, lay'd a guinea that I should not catch the

JOSEPH NOLLEKENS

venereal disorder for three years, which bet I had most certainly lost
and now was paying. We drank a great deal till I was so much intoxicated
that instead of going home, I went to a low house in one of the alleys of
Edinburgh, where I knew a common girl lodged and like a brute as I was,
I lay all night with her. . . . Next morning I was like a man ordered for
ignominous execution. But by noon I was worse; for I discovered that
some infection had reached me. Was not this dreadful? I had an assignation
in the evening with my charmer. How lucky was it that I knew my misfortune in time. I might have polluted her sweet body. Bless me! What a
risque! But how could I tell her my shocking story? I took courage. I
told how drunk I had been. I told the consequences. I lay down and kist
her feet. I said I was unworthy of any other favour. But I took myself. I
gloried that I had ever been firmly constant to her while I was myself.
I hoped she would consider my being drunk as a fatal accident which I

should never again fall into. I called her my friend in whom I had confidence and intreated she would comfort me—

How like you the eloquence of a young barrister? It was truly the eloquence of love. She bid me rise; she took me by the hand. She kist me. She gently upbraided me for entertaining any unfavourable ideas of her. She bid me take great care of myself and in time coming never drink upon any account. Own to me, Temple, that this was noble—and all the time her beauty enchanted me more than ever. May I not then be hers? In the meantime I must shut up, and honest Thomas must be my guardian.

5 January 1767

There is a handsome maid at this inn (at Grantham) who interrupts me by coming sometimes into the room. I have no *confession* to make, my *priest;* so be not curious, I am *too many* as the phrase is, for one woman; and a certain transient connection I am persuaded does not interfere with that attachment which a man has for a *wife* and which I have as much as any man that ever lived, though *some* of my qualifications are not valued by her, as they have been by other women—ay, and well educated women too. Concubinage is almost universal. If it was *morally* wrong why was it permitted to the most pious men under the old Testament? Why did our Saviour never say a word against it?

18 March 1775

My promise under the solemn yew I have observed wonderfully, having never infringed it until the other day, that a very jovial company of us dined superbly at a tavern; and I unwarily exceeded my bottle of old hock; and, having once broken over the pale, I ran wild. But I did not get drunk. I was, however, intoxicated, and very ill next day. I ask your forgiveness, and I shall be more strictly cautious for the future. The drunken manners of this country (Scotland) are very bad.

LETTERS TO THE REV. WILLIAM TEMPLE
12 August 1775

On the day after your departure, that most friendly fellow Courtenay (begging the pardon of an M.P. for so free an epithet) called on me, and took my word of honour that, till the 1st of March, my allowance of wine *per diem* should not exceed four good glasses at dinner, and a pint after it: and this I have kept, though I have dined with Jack Wilkes; at the London Tavern, after the launch of an Indiaman; with dear Edwards;

Dilby; at home with Courtenay; Dr Barrow; at the Mess of the Cold-stream; at the Club; at Warren Hasting's; at Hawkins, the Cornish member's; and at home with a Colonel of the Guards, etc. This *regulation* I assure you is of essential advantage in many respects.

LETTER TO EDMOND MALONE
4 December 1790

Saturday, 25th September.

Dr Johnson went to bed soon. When one bowl of punch was finished, I rose, and was near the door, in my way up stairs to bed; but Corrichatachin said, it was the first time Col had been in his house, and he should have his bowl;—and would not I join in drinking it? The heartiness of my honest landlord, and the desire of doing social honour to our very obliging conductor, induced me to sit down again. Col's bowl was finished; and by that time we were well warmed. A third bowl was soon made, and that too was finished. We were cordial, and merry to a high degree; but of what passed I have no recollection, with any accuracy. I remember calling Corrichatachin by the familiar appellation of Corri, which his friends do. A fourth bowl was made, by which time Col, and young M'Kinnon, Corrichatachin's son, slipped away to bed. I continued a little with *Corri* and *Knockow*; but at last I left them. It was near five in the morning when I got to bed.

Sunday, 26th September.

I awaked at noon, with a severe head-ach. I was much vexed that I should have been guilty of such a riot, and afraid of a reproof from Dr Johnson. I thought it very inconsistent with that conduct which I ought to maintain, while the companion of the Rambler. About one he came into my room, and accosted me, 'What, drunk yet?'—His tone of voice was not that of severe upbraiding; so I was relieved a little.—'Sir, (said I), they kept me up.'—He answered, 'No, you kept them up, you drunken dog':—This he said with good-humoured *English* pleasantry. Soon afterwards, Corri-chatachin, Col, and other friends assembled round my bed. *Corri* had a brandy-bottle and glass with him, and insisted I should take a dram.— 'Ay, (said Dr Johnson), fill him drunk again. Do it in the morning, that we may laugh at him all day. It is a poor thing for a fellow to get drunk at night, and sculk to bed, and let his friends have no sport.'—Finding him thus jocular, I became quite easy; and when I offered to get up, he very good-naturedly said, 'You need be in no such hurry now'.—I took my host's advice, and drank some brandy, which I found an effectual cure for my head-ach. When I rose, I went into Dr Johnson's room, and taking up Mrs M'Kinnon's Prayer-book, I opened it at the twentieth Sunday after Trinity, in the epistle for which I read, 'And be not drunk with wine, wherein there is excess'. Some would have taken this as a divine interposition.

THE JOURNAL OF A TOUR TO THE HEBRIDES WITH SAMUEL JOHNSON, LL.D.
by James Boswell Esq., 1785

THE DUKE OF NORFOLK (1746–1815)

The last time Kemble had dined with us at the Beef-Steaks, was when his friend the late Duke of Norfolk was present. The place, the chair formerly occupied by his Grace, were so many links in a chain of agreeable association, to one who remembered him so well, and loved to cherish that remembrance; for Kemble had received many substantial kindnesses from his Grace. John told us that he had seldom, in the whole course of his life, erred on the side of convivial intemperance; but in his Grace's society, whose powers of carrying off a great quantity of wine, and the charms of whose conversation, (seducing others into the same excess,) were, he said, never equalled by man,—a long sitting seemed miraculously to comprise itself into a most inconsiderable space; and it was impossible, even for those who practised the austerest temperance, to wish to get away.

It sometimes happened, at the close of the evening, that the Duke, without exhibiting any symptom of inebriety, became immoveable in his chair, as if deprived of all muscular volition. He would then request the bell to be rang three times; this was a signal for bringing in a kind of easy litter, consisting of four equi-distant belts, fastened together by a transverse one, which four domestics placed under him, and thus removed his enormous bulk, with a gentle swinging motion, up to his apartment. Upon these occasions, the Duke would say nothing; but the whole thing was managed with great system, and in perfect silence.

THE CLUBS OF LONDON. 1828

JOHN HAMILTON MORTIMER (1741–1829)

He was employed by Lord Melbourne to paint a ceiling at his seat of Brocket Hall, Herts; and taking advantage of permission to angle in the fish-pond, he rose from a carousal at midnight, and seeking a net, and calling on an assistant painter for help, dragged the preserve, and left the whole fish gasping on the bank in rows. Nor was this the worst: when reproved mildly, and with smiles, by Lady Melbourne, he had the audacity to declare, that her beauty had so bewitched him he knew not what he was about.

THE LIVES OF THE MOST EMINENT BRITISH PAINTERS, SCULPTORS, AND
ARCHITECTS. Allan Cunningham. 1832

SIR JOHN DANVERS

Sir John Danvers lived well, as the gout in his left leg testified. He usually took his three bottles, which he called his three friends: the first, his encourager; the second, his adviser; and the third, his consoler. He had also a humourous knack of bestowing upon wine a regal appellation, and making its various species represent, when placed upon the table, the sovereigns of the countries that produced them:—thus, a bottle of port stood for the King of Portugal, champaigne for that of France, Madeira for his Spanish Majesty, whilst a bottle of porter, I believe, represented our beloved Monarch. If we turned, therefore, from one wine to another, he would exclaim, 'Now we have bled the King of Spain to death, what if we decapitate the King of France!'

RETROSPECTIONS OF THE STAGE
John Bernard, 1830

RICHARD BRINSLEY SHERIDAN (1751–1816)

Sheridan did not display his admirable powers in company till he had been warmed by wine. During the earlier part of dinner he was generally heavy and silent; and I have heard him, when invited to drink a glass of wine, reply, 'No, thank you; I'll take—a little small beer'. After dinner, when he had had a tolerable quantity of wine, he was brilliant indeed. But when he went on swallowing too much, he became downright stupid: I once, after a dinner-party at the house of Edwards, the bookseller in Pall Mall, walked with him to Brookes's, when he had absolutely lost the use of speech.

TABLE TALK
Samuel Rogers (1763–1855)

GEORGE FREDERICK COOKE (1756–1811)

During the short residence Mr Cooke now made at Manchester, the curious scene took place which Riley has happily described in his Itinerant. 'One evening, in Manchester, we were in a public bar, amongst promiscuous

135

MR COOKE
of the Theatre Royal, Covent Garden

company, where Cooke was, as usual, the life of the party. Mirth and good humour prevailed till about ten o'clock, when I perceived a something lurking in his eye, which foretold a storm. Anxious to get him home before it burst forth, I pressed our departure under the plea of another engagement; but, instead of having the desired effect, it precipitated what I had foreseen. With a haughty supercilious look, he said, "I see what you are about, you hypocritical scoundrel! you canting methodistical thief! Am I, George Frederick Cooke, to be controlled by such a would-be puritan as you? I'll teach you to dictate to a tragedian". Then, pulling off his coat, and holding his fist in a menacing attitude, "Come out," continued he, "thou prince of deceivers; though thou hast faith to remove mountains, thou shalt not remove me—Come out, I say!" With some difficulty he was pacified, and resumed his coat.

'There was a large fire in the bar, before which stood, with his skirts under each arm, a pitiful imitation of *Buckism*, very deficient in cleanliness and costume. His face was grimy, and his neckcloth of the same tint, which nevertheless was rolled in various folds about his throat; his hair was matted and turned up under a round greasy hat, with narrow brims, conceitedly placed on one side of his head, which nodded under it like a shaking mandarin. Thus equipped the filthy fop straddled before the fire, which he completely monopolized. At length, he caught the eye of our tragedian, who, in silent amazement, for the space of half a minute, examined him from top to toe; then, turning to me, he burst into a horse laugh, and roared out, *"Beau nasty*, by ——" Perhaps intimidated by Cooke's former bluster, this insensible puppy took little notice; but I knew George would not stop here, and indeed I thought the stranger fair game. Cooke now rose from his seat, and taking up the skirts of his coat in imitation of the other, turned his back to the fire. "Warm work in the *back settlements*, Sir," said he; then approaching still nearer, as if he had some secrets to communicate, whispered, though loud enough for every one to hear,—

"Pray, Sir, how is soap?"

"Soap?"

"Yes, Sir, soap. I understand it is coming down."

"I am glad of it, Sir."

"Indeed, Sir, you have cause, if one may judge from your appearance."

'Here was a general laugh, which the stranger seemed not to regard; but nodding his head, and hitting his boots with a little rattan, rang the bell with an air of importance, and inquired if he could have a *weal kitlet*, or a *mutten chip*?

"What do you think", says Cooke, "of a *roasted puppy*? because", taking up the poker, "I will spit you and roast you in a minute."

'This had a visible effect upon the dirty beau; he retreated towards the door, Cooke following: "Avaunt, and quit my sight, thy face is dirty, and thy hands unwashed. Avaunt, avaunt! I say!" then replacing the poker, and returning to his seat, he continued, "being gone, I am a man again".

'It happened that Perrins, the noted pugilist, made one of the company this evening; he was a remarkably strong man, and possessed of great modesty and good nature: the last scene took such effect on his imagination, that he laughed immoderately—Cooke's attention was attracted, and turning towards him, with his most bitter look; "What do you laugh at, Mr Swabson? hey? Why, you lubber-headed thief, Johnson would have beat two of you! laugh at me! at George Frederick Cooke! Come out, you scoundrel!"

'The coat was again off, and putting himself in an attitude, "This is the arm that shall sacrifice you." Perrins was of a mild disposition, and, knowing Cooke's character, made every allowance, and answered him only by a smile, till aggravated by language and action the most gross, he very calmly took him in his arms, as though he had been a child, set him down in the street, and bolted the door. The evening was wet, and our hero, without coat or hat, unprepared to cope with it; but entreaty for admission was vain, and his application at the window unattended to. At length, grown desperate, he broke several panes, and inserting his head through the fracture, bore down all opposition by the following witticism: "Gentlemen, I have taken some *pains* to gain admittance; pray let me in, for *I see through my error.*" The door was opened, dry clothes procured; and about one o'clock in the morning we sent him home in a coach. . . .'

Mr Matthews, (Charles Matthews 1776–1835) now and for some years a distinguished favourite with the London audience, at that time a very young man and actor, was a member of Daly's company, and lodged in the same house with Cooke. One night after play and farce, in the latter Matthew's having played Mordecai to Cooke's Sir Archy, and to the satisfaction of the veteran, was invited by him to take supper in his room *tête-a-tête*, and drink whiskey punch. This high honour was gratefully received and accepted by the young comedian, who anticipated both pleasure and instruction from the society of the celebrated actor. Supper over, and Cooke's spirits elevated, the fatigues of the evening were forgotten; he was pleased with his young companion, whose tongue, freed from all shackles by the smoking liquor, glibly poured forth those praises which Cooke's superior talents prompted. One jug of whiskey punch was quickly emptied, and while drinking the second, George Frederick in his turn begins to commend young Matthews.

'You are young, and want some one to advise and guide you: take my word for it, there is nothing like industry and sobriety—Mrs Burns! Another jug of whiskey punch, Mrs Burns—you make it so good, Mrs Burns, another jug.'

'Yes, Mister Cooke.'

'In our profession, my young friend, dissipation is too apt to be the bane of youth—Villainous company, low company, leads them from studying their business and acquiring that knowledge which alone can make them respectable.'

Thus he proceeded drinking and uttering advice (not the less valuable because in opposition to his own practice), and assuring Matthews of his protection, instruction, and all his influence to forward his views, while

138

the whiskey punch, jug after jug, vanished, and with it all semblance of the virtues so eloquently praised. Though maddened by the fumes of the liquor, the chain of his ideas continued still unbroken, and he began a dissertation on the histrionic art, proceeding from first principles to a detail of the mode of exhibiting the passions, with a specimen of each by way of illustration.

It is impossible to describe, but the reader may perhaps imagine, the ludicrous effect of this scene. The power of the whiskey operating in diametric opposition to the will on his strong and flexible features, produced contortions and distortions, of which he was insensible, while Matthews sat gazing with astonishment and at times in an agony, from the effort to restrain his risible faculties; but to add to his torture, Cooke began to question him, after each 'horrible face', as to the meaning of it, or the passion expressed. Matthews, totally in the dark as to *Cooke's meaning*, made every possible mistake; and when set right by Cooke, excused himself by charging his stupidity on the whiskey.

'There—what's that?'

'Very fine, Sir.'

'But *what* is it?'

'O—anger—anger, to be sure.'

'To be sure you're a blockhead—Fear! fear, Sir!'

But when the actor, after making a hideous face, compounded of satanic malignity and the brutal leering of a drunken satyr, told his pupil that *that* was *love*, poor Matthews could resist no longer, but roared with convulsive laughter.

Cooke was surprised and enraged at this rudeness in his young guest, but Matthews had address enough to pacify him.

Mistress Burns, in the mean time, had protested against making any more whiskey punch, and had brought up the last jug, upon Cooke's solemn promise that he would ask for no more. The jug is finished; and Matthews, heartily tired, thinks he shall escape from his tormentor, and makes a move to go.

'Not yet, my dear boy, one jug more.'

'It's very late, Sir.'

'Only one more.'

'Mistress Burns will not let us have it.'

'Wo'nt she? I'll show you that presently.'

Cooke thunders with his foot, and vociferates repeatedly 'Mistress Burns!' at length honest Mrs Burns, who had got to bed, in hopes of rest, in the chamber immediately under them, answers,

'What is it you want, Mister Cooke?'

'Another jug of whiskey punch, Mistress Burns.'

'Indeed, but you can have no more, Mister Cooke.'

'Indeed but I will, Mistress Burns.'

'Remember your promise, Mister Cooke.'

'Another jug of punch, Mistress Burns.'

'Indeed, and I will not get out of my own bed any more at all, Mister Cooke, and so there's an end of it!'

'We'll see that, Mistress Burns.'

When, to Matthews's further astonishment, he seized the jug and smashed it on the floor over the head of *Mistress Burns*, exclaiming,

'Do you hear that, Mistress Burns?'

'Yes I do, Mister Cooke.'

He then proceeded to break the chairs, one by one, after each, exclaiming, 'Do you hear that, Mrs Burns?' and receiving in reply,

'Yes I do, Mister Cooke, and you'll be very sorry for it to-morrow, so you will.'

He then opened the window, and very deliberately proceeded to throw the looking-glasses into the street, and the fragments of broken tables and chairs. Matthews had made several attempts to go, and had been detained by Cooke: he now ventured something like an expostulation; on which his Mentor ordered him out of his apartment, and threw the candle and candlestick after him. Matthews, having departed, the wretched madman sallied out, and was brought home next day, beaten and deformed with bruises.

On the 7th of October, the public attention was excited by bringing out Pizarro, for the first time at Covent-Garden, and the bills announced,

Pizarro	...	Mr Cooke,
Rolla	...	Mr Kemble,
Elvira	...	Mrs Siddons

But alas! Mr Cooke was *indisposed*.—He appeared, indeed, but only to render his shame more glaring. He was received with the usual testimonies of distinguished favour; but, as soon as he began to speak, his state was too evident. After a few ineffectual attempts to proceed, he made an effort to address the audience, and began—pressing his hand upon his chest, and making a lamentable face,

'Ladies and Gentlemen—my old complaint—my old complaint—'

This was irresistible—the laughter caught instantaneously through the house, and amidst roars, shouts, and hisses, he retired. . . .

Having received the amount of a benefit and the proceeds of an engage-ment at Manchester, he pocketed the whole, three or four hundred pounds, and that evening fell into company at a public-house with some republican manufacturers of the neighbourhood. The loyalty of our hero was always great, but increased in warmth thermometrically with his stomach and head. One of the mechanics entered the field of political disputation with George Frederick, who soon became intemperate in words as well as conduct, and finally challenged his antagonist to determine the controversy by the fist. The man, who knew him and his reputation, endeavoured to avoid the necessity of beating him, and excused himself by 'Nah now, Mr Cooke, you know I would not harm you if I could; you take the liberty of abusing me and challenging me, because you are rich, and know I am a poor man.'

'Do I?' says George, 'I'll show you that. There look,' pulling all the bank notes from his pocket, 'there—that's all I have in the world—there,' putting them in the fire. 'Now I am as poor as you are—now, damn you, come on!' . . .

The trouble which Mr Cooke's behaviour about this time, and perhaps before, gave to the managers of the theatre, must have been immeasurable. They could not calculate upon him from one hour to another. Sometimes when they supposed him to be sober, he came to the theatre, and created a riot and confusion, by insisting upon going before the public, utterly incompetent to perform that for which he was pledged; and sometimes when he was in a state of comparative sanity, he would deliberately de-termine that he would not play, and either go to some place where he would not easily be found, or send word that he could not, or would not, act that evening.

It is related of him, that with predetermination he once had his Richard's dress removed privately from the theatre to his lodgings, being advertized for that character, to be performed the next night, and instead of going to dress for the part as usual, he prepared himself at home, and rode to a place near the theatre, where he waited until the very moment of ringing up the curtain, knowing full well *what the feelings* of his friend John would be; and then, at the moment when Mr Kemble was preparing to step forward with an apology, and perhaps to offer his own Richard, as a substitute, in marches the true Richard, and takes his place at the side, ready to begin.

He has told me that once he dined alone at a coffee-house in the vicinity of the theatre on the day of his performing, with the full intention of going early to his dressing-room; but after dinner, the thought suggested itself that he would not play that night, and he determined that he would not play. 'I had not been drinking at the time', said he, 'but I felt the humour come over me, and I indulged it—a kind of madness—and there I sate indulging in a kind of reverie, but determined that I would not go to the theatre. Mr Kemble, however, heard that I was not in my dressing-room; the alarm spread, and after a time he found out where I was; so he came in, and after a little chat I gave up the whim, and went with him and acted as well as ever I did.

On the 8th of January, 1810, Mr Cooke was again announced, and for Richard the Third. The house was crowded and an apology was expected. Accordingly he came forward previously to assuming the lofty demeanour of the triumphant Duke of Gloster, as a pitiful suppliant to crave indulgence, and to promise what he could never hope to perform. He addressed the audience and entreated their indulgence, but when he came to 'If you will restore me once more to the favour I enjoyed, I promise——' he was interrupted by plaudits, and dismissed, to assume a more brilliant, if not more virtuous, character. Poor Cooke! it was time that you should be removed from the scene of such humiliation; for in removal was the only hope that now remained of reformation.

He continued to play very steadily, and with his usual excellence, those great parts, in which he shone with an unrivalled lustre, but his attraction had in a degree ceased; and no actress's husband, or dramatic author, or dramatic author's friend, thought it worth their trouble to make particular mention of him in the way of praise, and to dispraise that which all had concurred to admire, they dared not. But on the 5th of May, Mr Cooke appeared in a new character, and the opportunity was eagerly seized to write him still further down with the public.

The opportunity offered was his playing the character of Henry the Eighth. Public opinion did not shield him from a blow in this part, and those who had been shooting the pointless shafts of *their* wit at him for some time past, now hurled venom and filth on his head with the most shameless effrontery.

On the 5th of June Mr Cooke played Falstaff, in the 1st part of Henry Fourth. This was the last time he played in London. He soon after left the metropolis of England, never more to return.

MEMOIRS OF GEORGE FREDERICK COOKE, ESQ.
William Dunlap, 1813

JOHN PHILIP KEMBLE (1757–1823)

About this period, these friends had been dining together at Mr Charles

Kemble's house. Mr John Kemble had taken much wine, and when the party broke up, Mr Mathews determined to accompany the tragedian to his own door. Giving him his arm, therefore, they proceeded slowly to Mr Kemble's house in Great Russell-street, Bloomsbury. The tragedian was full of talk, and 'very happy', as it is called; and although the hour was late, his pressing invitation to his friend to enter the house with him, induced my husband to obey. It was evident that the man who opened the door was the only person who remained up in the establishment. Mr Kemble went into his library, accompanied by Mr Mathews, and desired the attendant to bring a tray, at the same time, with great formality, introducing him to the notice of his guest as the 'gentleman who did him the honour to take care of his wine', &c. It was in vain that Mr Mathews protested against further hospitality. Mr Kemble was too much excited to have his spirit easily laid, and, surrounded as he was with books, he began a disquisition upon their authors, above all, his 'belov-ed Shakspeare!,' on whom he discoursed most eloquently, after taking a volume from the shelf, and devoutedly kissing the binding. At length the tray was brought in with wine and water, &c., and with it entered an enormous cat, decorated with a red collar and a bell. The appearance of his favourite cat called forth its master's most affectionate notice, and many relations of its extraordinary powers of understanding, its devoted attachment to its master's person, &c., were detailed to Mr Mathews. Mustapha, Mr Kemble declared, had much of human feeling of the best kind in his composition; he described how he watched his return home, mourned his absence, &c., and grew maudlin in its praise. The animal seemed, indeed, happy in its master's presence, and it looked up in his face as it composedly lay down before him. Mr Mathews mewed; Mr Kemble, turning round at this sound, which he believed to proceed from the cat, observed, 'There, my dear Mathews, do you hear that? Now, that creature knows all I say of him, and is replying to it'. This amused my husband, and he repeated the experiment in all the varieties of feline intonation, mewing, purring, &c. Mr Kemble at last said to him, in his slow and measured tones, 'Now, you don't know what he means by that, but I do. Mus!—Mus!' (on every reiteration of this affectionate diminutive, raising his voice to its most tragic expression of tenderness)—'umph! My dear sir, that creature knows that it is beyond my usual time of sitting up, and he's uneasy! Mus! Mus!' But Mus was sleepy and inattentive, and his master resumed his criticisms upon the different readings of Shakspeare, talked also of Lope de Vega, and was again interrupted by a mew, as he believed, from the dissatisfied Mus. 'What', asked his fond master, looking down upon him, 'what is it you desire, my good friend?' (Mus, alias Mathews, mewed once more, in a more supplicating and more touching tone.) 'Well, well! I understand you: you want to go to bed. Well, I suppose I must indulge you.' Here Mr Kemble deliberately arose, put down his book upon the table, took a measured pinch of snuff, and somewhat tottered to the door, which he with difficulty opened. He then awaited Mustapha's exit, but Mustapha having no *voice* in the affair, preferred remaining where he was; and his master kindly reproached him with being a 'little capricious in first asking to go, and then preferring to stay'. With a smile and look at my husband of the gentlest indulgence towards his favourite's humour, he tottered back again to his chair, resumed his declamatory observations upon the relative powers of dramatic writers and their essential requisites, till the troublesome Mustapha again renewed his mewing solicitations. Mr Kemble once more stopped, and looking again at the imaginary cause of his interruption with philo-sophic patience, asked, 'Well, Mus, what would you have?' Then, after another pause, turning to his guest, said: 'Now, my dear Mathews, you are fond of animals, and ought to know this one; he's a perfect character for you to study. Now, sir, that cat knows that I shall be ill to-morrow, and he's uneasy at my sitting up'. Then benevolently looking at the cat, added, 'Umph! my dear Mus. I must beg your indulgence, my good friend; I really can-*not* go to bed yet.' Mus whined his reply, and his master declared that the cat asked to be allowed to go away. On the door being a second time opened, after similar exertion on Mr Kemble's part to effect this courtesy, and several grave chirpings in order to entice Mus from the fire-place, the animal at length left the room. Mr Kemble then returned, as before, to his seat, drank another glass of wine and water, and, just as he was comfortably re-established, the incorrigible Mus was heard in the passage again, in loud lament, and importunate demand for re-admittance. 'Umph!' said Mr Kemble, with another pinch of snuff—'now, that animal, sir, is not happy, after all, away from me.' (Mus was louder than ever at this moment.) 'Why, what ails the creature? Surely there is more in this than we dream of, Mathews. You, who have studied such beings, ought to be able to explain.' Poor Mus made another pathetic appeal for re-admission, and his master's heart was not made of flint. Mr Kemble apologized to his guest for these repeated interruptions, and managed once more to make his way to the door. After opening it, and waiting a minute for the re-entrance of his favourite, but not seeing it, he smiled at my husband with the same indulgent expression as before, and remarked, 'Now, would you believe it, Mathews, that extrordinary animal was affronted at not being let in again on his first appeal?—and now it is his humour not to come at all! Mus!—Mustapha!—Mus!' But as no Mus appeared, the door was closed with the same deliberation, and Mr Kemble once more contrived to regain his chair, and recommenced his comments, quite unobservant of the almost hysterical fit of laughter to which my husband was by this time reduced at the imposition he had so successfully, though in the first place so unintentionally, practised upon the credulity of his grave and unsuspecting friend. But it did not end here, for Mr Mathews reiterated his imitations, and Mr Kemble again remarked upon his favourite's peculiarities of temper, &c. Again he went to the door, again returned, till even 'Mr Midnight' (as some friends of ours christened Mr Mathews, from his love of late hours) felt it time to retire, and leave Mr Kemble, which he did as he saw him fall asleep, in the act of representing his idea of the scene of the sick king in Henry IV., with his pocket-handkerchief spread over his head as a substitute for the characteristic drapery of the dying monarch.

> THE LIFE AND CORRESPONDENCE OF CHARLES MATHEWS, THE ELDER,
> COMEDIAN. By Mrs Mathews
> (Abridged by Edmund Yates, 1860)

RICHARD PORSON (1759–1808)

Porter was his favourite beverage at breakfast. One Sunday morning meeting Dr Goodall (Provost of Eton), he said, 'Where are you going?' 'To church.'—'Where is Mrs Goodall?' 'At breakfast.'—'Very well; I'll go and breakfast with her.' Porson accordingly presented himself before Mrs Goodall; and being asked what he chose to take, he said 'porter'. It was sent for, pot after pot; and the sixth pot was just being carried into the house when Dr Goodall returned from church. . . . Porson would sit up drinking all night, without seeming to feel any bad effects from it. . . .

Tooke used to say that 'Porson would drink ink rather than not drink at all'. Indeed, he would drink anything. He was sitting with a gentleman, after dinner, in the chambers of a mutual friend, a Templar, who was then ill and confined to bed. A servant came into the room, sent thither by his master for a bottle of embrocation which was on the chimney-piece. 'I drank it an hour ago', said Porson.

When Hoppner the painter was residing in a cottage a few miles from London, Porson, one afternoon, unexpectedly arrived there. Hoppner said that he could not offer him dinner, as Mrs H. had gone to town, and had carried with her the key of the closet which contained the wine. Porson, however, declared that he would be content with a mutton-chop,

RICHARD PORSON

and beer from the next ale-house; and accordingly stayed to dine. During the evening said, 'I am quite certain that Mrs Hoppner keeps some nice bottle, for her private drinking, in her own bedroom; so, pray, try if you can lay your hands on it'. His host assured him that Mrs H. had no such secret stores; but Porson insisting that a search be made, a bottle was at last discovered in the lady's apartment, to the surprise of Hoppner,

146

and the joy of Porson, who soon finished its contents, pronouncing it to be the best gin he had tasted for a long time. Next day, Hoppner, somewhat out of temper, informed his wife that Porson had drunk every drop of her concealed dram. 'Drunk every drop of it!' cried she: 'my God, it was spirits of wine for the lamp!'. . . .

Gurney (the Baron) had chambers in Essex Court, Temple, under Porson's. One night (or rather, morning) Gurney was awaked by a tremendous thump in the chambers above. Porson had just come home dead drunk, and had fallen on the floor. Having extinguished his candle in the fall, he presently staggered down stairs to relight it; and Gurney heard him keep dodging and poking with the candle at the staircase-lamp for about five minutes, and all the while very lustily cursing the nature of things.

Porson was fond of smoking, and said that when smoking began to go out of fashion, learning began to go out of fashion also. . . .

When Porson dined with me, I used to keep him within bounds; but I frequently met him at various houses where he got completely drunk. He would not scruple to return to the dining-room, after the company had left it, pour into a tumbler the drops remaining in the wine-glasses, and drink off the omnium gatherum.

PORSONIANA
Samuel Rogers (1763–1855)

EDMUND KEAN (1787–1833)

The next scene in our hero's changeful life lies in the island of Guernsey. He went to this place, with the rest of Hughes's company, about the early part of May, 1812. Mrs Kean followed shortly afterwards; and, on landing, was accosted by the tragedian, who was in tip-toe spirits, with— 'My dear Mary, what do you think? I can get brandy here for eighteen-pence a bottle! I can drink it instead of beer'.

(1814, 1815).

At the close of his first London season, Kean set off for Dublin. He had entered into an engagement with Mr Jones, the Dublin manager, to act four times a week for three weeks, and to divide the profits of the House with him, after a deduction of £80 for the current expenses. He opened in Richard the Third, and played all his successful characters, with even more than his former success. Thundering applause, compliments of all sorts, and the sum of £1,370 in money, rewarded his twelve nights' exertions. Mr Grattan, the celebrated Irish orator, invited him to his house, and gentlemen of all creeds (in politics and religion) vied with each other in showing him attention. Nothing stood in the way of his popularity (not even his own jovialities), and he came off, by universal assent, a conquerer of all the warm hearts in Dublin.

Yet, he had nearly been vanquished at the outset. Bold spirit as he was, the spirit 'Whiskey' was of a more potent order; and on his first setting foot in Ireland, its effects upon him were rapid and alarming, accustomed as he was to liquors falsely termed generous. One night, in particular, after having acted with applause at the theatre, he encountered the malevolent Whiskey, and the result of the contest was so decisive, that, at some indefinite hour of the morning (about the time probably when
'The morning cock crew loud),'
the tragedian was brought home, by a competent number of watchmen, (our history says six), and deposited, in a state of apparent insensibility, on the floor of the hall. The actor, however, was still acting; for, as soon as his enemies were off their guard, he started up and took to flight, followed by his custodians, who, in the true spirit of their country, began to shout 'murder!' immediately their man was restored to life. After a hot pursuit, the victim of whiskey was recaptured, and conducted to the watch-house. But when they were about to accommodate him with a lodging (free of all expense) until morning, he contrived to secrete the key of the prison door, and once more set off at full speed. It would be difficult to describe this night-hunt; but one may imagine the mischievous player, running off at a pace of ten knots an hour, and the hounds of justice loud behind him (loud, but not swift, for we know them:

'*Our* hounds are bred out of the Irish kind;
.   .   .   and their heads are hung
With ears that sweep away the morning dew;
Crook-knee'd and dewlap'd, like Thessalian bulls,
Slow in pursuit, but matched in mouth like bells,
Each under each——')

One may imagine the tumult of the pursuit, the stamping of feet, the clattering of lanterns, the flourishing of shillelahs, the floating 'wrap-rascals', and finally the yells and cries and denunciations (to which no English translation could do justice) of the rogues whose dexterity had been outwitted by a stranger, and whose hearts no 'tinpinny' had softened. The tragedian escaped, and, as we have reason to apprehend, considered himself aggrieved at having been seized upon, *vi et armis*, and sentenced to prison, for so simple and everyday a matter, in hospitable Ireland, as moistening his clay with the mountain dew of the country.

THE LIFE OF EDMUND KEAN
Bryan Waller Proctor, 1835

WILLIAM PITT (1759–1806)

During his boyhood, Pitt was very weakly; and his physician, Addington (Lord Sidmouth's father) ordered him to take port wine in large quantities: the consequence was, that, when he grew up, he could not do without it. Lord Grenville has seen him swallow a bottle of port in tumblerfuls, before going to the House. This, together with his habit of eating late suppers (indigestible cold veal-pies, etc.), helped undoubtedly to shorten his life. Huskisson, speaking to me of Pitt, said that his hands shook so much, that, when he helped himself to salt, he was obliged to support the right hand with the left.

Stothard the painter happened to be one evening at an inn on the Kent Road, when Pitt and Dundas put up there on their way from Walmer. Next morning, as they were stepping into their carriage, the waiter said to Stothard, 'Sir, do you observe these two gentlemen?'—'Yes,' he replied; 'and I know them to be Mr Pitt and Mr Dundas'.—'Well, sir, how much wine do you suppose they drank last night?'—Stothard could not guess.— 'Seven bottles, sir'.

TABLE TALK
Samuel Rogers (1763–1855)

ROBERT BURNS (1759–96)

Madam,

I dare say that this is the first epistle you ever received from this nether world. I write you from the regions of Hell, amid the horrors of the damn'd. The time and manner of my leaving your earth I do not exactly know, as I took my departure in the heat of a fever of intoxication, contracted at your too hospitable mansion; but, on my arrival here, I was fairly tried, and sentenced to endure the purgatorial tortures of this infernal confine for the space of ninety-nine years, eleven months and, twenty-nine days, and all on account of the impropriety of my conduct yesternight under your roof. Here am I, laid on a bed of pitiless furze, with my aching head reclined on a pillow of ever-piercing thorn, while an infernal tormentor, wrinkled, and old, and cruel, his name I think is *Recollection*, with a whip of scorpions, forbids peace or rest to approach me, and keeps anguish eternally awake. Still, Madam, if I could in any measure be reinstated in the good opinion of the fair circle whom my conduct last night so much injured, I think it would be an alleviation to my torments. For this reason I trouble you with this letter. To the men of the company I will make no apology.—Your husband, who insisted on my drinking more than I chose, has no right to blame me; and the other gentlemen were partakers of my guilt. But to you, Madam, I have much to apologize. Your good opinion I valued as one of the greatest acquisitions I had made on earth, and I was truly a beast to forfeit it. There was a Miss I—— too, a woman of fine sense, gentle and unassuming manners—do make, on my part, a miserable damn'd wretch's best apology to her. A Mrs G——, a charming woman, did me the honour to be prejudiced in my favour; this makes me hope that I have not outraged her beyond all forgiveness.—To all the other ladies please present my humblest contrition for my conduct, and my petition for their gracious pardon. O all ye powers of decency and decorum! whisper to them that my errors, though great, were involuntary— that an intoxicated man is the vilest of beasts—that it was not in my nature to be brutal to any one—that to be rude to a woman, when in my senses, was impossible with me—but—

.   .   .   .   .

Regret! Remorse! Shame! ye three hellhounds that ever dog my steps and bay at my heels, spare me! spare me!

Forgive the offences, and pity the perdition of, Madam,

Your humble Slave,
(Robt. Burns)

LETTER TO MRS ROBERT RIDDELL 1793 (?)

GEORGE COLMAN (1762–1836)

I have met George Colman occasionally, and thought him extremely pleasant and convivial. Sheridan's humour, or rather wit, was always saturnine, and sometimes savage; he never laughed, (at least that *I* saw, and I watched him,) but Colman did. If I had to *choose*, and could not have both at a time, I should say, 'Let me begin the evening with Sheridan, and finish it with Colman'. Sheridan for dinner, Colman for supper; Sheridan for claret or port, but Colman for everything, from the madeira and champagne at dinner, the claret with a *layer* of *port* between the glasses, up to the punch of the night, and down to the grog, or gin and water, of daybreak;—all these I have threaded with both the same. Sheridan was a grenadier company of life-guards, but Colman a whole regiment—of *light infantry*, to be sure, but still a regiment.

Lord Byron

LORD BYRON (1788–1824)

I am but just returned to town, from which you may infer that I have been out of it; and I have been boxing, for exercise, with Jackson for

GEORGE COLMAN

this last month daily. I have also been drinking, and, on one occasion, with three other friends at the Cocoa Tree, from six till four, yea, unto five in the matin. We clareted and champagned till two—then supped, and finished with a kind of regency punch composed of madeira, brandy, and *green* tea, no *real* water being admitted therein. That was a night for you! without once quitting the table, except to ambulate home, which I did alone, and in utter contempt of a hackney-coach and my own *vis*, both of which were deemed necessary for our conveyance. And so,—I am very well, and they say it will hurt my constitution.

I have also, more or less, been breaking a few of the favourite commandments; but I mean to pull up and marry, if any one will have me. In the meantime, the other day I nearly killed myself with a collar of brawn, which I swallowed for supper, and *in*digested for I don't know how long: but that is by the by. All this gourmandise was in honour of Lent; for I am forbidden meat all the rest of the year, but it is strictly enjoined me during your solemn fast. I have been, and am, in very tolerable love; but of that hereafter as it may be.

LETTER TO THOMAS MOORE
9 April, 1814

The supper, to which he here looks forward, took place at Watier's, of which club he had lately become a member; and, as it may convey some idea of his irregular mode of diet, and thus account, in part, for the frequent derangement of his health, I shall here attempt, from recollection, a description of his supper on this occasion. We were to have been joined by Lord R——, who however did not arrive, and the party accordingly consisted but of ourselves. Having taken upon me to order the repast, and knowing that Lord Byron, for the last two days, had done nothing towards sustenance, beyond eating a few biscuits and (to appease appetite) chewing mastic, I desired that we should have a good supply of, at least, two kinds of fish. My companion, however, confined himself to lobsters, and of these finished two or three, to his own share,—interposing, sometimes, a small liqueur-glass of strong white brandy, sometimes a tumbler of very hot water, and then pure brandy again, to the amount of near half a dozen small glasses of the latter, without which, alternatively with the hot water, he appeared to think the lobster could not be digested. After this, we had claret, of which having despatched two bottles between us, at about four o'clock in the morning we parted.

. . . Among other nights of the same description which I had the happiness of passing with him, I remember once, in returning home from some assembly at rather a late hour, we saw lights in the windows of his old haunt Stevens's, in Bond Street, and agreed to stop there and sup. On entering, we found on old friend of his, Sir G—— W——, who joined our party, and the lobsters and brandy and water being put in requisition, it was (as usual on such occasions) broad daylight before we separated.

Yesterday, I dined out with a large-ish party, where were Sheridan and Colman, Harry Harris of C.G., and his brother, Sir Gilbert Heathcote, Ds. Kinnaird, and others, of note and notoriety. Like other parties of the kind, it was first silent, then talky, then argumentative, then disputatious, then unintelligible, then altogethery, then inarticulate, and then drunk. When we had reached the last step of this glorious ladder, it was difficult to get down again without stumbling; and to crown all, Kinnaird and I had to conduct Sheridan down a d——d corkscrew staircase, which had certainly been constructed before the discovery of fermented liquors, and to which no legs, however crooked, could possibly accommodate themselves. We deposited him safe at home, where his man, evidently used to the business, waited to receive him in the hall.

Both he and Colman were, as usual, very good; but I carried away much wine, and the wine had previously carried away my memory; so that all was hiccup and happiness for the last hour or so, and I am not impregnated with any of the conversation. Perhaps you heard of a late answer of Sheridan to the watchman who found him bereft of that 'divine particle of air', called reason, . . . He, the watchman, who found Sherry in the street, fuddled and bewildered, and almost insensible. 'Who are *you*, Sir?'—no answer. 'What's your name?'—a hiccup. 'What's your name?'—Answer, in a slow, deliberate and impassive tone—'Wilberforce ! ! !' Is not that Sherry all over?—and, to my mind, excellent. Poor fellow, *his* very dregs are better than the 'first sprightly runnings' of others.

My paper is full, and I have a grievous headache.

LETTER TO THOMAS MOORE
31 October, 1815

We went down to Newstead together, where I had got a famous cellar, and *Monks'* dresses from a masquerade warehouse. We were a company of some seven or eight, with an occasional neighbour or so for visitors, and used to sit up late in our frairs' dresses, drinking burgundy, claret, champagne, and what not, out of the *skull-cup*, and all sorts of glasses, and buffooning all round the house, in our conventual garments. Matthews always denominated me 'the Abbot', and never called me by any other name in his good humours, to the day of his death. The harmony of these our symposia was somewhat interrupted, a few days after our assembling, by Matthews's threatening to throw —— out of a *window*, in consequence of I know not what commerce of jokes ending in this epigram. —— came to me and said, that 'his respect and regard for me as host would not permit him to call out any of my guests, and that he should go to town next morning.' He did. It was in vain that I represented to him that the window was not high, and that the turf under it was particularly soft.

LETTER TO JOHN MURRAY
9 December, 1820
LIFE OF BYRON, Thomas Moore, 1829

A MEETING BETWEEN MEN OF BUSINESS

CHARLES LAMB (1775–1834)

My head is playing all the tunes in the world, ringing such peals! It has just finished the 'Merry Christ Church Bells', and absolutely is beginning 'Turn again Whittington', Buz, buz, buz, bum, bum, bum, wheeze, wheeze, feu, feu feu, tinky, tinky, tinky, *cr'annch*. I shall certainly come to be damned at last. I have been getting drunk two days running, and I find my moral sense in the last stage of consumption, my religion burning blue and faint as the tops of burning bricks. Hell gapes and the Devil's great guts cry 'cupboard' for me. In the midst of these infernal larums,

154

conscience (and be damned to her) barking and yelping as loud as any of them.

TO SAMUEL TAYLOR COLERIDGE
14 August, 1800

My habits are changing, I think i.e. from drunk to sober. Whether I shall be happier or not remains to be proved. I shall certainly be more happy in a morning; but whether I shall not sacrifice the fat, and the marrow, and the kidneys, i.e. the night, glorious care-drowning night, that heals all our wrongs, pours wine into our mortifications, changes the scene from indifferent and flat to bright and brilliant! O Manning, if I should have formed a diabolical resolution, by the time you come to England, of not admitting any spirituous liquors into my house, will you be my guest on such shameworthy terms? Is life, with such limitations, worth trying? The truth is, that my liquors bring a nest of friendly harpies about my house, who consume me.

TO THOMAS MANNING
24 September, 1802

Last night I had been in a sad quandary of spirits, in what they call the evening; but a pipe, and some generous Port, and *King Lear* (being alone), had their effects as solacers. I went to bed pot-valiant.

TO SAMUEL TAYLOR COLERIDGE
20 March, 1803

Mary has left a little space for me to fill up with nonsense, as the geographers used to cram monsters in the voids of the maps, and call it Terra Incognita. She has told you how she has taken to water like a hungry otter. I too limp after her in lame imitation, but it goes against me a little at first. I have been acquaintance with it now for full four days, and it seems a moon. I am full of cramps, and rheumatisms, and cold internally, so that fire won't warm me; yet I bear all for virtue's sake. Must I then leave you, gin, rum, brandy, aqua-vitæ, pleasant jolly fellows? Hang temperance, and he that first invented it!—some Anti-Noahite. C—— has powdered his head, and looks like Bacchus, Bacchus ever sleek and young. He is going to turn sober, but his clock has not struck yet; meantime he pours down goblet after goblet, the second to see where the first is gone, the third to see no harm happens to the second, a fourth to say there is another coming, and fifth to say he is not sure he is the last.

TO DOROTHY WORDSWORTH (about 1822)

155

I long to see Wordsworth once more before he goes hence, but it would be at the expence of health and comfort my infirmities cannot afford. Once only have I been at a dinner party, to meet him, for a whole year past, and I do not know that I am not the worse for it now. There is a necessity for my drinking too much (don't show this to the Bishop of ——, your friend) at and after dinner; then I require spirits at night to allay the crudity of the weaker Bacchus; and in the morning I cool my parched stomach with a fiery libation. Then I am aground in town, and call upon my London friends, and get new wets of ale, porter, etc; then ride home, drinking where the coach stops, as duly as Edward set up his Waltham Crosses. This, or near it, was the process of my experiment of dining at Talfourd's to meet Wordsworth, and I am not well now. Now let me beg that we may meet here with assured safety to both sides. Darley and Procter come here on Sunday morning; pray arrange to come along with them. Here I can be tolerably moderate. In town, the very air of town turns my head and is intoxication enough, if intoxication knew a limit. I am a poor country mouse, and your cates disturb me. Tell me you will come. We have a bed, and a half or three quarters bed, at all your services; and the adjoining inn has many. If engaged on Sunday, tell me when you will come; a Saturday will suit as well. I would that Wordsworth would come too. Pray believe that 'tis my health only, which brought me here, that frightens me from the wicked town. Mary joins in kind remembrances to Mrs Cary and yourself.

TO THE REV. HENRY F. CARY
10 June, 1828

It is an observation of a wise man, that 'Moderation is best in all things'. I cannot agree with him 'in liquor'. There is a smoothness and oiliness in wine that makes it go down by a natural Channel, which I am positive was made for that descending. Else, why does not wine choke us? Could Nature have made that sloping lane, not to facilitate the down-going? She does nothing in vain. You know that better than I. You know how often she has helped you at a dead lift, and how much better entitled she is to a fee than yourself sometimes, when you carry off the credit. Still, there is something due to manners and customs, and I should apologise to you and Mrs Asbury for being absolutely carried home upon a man's shoulders thro' Silver Street, up Parsons Lane, by the Chapels (which might have taught me better) and then to be deposited like a dead log at Gaffer Westwood's, who, it seems, does not 'insure' against intoxication. Not that the mode of conveyance is objectionable. On the contrary, it is more easy than a one horse chaise.

Ariel, in the 'Tempest' says:

> On a Bat's back do I fly
> After Sunset merrily.

Now I take it, that Ariel must sometimes have stayed out late of nights. Indeed he pretends that 'where the bee sucks, there lurks he'—as much as to say that his suction is as innocent as that little innocent (but damnably stinging when he is provok'd) winged creature. But I take it, Ariel was fond of metheglin of which the Bees are notorious Brewers. But then you will say, what a shocking sight to see a middle-aged-gentleman-and-a-half riding upon a Gentleman's back up Parsons Lane at midnight. Exactly the time for that sort of conveyance when nobody can see him, nobody but Heaven and his own Conscience; now Heaven makes fools, and don't expect much from her own creation; and as for Conscience, she and I have long since come to a compromise. I have given up false modesty, and she allows me to abate a little of the true. . . . By the way, is magnesia good on these occasions? ℥III pol. med. sum. antenoct. in rub. can. I am no licentiate, but know enough of simples to beg you to send me a draught after this model. But still you'll say (or the men and maids at your house will say) that it is not a seemly sight for an old gentleman to go home a pick-a-back. Well, maybe it is not. But I have never studied grace. I take it to be a mere superficial accomplishment. I regard more the internal acquisitions. The great object after supper is to get home, and whether that is obtained in a horizontal posture, or perpendicular (as foolish men and apes affect for dignity) I think is little to the purpose. The end is always greater than the means. Here I am, able to compose a sensible rational apology, and what signifies how I got here? I have just sense enough to remember I was very happy last night, and to thank our kind host and hostess, and that's Sense enough, I hope. N.B. what is good for a desperate head-ache? why, Patience, and a determination not to mind being miserable all day long. And that I have made my mind up to. . . .

TO DR J. V. ASBURY
(no date)

I protest I know not in what words to invest my sense of the shameful violation of hospitality which I was guilty of on that fatal Wednesday. Let it be blotted from the calendar. Had it been committed at a layman's house, say a merchant's or manufacturer's, a cheesemonger's or greengrocer's, or, to go higher, a barrister's, a member of Parliament's, a rich banker's, I should have felt alleviation, a drop of self-pity. But to be seen deliberately to go out of the house of a clergyman drunk! a clergyman of the Church of England too! not that alone, but of an expounder of that dark Italian Hierophant, an exposition little short of *his* who dared, unfold the Apocalypse: divine riddles both; and, without supernal grace vouchsafed, Arks not to be fingered without present blasting to the touchers. And then, from what house! Not a common glebe or vicarage, (which yet have been shameful,) but from a kingly repository of sciences, human and divine, with the primate of England for its guardian, arrayed in public majesty, from which the profane vulgar are bid fly. Could all those volumes have taught me nothing better! With feverish eyes on the succeeding dawn I opened upon the faint light, enough to distinguish, in a strange chamber, not immediately to be recognised, garters, hose, waistcoat, neckerchief, arranged in dreadful order and proportion, which I knew was not mine own. 'Tis the common symptom on awaking, I judge my last night's condition from. A tolerable scattering on the floor I hail as being too probably my own, and if the candlestick be not removed I assoil myself. But this finical arrangement, this finding every thing in the morning in exact diametrical rectitude, torments me. By whom was I divested? Burning blushes! not by the fair hands of nymphs, the Buffam Graces? Remote whispers suggested that I *coached* it home in triumph. Far be that from working pride in me, for I was unconscious of the locomotion; that a young Mentor accompanied a reprobate old Telemachus; that, the Trojan like, he bore his charge upon his shoulders, while the wretched incubus, in glimmering sense, hiccuped drunken snatches of flying on the bats' wings after sunset. An aged servitor was also hinted at, to make disgrace more complete, one, to whom my ignominy may offer further occasions of revolt (to which he was before too fondly inclining) from the true faith; for, at a sight of my helplessness, what more was needed to drive him to the advocacy of independency? Occasion led me through Great Russell Street yesterday. I gazed at the great knocker. My feeble hands in vain essayed to lift it. I dreaded that Argus Portitor, who doubtless lanterned me out on that prodigious night. I called the Elginian marbles. They were cold to my suit. I shall never again, I said, on the wide gates unfolding, say, without fear of thrusting back, in a light but peremptory air, 'I am going to Mr Cary's'. I passed by the walls of Balclutha. I had imaged to myself a zodiac of third Wednesdays irradiating by glimpses the Edmonton dulness. I dreamed of Highmore! I am de-vited to come on Wednesdays. Villanous old age, that, with second childhood, brings linked hand in hand her inseparable twin, new inexperience, which knows not effects of liquor. What I was to have sate for a sober, middle-aged-and-a-half gentleman, literary too, the neat fingered artist can educe no notions but of a dissolute Silenus, lecturing natural philosophy to a jeering Chromius, or a Mnasilus. Pudet. From the context gather the lost name of——.

TO REV. HENRY F. CARY
18 October, 1834
LETTERS OF CHARLES LAMB

Scott was a stout walker, Lamb was a *porter* one. He calculated Distances, not by Long Measure, but by Ale and Beer Measure. 'Now I have walked a pint.' Many a time I have accompanied him in these matches against Meux, not with out sharing in the stake.

Allan Cunningham

JOHN MYTTON (1796–1834)

There is but one excuse for a man being almost perpetually intoxicated, and prostituting the reason of the man to the appetite of the brute; and that is, the attempt to divert grief which he has found it impossible to subdue. As a balm for wounds which can never heal, or under the accumulated pressure of pecuniary difficulties, the bottle will be resorted to so long as the world shall stand; and who can condemn the wretch that tries the experiment? But the subject of this memoir had not such excuses to plead for his excess in drinking; neither will I endeavour to find them for him. It was, however, to him the Circean cup—the bane of his respectability, his health, his happiness, and everything that was dear to him as a man and a gentleman; and can this be marvelled at? It is written of Hercules, that he acquired his immense strength by feeding on the marrow of lions; and how powerful must have been the stimulus of the almost unheard-of quantity of from *four* to *six* bottles of port wine *daily*, on that volcanic excitability of mind which was, not only by nature, Mr Mytton's, but which had been acted upon, and increased, by a severe affection of the brain at an early period of life! Thus, then, although I offer no excuse for his drinking, his drinking—for men are tried by wine, says the proverb, as metals are by fire— furnishes excuses, I should rather have said apologies, for his conduct, inasmuch as his reason was, to a certain extent, lost in delirium, caused by the fumes of wine on an already somewhat distempered brain. Many of his acts were not the acts of John Mytton,

Woodward del   Rowlandson scul

DRUNKEN HEAD.

but of a man *mad, half by nature, and half by wine;* and I think his best and
dearest friends are decidedly of my opinion.

From this account of its host, it may be supposed that Halston was a
scene of general dissipation and riot. By no means. In short, I cannot
bring to my recollection a single instance of being one of what may be
termed a drunken party during my frequent visits to the house. But this
is accounted for in more ways than one. The host had always the start of
his friends, in the first place; and in the next, long sittings were not in
accordance with his restless disposition. In the summer, he would jump
out of the window, and be off. In the winter, he was anxious to get to the
billiard-table, which was always lighted up after coffee, for the amusement
of himself and his friends; and here he was in his element. How then, it

may be asked, did he consume that quantity of port wine? Why this question is easily answered. He shaved with a bottle of it on his toilet; he worked steadily at it throughout the day, by a glass or two at a time, and at least a bottle with his luncheon; and the after-dinner and *after-supper* work—not losing sight of it in the billiard-room—completed the Herculean task. No wonder, then, that Alexander the Great has been called a 'fool to him' in his Bacchanalian feats; at all events, he would have been a good playfellow for him at Persepolis; or that—as Cicero said of Piso—'his breath smelt like a vintner's vault'. He is, however, a memorable example of the comparatively harmless effects of *very good wine*, which he always had, and just of a proper age—about eight years old—for, assisted by exercise, such as he took, it was many years before it injured him. But, alas! wine at length lost its charms; brandy—which he was a stranger to when I was last at Halston—was substituted, and the constitution of John Mytton, *perhaps the hardest ever bestowed upon man*, was not proof against that.

THE LIFE OF JOHN MYTTON, ESQ. OF HALSTON, SHROPSHIRE
Nimrod, 1835

Alcoholic
Questions and Answers

RED NOSES

Q. Apollo, *Pray answer,*
That is, if you can, Sir,
The Question I'm about to propose:
If you please, you may banter,
If you cannot answer,
Why drinking strong Liquors should cause a red Nose?
A. 'Tis the Fumes of your Wine,
Make your *Boltsprit* thus shine,
Which ascending the Top of your *Cranium:*
Nature Healthfully throws
On your prominent Nose,
And proclaims you a jolly Companion.

Q. *Having a red Nose, which, possibly, was occasioned by drinking too much Wine, I desire to know, whether living more abstemiously, as to drinking, for the future, or by any other easier way, I may probably reduce my Nose to its former Colour.*

A. Your Abstinence from the immoderate use of Wine, may, perhaps somewhat lessen the splendor of your Nose, or, at least, prevent the increase of it, as also the bulk of your Nose itself. For *Bacchus,* as well as *Venus,* claim a residence in that part, and his Vassals are as eminently display'd by the Augmentation, as her's are by the diminution of it; and therefore, if *Apollo* may advise you, keep your Hand from your Head, lest your Nose and Pocke prove both Heteroclites, and you become in a literal Sense, entituled to the following Epigram:

Tongilian hath a *Nose,* 'tis true,
And nothing else but *Nose* can shew.

BUYER AND CELLAR—LIGHT WINE

DRINK AND SUICIDE

Q. *I must desire you to answer this Question, which is the greatest Sin, for a Man to kill himself immediately upon the spot, or to drink to Excess, so that, he knows, it impairs his health, and will most certainly shorten his days.*

A. Tho' Drinking to Excess be no Inconsiderable Crime, with regard to Self-murder, as well as other Imputations, yet it is not upon the Level with the notorious iniquity of an Immediate dispatch. And this will appear upon these Reflections.

1. Self-murder suffers the guilty wretch *to find no place for repentance, tho' he should seek it carefully with tears.* But the Drunkard may Repent and Live.

2. The Principal Ingredient to the Heinousness of Self-murder takes it's origin from hence, that to quit our Station before our appointed time, is an unworthy encroachment upon His Prerogative, who has an absolute dominion over us. The more Immediately therefore we quit our Station, the greater is our Sin.

3. To dispatch our selves at once has something of more *Daring* Impiety, than to cause our Lives to wear away by more Insensible Decays.

4. Tho' Excessive Drinking may daily impair our Bodies, yet before it prove the occasion of our Death, we may be snatcht away by some *Foreign* Cause. And then the very Fact of Self-murder is not chargeable upon us. But tho' this by way of Comparison may Extenuate, yet it cannot Excuse the Crime. For as we ought not to put so important an affair upon so Precarious an issue, so we are Imputatively guilty of Self-murder, while we venture upon such forbidden ways, as will infallibly retrench the number of our days, unless something interpose to prevent the Consequence.

OVER THE LEFT THUMB

Q. *Say, whence, Great Apollo,*
The Custom we follow,
When drinking brisk Liquors per Bumper:
In a Circular Pass,
We quaff e'ry Glass
And why it is o'er the left Thumb sir?

A. When Mortals with Wine,
Make their Faces to shine,
'Tis to look like *Apollo* in Luster;
And Circulatory.
To follow his Glory,
Which over the left Thumb they must Sir.

DRINK AND SPEECH

Q. *Great Sons of Apollo,*
Whom Multitudes follow,
For solution of difficult Doubts;
Pray tell me at pleasure,
When I've drank out of measure,
Why my words in such Clusters come out.
When I'm free from Grape's Juice,
My Tongue will produce,
Plain English as taught by the Grammer;
But a Pint of that same,
Makes it falter and lame,
And speak thick, like a Man that does stammer?

164

THE DEBATING SOCIETY, 1809

A. Since your Volatile Head,
By one Pint's thus misled,
And your Grammar does suffer so plainly;
To the Glass be not prone,
But let Tippling alone,
Or 'twill shatter your Poetry mainly.
For the Fumes of your Wine,
To the Spirits Assign,
Perverse and inordinate Motions,
Whence the Nervous default,
Makes your Clapper thus halt,
And express such impalpable Notions.

DRINK AND VIOLENCE

Q. *The uneasiness that a late ill Accident has brought on me, is the Author of this Address to you. The Accident was this:*

Some months since, through the Excess of Drinking, I was seiz'd with a very high Fever, and in the Delirium, I gave my Wife a Blow upon her left Breast, as she was offering me something to drink which (in the Judgment of her Physicians) produc'd a Cancer, of which she lately dy'd,

Now, I desire to know whether I am accountable for any Action committed without Consciousness, altho' it's the Consequent of a Crime committed with.

A. Where there is a melancholy Consequence of any Crime, we have been guilty of, which is entirely accidental, and could not possibly be fore-seen, we are chargeable with no other Guilt, than that of the Crime it self. But Drunkenness is attended with many terrible Consequences, which strangely aggravate its Sinfulness, and render it the more exceeding sinful. A Fever frequently proceeds from drinking to Excess, a consequent Delirium from such Excess, and unaccountable Actions from such Delirium. Whence we become the more strictly bound religiously to abstain from those Offences, of which, we know not what may be the dismal issue. And therefore you do well to be uneasy, so you be but careful, that your Uneasiness advance not to any, the least degree of unwarrantable Desperation. For you must not look upon your self as a Murderer, but as a kind of inadvertent Accessory. And indeed all Drunkards are equally guilty with your self, since, however, they might have been more happy than to have met so fatal a Circumstance ensuing from their Drunkenness, yet they could no more than you, warrant to themselves so undeserv'd an Happiness. Not but that you are yet oblig'd

166

more severely to bewail your Drunkenness, since the Tragedy that ensued, must have given you a more lively Sense of so dangerous a Sin. And upon the same Account you are under a stricter Obligation never to repeat the Crime, never more to be *drunk with Wine, wherein is Excess*.

DRUNKENNESS OR FORNICATION

Q. *Having had a great Dispute with one, (a single Person, as I am) whether Drunkenness, or Fornication, are Sins of an equal degree, I desire you therefore to inform me, which is the greatest before God?*

A. They are both Sins of so deep a dye, as to be stigmatiz'd in the Sacred Oracles, with the severest Censures. But tho' each of them is inclusive of so peculiar a Turpitude, that Fornication in some respects, and Drunkenness in other, may seem chargeable with the highest Guilt, yet from that memorable Passage in 1 *Cor.* 6. from the 13*th Verse*, to the end of the *Chapter*, one wou'd be apt to conclude, that Fornication, in the general were the most aggravated Sin. And since the foresaid Passage includes very powerful and persuasive Arguments against so enormous a Transgression, you would do well to peruse it with an attentive Seriousness. But if it be objected, That by some other unlawful Actions, we sin also against our own Bodies, we answer, That the Apostle, in the cited Passage, intends not the Argument as utterly exclusive of all, but most other Sins, and perhaps with regard to Drunkenness, inclusive of a more eminent degree. It must be confest, that Drunkenness is attended with a large Train of very fatal Consequences, that balance many Arguments on the other side.

But, after all, in Sins of so great a Magnitude, and at least very nearly equal in their Guilt, you should not make it matter of concern, nicely to distinguish which of them is the greatest, but rather, with equal Care, with equal Solicitude to avoid them both.

THE FUMES OF YOUR LIQUOR

Q. *Oh wonderful* Phoebus:
   In omnibus rebus,
So diverting, so pleasant and witty,
   So ready to answer
   Each Poetick Advancer,
That attacks you from Suburbs or City.

Pray tell me the reason,
Ev'n at any Season,
If I toss off but one Pint of Tipple;
When in Wezon 'tis gone,
For another I bone,
As much as a Child does for the Nipple;
And so for a Third,
And yet, on my Word,
I protest I'm as sound as a Roach:
No diseases nor Aches,
The Plagues of poor Wretches,
Did ever my Body approach.
If you say I'm a Sot, you do me Injustice,
For a Truth I affirm it, or in Mortal no trust is.
   A. Since so pleasant you deem us,
    Tibi gratias agemus,
And your Fuddling Proposal we'll Answer,
    And will totally rout,
    This particular Doubt,
Be you Tippler, Sot, or Romancer,
    'Tis the Fumes of your Liquor,
    That makes your Tongue quicker,
And engender a Heat in your Wezon,
    Which does certainly cause,
    That great Drowth in your Jaws,
And your *Cranium* does frequently seize on.
    For, tho' you pretend,
    Your Health to commend,
And seem free from Distemper in *Ano*;
    Yet we safely dare swear,
    You don't always appear,
With *Mens Sana in Corpore Sano.*
But here as a Toper we do not accuse ye,
Tho', did we, 'tis doubted, we should not abuse ye.

THE WATER DRINKER

Q. *Whether Water, if drank from Youth, would not be more agreeable to the Man than any Artificial Liquors.*

A. The Drinking of Water may be beneficial to some Constitutions, but destructive to others; and more especially to those, who inhabit cold Countries; nor do we find it agreeable in the Hotest Countries; for there the Transpirations are so great, that the strongest Liquors are scarcely powerful enough to supply the Great Expence of Spirits.

THE BRITISH APOLLO
Second Edition, 1711

DRINKING AND BLINDNESS

Q. I am under a very great Misfortune, and humbly beg your Advice; I have by long and hard drinking almost lost my Eyes, yet I hope if I forsake it, it would much conduce to the Recovery of my sight, but I am so much influenced by bad Company and a bad Habit, that I find it too hard to do, though 'tis like to cost me so dear as my Eyes; I beg your speedy Advice, which, by God's Assistance, I do resolve to follow. I pray don't fail, and you will very much oblige, etc.

A. Nay, if you have more Respect for our Judgment than for your own Eyes, we may do some good upon you; this ill Habit is generally more difficult to quit than any, yet since you seem to be sensible of the ill Effects on't, and the Necessity of leaving it, 'tis probable you may in Time get rid on't; but as it has been long contracting, so you cannot expect to forsake it presently; you must not only resolve against it, but likewise take such Measures as may make your Resolution effectual. Begin with spending one Hour in a Day less in this lewd Company and Drinking than is your usual Custom, and if possibly you can command yourself so far, drink something less; thus make strong Resolutions every Morning: And though you should fail once or twice, or more, let not that discourage you, but still pursue them, and in some time you'll make it easy to you; and having gained thus much, go on and make it two Hours, and so till you have got the entire Conquest. And if you are so happy as to be successful in the Attempt, be sure never to admit of any such Acquaintance again: But 'tis not only your Eyes that lie at Stake, but your Conscience, your Heaven, your All, your Interest and Duty are both Advocates; think of this, and then act as you think fit.

THE PUBLICAN'S DILEMMA

Q. One that keeps a Public-house desires to know what Rules to follow, that he may not displease God, nor offend his Guests, as to the Season of Time, and Quantity of Liquors?

The GIN Shop.

" " now Oh dear, how shocking the thought is   They do it on purpose folks lives to shorten.
  They makes the Gin from aquafortis :   And tickets it up at two-pence a quartern.   "

                                                                                      New Ballad

Designed Etch'd & Publ.ed by Geo Cruikshank — November 1.st 1829.

A. 'Tis an unanswerable Question; for 'tis impossible for a Person that keeps a Public-house, to carry himself so (under the fore-mentioned Circumstances) that he should not offend God, and yet gratify his Guests (generally speaking); but thus far may be done, which is the most that can be expected—viz. That no just Cause of Offence may be given; and such People as think they have cause, when they have not, you have this satisfaction, That you do 'em Friendship, and such as all honest Men must applaud, nay, themselves, when they come to be sober. The Method to be taken in such a management (we conceive) is this, As to the Quantity of Liquors to be vended to particular Persons, no Limits can be assigned, since Persons are of so different Constitutions, that what is necessary to the Refreshment of Nature in some Persons may be Intemperance in others; so that the Rule here is: You may let all Persons call on till you find they begin to exceed their due Limits; and when you perceive 'em entering the Confines of Drunkenness, 'tis Wickedness in you to let 'em proceed any further, since thereby you become accessory to all the Irregularities they shall commit in their Drunken Humours; and how great ones some have been guilty of then is Argument enough to deter all thinking Persons. As to the Time, you may (as near as you can) safely observe the Custom of your civilised Neighbours; to exceed may be Scandalous, and bring an ill Repute upon you, and to do less may be against an honest Interest.

THE ATHENIAN ORACLE
John Dunton, 1728

They Also Serve

THE WICKED BREWERS

You have already began a charitable work amongst you, I mean your common town brewhouse, the profit of which you intend shall be wholly employed for the supply of the poor and impotents which live in your city; from which sort of people, being such a multitude, the brewers there have found their best custom; for no doubt but the meanest beggar amongst you is, in some sort, more valiant than the richest man, because the one dares to spend all he hath at the ale-house, so dares not the other; for the poor man drinks stifly to drive care away, and hath nothing to lose, and the rich man drinks moderately, because he must bear a brain to look to what he hath. And of all traders in the world, a brewer is the loadstone, which draws the customers of all functions unto it. It is the mark or upshot of every man's aim, and the bottomless whirlpool that swallows up the profits of rich and poor. The brewer's art, like a wild kestrel or unman'd hawk, flies at all games; or like a butler's box at Christmas, it is sure to win, whosoever loses. In a word, it rules and reigns, in some sort, as Augustus Caesar did, for it taxeth the whole earth. Your inns and alehouses are brooks and rivers, and their clients are small rills and springs, who all, very dutifully, do pay their tributes to the boundless ocean of the brewhouse. For all the world knows that if men and women did drink no more than sufficed nature, or if it were but a little extraordinary now and then upon occasion, or by chance as you may term it; if drinking were used in any reason, or any reason used in drinking, I pray ye what would become of the brewer then. Surely we do live in an age, wherein[1] the seven deadly sins are every man's trade and living. Pride is the maintainer of thousands which would else perish, as mercers, tailors, embroiderers, silkmen, cutters, drawers, sempsters, laundresses, of

[1] Some make a profit of quarreling, some pick their living out of contentions and debate, some thrive, and grow fat by gluttony, many are bravely maintained by bribery, theft, cheating, roguery, and villany; but put all together, and join to them all sorts of people else; and they all in general are, drinkers and consequently the brewers, clients, and customers.

172

which functions there are millions which would starve but for madam pride with her changeable fashions. Lechery, what a continual crop of profit it yields, appears by the gallant thriving and gawdy outsides of many he and she, private and public sinners, both in city and suburbs. Covetousness is embroidered with extortion, and warmly lined and furred with oppression. And though it be a devil, yet is it most idolatrously adored, honoured, and worshipped by those sheep-headed fools, whom it hath undone and beggared. I could speak of other vices, how profitable they are to common-wealth; but my invention is thirsty and must have one carouse more at the brewhouse, who, as I take it, hath a greater share than any in the gains which spring from the world's abuses; for pride is maintained by the humble, yet one kind of pride doth live and profit by another. Lechery is supported by the cursed swarm of bawds, panders, pimps, applesquires, whores, and knaves; and so every sin lives and thrives by the members, agents, ministers, and clients, which do belong unto them, but drunkenness plays at all; all trades, all qualities, all functions and callings can be drunk extempore. Note at any great feast, or but at every ordinary dinner or supper almost, when men are well satisfied with sufficiency, that then the mystery of quaffing begins with healths to many an unworthy person, who perhaps, would not give the price of the reckoning to save all them from hanging, which make themselves sick with drinking such unthankful healths. I myself have oftentimes dined or supped at a great man's board, and when I have risen, the servants of the house have enforced me into the cellar or buttery, where, in the way of kindness, they will make a man's belly like a souse-tub, and enforce me to drink, as if they had a commission under the devil's great seal to murder men with drinking with such a deal of complimental oratory, as off with your lap, wind up your bottom, up with your tap-lash, and many more eloquent phrases which Tully or Demosthenes never heard of; that in conclusion I am persuaded three days fasting would have been more healthful to me than two hours feeding and swilling in that manner.

If any man hang, drown, stab, or by any violent means make away his life, the goods and lands of any such person are forfeit to the use of the king; and I see no reason but those which kill themselves with drinking should be in the same estate, and be buried in the highways with a stake drove through them. And if I had but a grant of this suit, I would not doubt but that in seven years, if my charity would agree with my wealth, I might erect almshouses, free-schools, mend highways, and make bridges; for I dare swear that a number, almost numberless, have confessed upon

THE CALL

their death-beds that at such and such a time, in such and such a place, they drank so much which made them surfeit, of which they languished and died.[1] The main benefit of these superfluous and man-slaughtering expenses comes to the brewer, so that if a brewer be in any office, I hold him to be a very ungrateful man if he punish a drunkard; for every stiff pot-valiant drunkard is a post, beam, or pillar, which holds up the brew-house; for as the bark is to the tree, so is a good drinker to a brewer.

A NEW DISCOVERY BY SEA WITH A WHERRY FROM LONDON TO SALISBURY
John Taylor, 1623
[1] Let these lines be considered if I lie or not.

THE RIVAL BREWERS

Concerning a pair of brewers, and a piece of justice. Another short Norfolk tale is not impertinent. There was one Master Fen, a brewer at Fensham, and one Master Francis Dix, a brewer at Sapham. This Dix was riding in the country amongst his customers, the inn-keepers and victuallers, and he called for a pot of ale or beer as he rode by. Now that ale-house was a customer to Fen, as soon as Dix had drank he asked who brewed that drink, to whom the hostess said that Master Fen of Fensham brewed it. 'Well', said Dix, 'I dare lay a wager, that I will give my mare but a peck of malt, and she shall piss better drink than this'; at the last these words came to Fen's hearing, for the which disparagement he sued Dix, and recovered from him twenty pound damage, besides cost, at the Assizes last at Norwich, 1639.

NEWS FROM HELL, HULL, AND HALIFAX
John Taylor, 1639

THE LICENSING MAGISTRATES

What shall the poor drink? How shall they drink it—in pint cups or quart mugs—hot or cold—in the morning or the evening. Whether the Three Pigeons shall be shut up, and the Shoulder of Mutton be opened. Whether the Black Horse shall continue to swing in the air, or the White Horse, with animated crest and tail, no longer portend spirits within. All these great questions depend upon little clumps of squires and parsons gathered together in alehouses in the month of September—so portentous to publicans and partridges, to sots and sportsmen, to guzzling and game. There are two alehouses in the village, the Red Horse and the Dun Cow. It is common sense to suppose these two publicans are not desirous of gaining customers from each other?—and that the means they take are not precisely the same as those of important inns—by procuring good articles, and retailing them with civility and attention. We really do not mean to accuse English magistrates of ill-nature, for in general there is a good deal of kindness and consideration among them, but they do not drink ale, and are apt to forget the importance of ale to the common people. When wine-drinkers regulate the liquor and comfort of ale-drinkers, it is much as if carnivorous animals should regulate the food of gramini-vorous animals—as if a lion should cater for an ox, or a coach-horse order dinner for a leopard. There is no natural capacity or incitement to do the thing well—no power in the lion to distinguish between clover and cow thistles—no disposition in the coach-horse to discriminate between the succulence of a young kid and the distressing dryness of a superannuated cow. The want of sympathy is a source of inattention and cause of evil. The immense importance of a pint of ale to a common person should never be overlooked; nor should a good-natured justice forget that he is acting for Liliputians, whose pains and pleasures lie in a very narrow compass, and are but too apt to be treated with contempt and neglect by their superiors. Public houses are not only the inns of the travelling poor, but they are the cellars and parlours of the stationary poor. A gentleman has his own public-house, locked up in a square brick bin; *London Particular —Chalier 1802—Carbonell 1803 Sir John's present of Hock at my marriage; bought at the Duke's sale—East India Madeira—Lafitte—Noyau—Maraschino.* Such are the domestic resources of him who is to regulate the potations of the labourer. And away goes this subterraneous Bacchanalian, greedy of the grape, with his feet wrapped up in flannel, to increase, on the licensing day, the difficulties of obtaining a pot of beer to the lower orders of mankind!—and believes, as all men do who are deciding upon other person's pleasures, that he is actuated by the highest sense of duty, and the deepest consideration for the welfare of the lower orders. In an advanced state of civilisation, there must be always an advanced state of misery. In the low public-houses of great cities very wretched and very criminal persons are huddled together in great masses. But is a man to die supperless in a ditch because he is not rich, or even because he is not innocent? A pauper felon is not to be driven into despair and turned into a wild beast. Such men must be, and such men must eat and sleep, and if laws are wise and police vigilant we do not conceive it to be any evil that the haunts of such men are known, and in some degree subject to inspection. What is meant by respectable public-houses are houses where all the customers are rich and opulent. But who will take in the refuse of mankind, if monopoly allows him to choose better customers? There is no end to this mischievous meddling with the natural arrangements of society. It would be just as wise to set magistrates to digest for mankind, as to fix for them in what proportion any particular wants of their class shall be supplied. But there are excellent men who would place the moon under the care of magistrates, in order to improve travelling, and make things safe and comfortable.

The Rev. Sydney Smith (1771–1845)

A TAVERN

A Tavern is a degree, or (if you will) a pair of stairs above an Ale-house, where men are drunk with more credit and apology. If the Vintner's nose be at door, it is a sign sufficient, but the absence of this is supplied by the Ivy-bush: The rooms are ill breath'd like the drinkers that have been

SPORTSMEN

washed well over night, and are smelt too fasting next morning; not furnished with beds apt to be defiled, but more necessary implements, stools, table, and a chamber-pot. It is a broacher of more news than hogsheads, and more jests than news, which are sucked up here by some spungy brain, and from thence squeez'd into a Comedy. Men come here to make merry, but indeed make a noise, and this musick above is answered with the clinking below. The drawers are the civilest people in it, men of good bringing up, and howsoever we esteem of them, none can boast more justly of their high calling. 'Tis the best theater of natures, where they are truly acted, not play'd and the business as in the rest of the world up and down, to wit, from the bottom of the celler to the great chamber. A melancholy man would find here matter to work upon, to see heads as brittle as glasses, and often broken; men come hither to quarrel, and come hither to be made friends: and if *Plutarch* will lend me his simile, it is even *Telephus's* sword that makes wounds and curses them. It is the common consumption of the afternoon, and the murderer or maker-away of a rainy day. It is the Torrid Zone that scorches the face, and tobacco the gunpowder that blows it up. Much harm would be done, if the charitable vintner had not water ready for these flames. A house of sin you may call it, but not a house of darkness, for the candles are never out; and it is like those countries far in the North, where it is as clear at mid-night as at mid-day. After a long sitting, it becomes like a street in a dashing shower, where the spouts are flushing above, and the conduits running below, while the *Jordans* like rivers overflow their banks. To give you the total reckoning of it; It is the busy man's recreation, the idle man's business, the melancholy man's sanctuary, the stranger's welcome, the Inns-of-Court man's entertainment, the scholar's kindness, and the citizen's courtesy. It is the study of sparkling wits, and a cup of Sherry their book, where we leave them.

MICROCOSMOGRAPHY, OR A PIECE OF THE WORLD CHARACTERIZ'D
John Earle, 1628

AN ENGLISH INN

An English inn is a house of so ancient standing, as 'tis ready to fall down again; only its sign-post is new, and in that consists its greatest gallantry. Within 'tis a great machine on four wheels, hostler, cook, tapster and chamberlain, with mine host and hostess, the main-springs that move all the rest. Being entered, they all fall to cozening you in their several vocations; the hostler your horses, the rest you; the cook with meat so tough and raw-roasted, as spite of teeth y'are forced to leave it to the house; the tapster in so miscounting his stone jugs, as you may as well count the stoneage as them; then the chamberlain uses such cozenage with his faggots, as the fire itself can scarcely bring to light. For your chamber it seems the press-yard by the pillar of bed, with a teastern[1] so heavy, as if it fall on you, Lord have mercy upon you; and for more exquisite torment and lingering pain, you have a heavy tapestry for coverlet, in summer kills you with heat, and in winter with cold as well as weight; with a feather-bed whose feathers (as if you'd flounced into the water) part on either side, and leave you in the midst to sink into the bottom. For mine host and hostess, who were wont to be good fellows in the days of jollity, their humours are spoiled in this time of godliness, and stunn'd sack, and religion has quite marred their mirth; only mine host will make a shift to be half drunk every day, and on market days outright, when he is wondrous kind: and his kindness chiefly consists in a pint of sack to the master, and a double jug unto the serving-man, always in order to the reckoning, which as a warning piece being discharged once, there follows a whole volley of welcomes, like small shot discharged on every side, and you are discharged too.

ENIGMATICAL CHARACTERS
Richard Flecknoe, 1665

[1] The upper part of a bed.

EDINBURGH TAVERNS

Mrs Flockhart's

This landlady seems to have been the 'Mrs Flockhart of Waverly'.

Mrs Flockhart, or as she was more ordinarily called, *Luckie* Fykie, was a neat, little, thin woman, usually habited in a plain, striped blue gown, and apron of the same stuff, with a white 'mutch', having a black ribbon round the head, and lappets brought down along the cheeks and tied under the chin. She was well to do in the world; as the umquhile John Flucker or Flockhart had left her a good deal of money, together with his whole stock in trade, consisting in a multifarious variety of articles, such as ropes, tea, sugar, whipshafts, porter, ale, beer, butter, sand, caum stane, herring, nails, cotton, wicks, papers, pens, ink, wafers, thread, needles, tapes, potatoes, rubbers, gundy, spunks, colored eggs in their seasons, etc., etc.,—constituting what was then called a 'merchant' and now a small grocer. Mrs Flockhart sat, moreover, in a 'front loft' in Mr Pattieson's ghostly chapel in Bristo street, and was well-looked-upon by all her neighbours, on account of the quality of her visitors.

179

Mrs Flockhart's customers were very numerous and respectable, including Mr Dundas, afterwards Lord Melville,—Lord Stonefield,—Lord Braxfield,—Sheriff Cockburn,—Mr Scott, father of Sir Walter—Mr Donald Smith, banker,—and Dr Cullen. The use and wont of these gentlemen, on ˙entering the shop, and finding Mrs Flockhart engaged with customers, was, to salute her with 'Hoo do ye doo, mem?' and a *coup de chapeau*, and then walk 'ben' to the room, where, upon the bunker seat of the window, they found three bottles, severally containing brandy, rum, and whiskey, flanked by biscuits and gingerbread; the latter, either in thin, crisp, square cakes, called 'Parliament'—in round pieces, denominated 'Snaps' or in thin soft cakes, chequered on the surface, and according to its colour, called white or brown 'Quality', and biscuits. The gentlemen seldom sat down, but, after partaking of what bottle they chose, walked quickly off. Upon certain occasions, there was provided more solid fare than these simple refreshments—such as a chop-steak stew, prepared by Mrs Flockhart's own skilful hands. This entertainment, termed a 'soss', was always laid out on the bunker seat in the closet, which was covered with a clean napkin, there being room besides only for a chair.

After the death of her first husband, Mrs Flockhart, despairing of another, her stock (£800) in the hands of a banker, who allowed her a certain annuity. But she afterwards *did* procure another husband—namely, a highland pedlar, who, finding his hands much cramped by the annuity affair, proceeded to dilapidate her stock in trade, and was at length caught stealing (ominous article!) a coil of ropes. The old lady's banker, who was also her relation, then ordered the hotel to be shut up; and she died afterwards in Middleton's Entry, while enjoying the said annuity.

Daunie's

Daniel Douglas's Tavern, or, as it was more commonly called, *Daunie's* Tavern, was situated in the Anchor close, near the Cross. The house of which it composed one flat is extremely ancient, and was probably built for some religious purpose, as over the door, which is the second on the left hand down the close, there is the following inscription—'o LORD IN THE IS AL MY TRAIST'. *Daunie's* Tavern has been shut up for many years, like a plague-cellar; and the door, and the long, tall, religious-looking windows are overgrown with dust. Of course, it is at present impossible to get admission into the very scene of the orgies of the Pleydells and Fairfords, the Hays and the Erskines, of the last century; but curiosity may be gratified by the sight of the outside of a long line of windows, indicating a gallery within, along which those votaries of bacchanalian glory formerly passed to their orgies.

During the period when it flourished, *Douglas's* was one of the most noted and respectable taverns in Edinburgh. It could only be reckoned inferior to the *Star and Garter*, in Writer's court, which was kept by *Clerihugh*, and which was the chief resort of the then magistrates of Edinburgh (who had all their regular parties there,) as well as of Dr Webster, Lord Gardenstone, David Hume, John Home, and James Boswell. The entrance into *Douglas's* was by a low narrow passage, and up a few steps—in every respect resembling the description of Pleydell's Saturday-night house in Guy Mannering. The guests, before getting to any of the rooms, had to traverse the kitchen—a dark, fiery Pandemonium, through which numerous ineffable ministers of flame were constantly flying about, like devils in a sketch of the valley of the Shadow of Death, in the Pilgrim's Progress. Close by the door of the kitchen sat Mrs Douglas, a woman of immense bulk, spendidly arrayed in a head-dress of stupendous grandeur, and a colored silk-gown, with daisies upon it like sunflowers, and tulips as big as cabbages. Upon the entry of guests, she never rose from her seat, either because she was unable from fatness, or that, by sitting, she might preserve the greater dignity. She only bowed as they passed; there were numerous waiters and slip-shod damsels, ready to obey her directions as to the rooms in which the customers should be disposed; and when they went out, another graceful bend of the head acknowledged her sense of gratitude.

Daunie himself (for so he was always called) was—in perfect contrast to his wife—limber, nimble, and insignificant. He precisely personified Shakespeare's *Francis*, with only a few more words, but fully as passive and inane. The genius and tongue of his helpmate had evidently been too much for him; she kept him in the most perfect subjection, and he acted under her as a sort of head-waiter. He spoke very seldom—only when he was obliged to do so by a question—and seemed to have no ideas further than what were required to make a monosyllabic answer. Quietness—humble, peaceful, noteless quietness—was the passion of the man. He did every thing quietly—walked quietly, spoke quietly, looked quietly, and even thought quietly. He lived under his breath. So completely was he imbued with the spirit of quietness, or such was the effect of his quiet habits, that he acquired a trick of interjecting the word 'quietly', whenever he opened his mouth, or adding it to the ends of all his little quiet sentences, without regard to the construction of the said sentences, or the turn which it sometimes gave to their sense. Nor could he restrain himself from uttering it, even when speaking of things which had no relation whatever to quietness. A gentleman one day on entering the house, and being attended by *Daunie*, asked him, in a trivial way, if there were any news to day, 'No—sir' lisped the weakling,—'though—I—believe—the—Castle has—been—firing—the—day,—*quietly*'. On another occasion, being met in the street, along which he glided like a ghost, he was asked how Mrs Douglas was to-day, 'Ou,—sir,—she's—aye—flytin—away—*quietly*.

Daunie's Tavern was remarkable, above all other things, for its cheap and comfortable suppers. Vast numbers of people of every rank and profession, not excepting noblemen and judges, used to frequent it on this account. Tripe, minced collops, *rizzared* haddocks, and *haches*, were the general fare; and, what will surprise modern hosts, as well as modern guests, sixpence a-head was the humble charge for all these plenteous purveyances! Yet, such were the effects of Daniel's good management, that he got rich upon these charges, and left Mrs Douglas, when he died, in very good circumstances.

The convivialities of the time appear to have often assumed the shape of supper-parties. Undisguised 'even down drinking' was not the habit of all. There was a considerable minority of respectable persons, who wished to have some excuse for their potations, and this was afforded by their professing to meet at supper. Nevertheless, perhaps, while they seemed to gather together, as by chance, in Mrs Douglas's, for the mere sake of the 'crumb o'tripe', or the 'twa-three peas', or the 'bit lug o'haddo' ' (for such were the phrases), social mirth was in true verity their only object. Nor was the supper without its use; for, though some partook of it only as an incentive to subsequent potations, it generally acted as a sort of ballast in steadying their over-crowded top-sails through the tempests of the night.

The rooms in *Daunie's* tavern were all in a string, the kitchen being placed in the first rank, like a fugle-man, and serving to remind the guests, at their entry, of certain treats and indulgences which their stomachs would not otherwise have thought of. Beyond this, there was a passage or gallery, from which the rooms were entered, as well as lighted, and at the end was a large room, lighted from both sides. The latter was the scene of many a game (similar to that of 'high jinks' described in Guy Mannering), played on Saturday-nights by a club of venerable compotators, who had met regularly for the better part of a century, and grown, not gray, but red, in each other's company.

THE YEAR BOOK
William Hone, 1839

AN IRISH INN

Shortly before our close at Sligo, a party of us proposed to take a ride into the country, the first fine Sunday morning, to view some adjacent spots of renowned picturesque, and return home to dinner. The weather proving favourable the ensuing Sabbath, we fulfilled our design. Having taken our fill of the beauties of Nature, we then began to think of satisfying another sense—the palate, and rode to a shebeen-house situated on one corner of a common, with the usual distinctions of a red stocking, pipe-stem, and certain characters chalked on a board, signifying to those who could read them, that entertainment was to be had within for man and beast.

The furniture of this caravansera consisted of a large iron pot, two oaken tables, two benches, two chairs, and a whiskey noggin: there was a loft above (attainable by a ladder), upon which the inmates slept; and the space below was divided by a hurdle into two apartments,—the one for their cow and pig, the other for themselves and guests.

On entering the house, we discovered the family at dinner, (eleven in number,)—the father sitting at the top, the mother at the bottom, and the children on each side of a large oaken board, which was scooped out in the middle like a trough, to receive the contents of the pot of 'para-tees'. Little holes were cut at equal distances to contain salt, and a bowl of milk stood on the table; but all the luxuries of meat and beer, bread, knives, and dishes were dispensed with. They ate as Nature dictated, and as God had given;—they ate, and were satisfied.

The landlord was of the ordinary broad-backed, black-browed breed, with a leg like an elephant's, a face as round as the shield of Douglas, and a mouth which, when open, bore the same proportion to his head, that the sea does to the land. His wife was a sun-browned but well-featured woman, and his young ones (but that they had a sort of impish hilarity about them) were chubby, and bare enough for so many Cupids.

When we asked the landlord what he had to eat,—he said, 'Whiskey!' —What he had to drink,—'Whiskey!'—'What we could contrive to stay our stomachs on,'—his answer was still—'Whiskey!' There was nothing to be had at this place of entertainment but the one commodity. Luckily, one of our party had brought some sandwiches with him, and though scanty when distributed among six, we contrived nevertheless to make them a stopgap, and washed them down very pleasantly with some of our host's whiskey.

RETROSPECTIONS OF THE STAGE
John Bernard, 1830

THE CHURCH AND THE ALEHOUSE

He was wont to say that he did not care to have his servants goe to church, for there servants infected one another to goe to the alehouse and learne debauchery; but he did bid them goe to see the executions at Tyburne; which worke more upon them than all the oratory in the sermons.

AUBREY'S BRIEF LIVES
Sir Henry Blount, Traveller (1602–82)

THE SUNDAY-SCHOOL AT THE PUBLIC-HOUSE

Mr Charles Ridings, of Manchester, at a late Beer-Act meeting, informed his hearers 'that Sunday-school children were trained to watch public-houses on the Sunday'. We presume that, according to the Solomons of Manchester, this is in obedience to the injunction,—'train up a child in the way he should go, and when he is old he will not depart from it'. Anyway the training has already brought forth most remarkable effects. We are enabled by the kindness of persons—the trainers—too modest to allow their names to appear—to give a couple of the reports of these ingenuous, simple-minded children, these young lambs, trained to watch wolves of bitter beer, and the equivocating foxes of half-and-half. The experience of the children is written; and, we must say, the style and penmanship do great credit to the Sunday-school trainers of the Sabbath spies.

Matilda Peepwit, *of St Margery's*

'Was at the Punch-Bowl—least ways at the corner—all the time I was out of school and church. Saw a good many women go into the Punch-Bowl. Mrs Davis, Mary Tomkins, Julia Cloggs above any others. All had a look of drink when they went in, and all redder when they came out. A man asked me what I did there, when I told him I was waiting for my father. Father's been dead these three year. Thought it was Maria Sneep that went into the Bowl; but wasn't sure. Went in making believe to ask what was o'clock. Saw it was Maria: she see me and stooped to speak to me. Smelt of rum, I'm sure; and—no doubt on it—is a confirmed drunkard. Which is shocking for any one that loves her neighbour as herself.'

Nehemiah Wiggles, *of St Juniper's*

'Went last Sunday after church and stood opposite the Spoon-and-Nutmeg-grater. Took dinner in my pocket that, as I was bid, I might

184

TO A PUBLICAN.

'Tis thus fat Publican and sinner,
You rob the poor man of a dinner;
He who joins your club must be
The "Greatest Goose" that one can see.

I'm not the goose to call you mine, so get some other Valentine.

AN EARLY VALENTINE

give my heart and soul to the good work. Hadn't been where I was ten minutes when I saw Jem Blowfly, the butcher's man, come out with his mouth *very wet*: all froth and such like. Could lay my hand upon my heart an say it was beer. Jem looked at me, but I wouldn't see him. In half-an-hour Jem comes again with a bottle. He went into the house, and come out again, with the bottle tucked in his breast, but with the neck of it looking out, like the neck of a serpent.'

'Wisdom'—says the poet—'is found with children at her knees.' But there is a sort of Manchester wisdom that sends forth children as spies and eavesdroppers'.

Reproduced by permission of the Proprietors of PUNCH
27 January, 1855

AN HOST

An Host is the kernel of a sign: or the sign is the shell, and mine host is the snail. He consists of double beer and fellowship, and his vices are the bawds of his thirst. He entertains humbly, and gives his guests power, as well of himself, as house. He answers all men's expectations to his power, save in the reckoning: and hath gotten the trick of greatness, to lay all mislikes upon his servants. His wife is the cummin-seed of his dove-house; and to be a good guest is the warrant for her liberty. He traffics for guests by men's friends, friends' friends, and is sensible only of his purse. In a word, he is none of his own: for he neither eats, drinks, or thinks, but at other men's charges and appointments.

CHARACTERS OR WITTY DESCRIPTIONS OF THE PROPERTIES OF SUNDRY PERSONS
Sir Thomas Overbury, 1614

A VINTNER

A Vintner hangs out his Bush to shew he has not good Wine; for that, the Proverb says, needs it not. If Wine were as necessary as Bread, he would stand in the Pillory for selling false Measure, as well as Bakers do for false Weight; but since it is at every Man's Choice to come to his House or not, those that do, are guilty of half the Injuries he does them, and he believes the rest to be none at all, because no Injury can be done to him, that is willing to take it. He had rather sell bad Wine, than good that stands him in no more, for it makes Men sooner drunk, and then they are the easier over-reckoned. By the Knaveries he acts above-board, which every Man sees, one may easily take a Measure of those he does under Ground in his Cellar; but he that will pick a Man's Pocket to his

Mr. Alderman Abell and Richard Kilvert,
the two maine Projectors for Wine 1641.

Face, will not stick to use him worse in private when he knows nothing of it. When he has poisoned his Wines he raises his Price, and to make amends for that abates his Measure, for he thinks it a greater Sin to commit Murder for small Gains, than a valuable Consideration. He does not only spoil and destroy his Wines, but an ancient reverent Proverb, with brewing and racking, that says, *In vino veritas*, for there is no Truth in his, but all false and sophisticated; for he can counterfeit Wine as cunningly as *Apelles* did Grapes, and cheat Men with it, as *he* did Birds. He brings every Bottle of Wine he draws to the *Bar*, to confess it to be a Cheat, and afterwards puts himself upon the Mercy of the Company. He is an *Anti-christian* Cheat; for Christ turned Water into Wine, and he turns Wine into Water. He scores all his Reckonings upon two Tables made like those of the ten Commandments, that he may be put in Mind to break them as oft as possibly he can; especially that of stealing and bearing false Witness against his Neighbour, when he draws him bad Wine and swears it is good, and that he can take more for the Pipe than the Wine will yield him by the Bottle, a Trick that a *Jesuit* taught him to cheat his own Conscience with. When he is found to over-reckon notoriously, he has one common Evasion for all, and that is, to say it was a Mistake, by which he means that he thought they had not been sober

187

enough to discover it; for if it had past, there had been no Error at all in the Case.

THE GENUINE REMAINS IN VERSE AND PROSE
Samuel Butler, 1759

THE LANDLORD OF A COUNTRY HOTEL

How varied are the receptions, styles of entertainment, and salutations at departure, of the several proprietors of hotels, or commercial inns, throughout the kingdom; and in what a multifarious way they manage their business, make provision for their friends, and regulate their conduct; or address themselves to their various guests and supporters, it will be in the recollection of every one accustomed to perambulate.

The character which I here intend to pourtray will consequently, at once, be recognized by those acquainted with the road; for there is no district or division of the kingdom without many such. It will be, nevertheless, requisite in some measure to individualise, leaving of course the identity to the imagination. Inn-keepers generally have a tolerable rotundity. The subject of my present paper, however, is above the average in corporal obesity; burly as a cask of his own XXX, with a Saracenic head and ponderous double chin; apparently fed up with smoking, drinking bitter beer, and better beverages, with a broad Pecksniff sort of frill always oozing from his waistcoat, a smirk always upon his countenance, too doubtful to have the credit of sincerity; an oily, soft sawder, Sam Slick sort of tongue; a wheezy, self-satisfied, but suppressed horse-laugh; and one general mode of reception for all arrivers. And this habit compels him, parrot-like, to repeat, in a whining, insincere tone, over and over again, to the same persons every time they cross his path, whether entire strangers to him or visitors of long standing to his house, 'Well, my dear Sir, and how are you?—and how d'ye do, Sir? Beautiful weather, Sir, aint it?—and how have you been, Sir, since I last had the pleasure of seeing you, Sir?—and how did you leave your good lady, Sir, and the family, Sir—eh, Sir?' This is so constantly his wording and style of address, without previous consideration as to whether the gentleman addressed may be a stranger to him or not, or knowing whether he may be married or single, induces a feeling of unpleasantness, almost of disgust, in the party thus accosted. And his sycophantish smile, canting voice, and unceremonious thrust of a fist as clumsy as a mutton leg, and clammy as a clay-clod, into the hand of every guest, every time he meets him, is disagreeable and offensive.

188

The PUBLICAN'S COAT of ARMS.
Explain'd and Figur'd

A liberty of this kind is unwarrantable; and experience proves that the more scarce a landlord makes himself to the friends and supporters of his inn the better they are pleased with him. Men of business ordinarily have something more important to engage their time and attention, too, than the fawning servility and common-place expressions of an indolent, bloated, ignorant, bacchanalian, Boniface. A man steps out of his province who is always seeking opportunities of familiarity, and finding occasion for small talk and a lounge. The most sensible, respected, and successful, have ever been retiring; producing, in lieu of a bold presumptuousness of manner, the more solid essentials for regard of excellent arrangement and bountiful provision, with economy, and a properly marked attention, without being fulsome, officious, or dissembling. Who, possessed of common sense, cares a rush for the repeated inquiries of—'I hope you like your dinner, gents? How's the wine, gents? How d'ye do, altogether, gents? It's a fine day, gents': or the mechanical and insincere farewell, with the wave of the hand, 'Good bye! thank ye! much obliged!—take care of yourself, I can't be with you always' nonsense; or who, but an addle-pated fop, regards the formally raised gossamer, cringing bow, parasitical smile, and forced unmeaning courtesy, with the ringing of every bell, and summoning every servant, at arrival or departure? No! value received is the acknowledgment commercial men generally approve, in preference to such 'blarney', if I may be excused the expression; and nothing short of this will satisfy; and from the competition and alteration which railroads have produced, houses, which originally had an exclusive family and posting trade, are now cultivating a commercial business; and these essentials will, from opposition, be procured to a much greater extent, and at a more moderate cost, too. But let me warn this class of inn-keepers, and tell them that travellers by rail, coach, or their own con-veyance, at the present day, who leave home upon business, differ materially from their former supporters, the ostentatious loungers in a rumble or escutcheoned family carriage, who wanted, while halting between stages, nothing at an inn, in addition to the relay of horses, but a glass of water, a biscuit, and fulsome acknowledgment of their superiority. No! travellers will be satisfied without such formality so long as the provision is ample and excellent (well remunerating for what they have) but will not be well content with anything short of an attention courteous, respectful, and sincere.

THE DIARY OF A COMMERCIAL TRAVELLER
Throne Crick, 1847

A HANDSOME HOSTESS

A Handsome Hostess is the fairer commendation of an Inn, above the fair sign, or fair lodgings. She is the loadstone that attracts men of iron, gallants and roarers, where they cleave sometimes long, and are not easily got off. Her lips are your welcome, and your entertainment her company, which is put into the reckoning too, and is the dearest parcel in it. No Citizen's wife is demurer than she at the first greeting, nor draws in her mouth with a chaster simper; but you may be more familiar without distaste, and she does not startle at bawdry. She is the confusion of a pottle of sack more than would have been spent elsewhere, and her little jugs are accepted to have her kiss excuse them. She may be an honest woman, but is not believed so in her parish, and no man is a greater infidel in it than her husband.

MICROCOSMOGRAPHY, OR, A PIECE OF THE WORLD CHARACTERIZ'D
John Earle, 1628

THE LANDLADY

Plump priestess of the temple where
   Thousands libate from poison'd chalice,
And thus, to drown their grief and care
   Leave their *huts* and seek your *palace*,

The Town will strive, in prose and rhyme,
   To dwell at length upon your merits—
'Sir, pray proceed—I shall not *whine*,
   Nor let your *gag* depress my *spirits*.'

'My fame is known and heard afar;
   I've nothing *legally* to fear,
While swells will *practice* at my *bar*,
   To gain but one *brief* artful leer.'

Madam, we rarely blameth the fair,
   However sinful their employment;
But still we feel that gin-shops are
   A bane to rational enjoyment.

191

We shall now proceed to dilate upon the subject-matter before us, viz., the wholesale poison-selling palaces of the metropolis.

> 'Black *spirits* and white,
> Blue *spirits* and grey,
> Mingle, mingle, mingle—
> You that mingle may.'

The song of the witches in *Macbeth* over their cauldron, we think, would be an allowable and suitable *stave* to be sung by the London gin-spinners, while mixing their poisons—in their significant phraseology, termed 'making up their *spirits*.' Some of these worthies, who carry the *spirit* of competition to a great length, advertise gin at seven shillings per gallon, while the price they have to pay the distiller is about twelve shillings per gallon. The deleterious compounds used in its adulteration, we shall not attempt to set forth, because they are as varied as are the advertised prices of the commodity. We have heard the sinners themselves aver, that they can 'make up' gin at any price; but, the fact is, that the genuine article cannot be retailed to return the dealer a profit, under twelve-and-sixpence a gallon. Rums and brandies, are, of course, more or less reduced and adulterated; but with less pernicious ingredients than those used for the same purpose in gin. There can be no doubt that vast quantities of British brandy are consumed in the adulteration of foreign. This, perhaps, is the most harmless imposition of the whole; for it cannot be denied that the indiscriminate admission of some chemical preparations into the stomach, must undermine the constitution and 'depose the archeus' to an incalculable extent. Knowing these things, and the wholesale price of gin, it is worse than madness to purchase the cheap rubbish advertised and placarded by the leading spirit-merchants in London and its suburbs.

Since the days of the celebrated 'Landlady Meg', whose praises were taken as the poet's theme in the old song commencing thus:—

> ' 'Twas Landlady Meg that made such rare flip—
> Pull away, pull away, my hearties!
> At Wapping she lived, at the sign of the Ship,
> Where tars met in such jolly parties.'

Since the days, the golden days, of Mistress Meg, as we were saying, many and many a thorough-bred, rapid-paced, blooming widow has flourished in every locality in and approximating modern Babylon. Some years back, it was a common trick with brewers to place a good-looking woman in a public-house, in order to draw custom; then it was disposed of at a great price; the attraction removed with her, and, of course, all the business: so that, if the unlucky wight who took the house happened to be blessed, or rather cursed, with an ugly wife—for in such a case it would be so—he lost all his cash by the speculation.

The beauty of Bacon-street, Spitalfields, some seventeen years back, startled the public, and, for the time being, made a good house of a bad one. This lady awakened the lyric spirit of the Grub-street ballad-writers of the day, in a ditty called 'The Beauty of Bacon-street'; the burthen of chorus of which ran as follows:—

> 'The young ones run and the old ones creep,
> To see the beauty of Bacon-street.'

Her career, however, was of a very ephemeral description, for it was a regular 'do', and no mistake; her personal attractions did not bear out the encomiums passed upon her by some of the daily press, who were undoubtedly in the pay of the crafty and ingenious brewers. But modern times supply us with many very charming landladies, who are not put forth by designing capitalists, but by their own proper, legitimate, and lawfully-married spouses, as sources of attraction to gain business, and thereby yield profit to the concern. Yet it must be conceded, that a lady behind a bar is much more agreeable to customers, generally, than a man; the proper department of the licensed victualler, himself, is the cellar, of a morning, and his parlour, of an evening: he who can and will stick to this system, may safely leave his better-half to manage the rest, and finally ensure independence in the evening of his life.

The act of parliament orders, that all persons having licenses as victuallers shall provide accommodation for persons whose pursuits, avocations, or business may render it necessary or convenient to dine at a public-house; they are expected to cook a steak, chop, or any other eatable for any person who may require them to do so, and to afford accommodation for them to eat the same. This part of the act few of the metropolitan gin-palace keepers adhere to, unless, indeed, it be about the licensing time; then, perhaps, some temporary convenience is afforded, so that their licenses may not be suspended upon that account.

But we are getting out of the ladies almost, before we have got into them. The charming Mrs Bill, at the Shades, not a hundred miles from the Obelisk, has strong claims upon our notice, as one of the most fascinating of her craft. It was rumoured, some time since, that she was fond of listening to the story of Abdallah, in the *Arabian Nights' Entertainments;* but, we believe this report was without foundation, and that the *Bill,*

o

at present, has not been dishonoured. We trust it will always keep a good name to its back.

Then we have Lord Waterford's especial favourite, Mrs Emerson, who, every night, reposes in his lordship's *arms*. To prevent evil construction, we may observe, that the house the lady keeps is called the Waterford Arms. *Mother* as she is called by the numerous swells who have affiliated themselves upon her, is the most glorious of all landladies, and one of the cleverest women of the business on town—at least, in her particular line, which is priestess-in-chief, of a temple dedicated to Momus, 'neath the shades of night'. Mother, though not a very young 'un has preserved all her points—her charms seem to bid old Time defiance; despite his scythe and glass, they will not quit the scene of their former redolence.

A *Gine*va palace has been recently erected in Rupert street, Coventry-street, where two or three sprightly daughters of the proprietor enliven the scene; and, in good truth, choice *spirits* abound within the dwelling. But we must not dwell; so many have we to remark upon, that our space will not allow us to be critical.

The Old Bailey boasts the pretty Mrs Sharp; Basing-lane, the delightful Mrs Younghusband; and Newgate Market, the charming Mrs Pusey. In Bishopsgate-street, a blooming flower is planted in the Flower Pot; and the Marlborough Head has a good-looking face. Billingsgate too, recalls pleasing recollections: Mrs Clarke is a remarkably 'tidy sort'; and honest Joe Tomlinson, of Saint Mary-at-Hill, has a better half equal to his ancient namesake, of the Bell, who espoused the 'blue-eyed Sue'. The rib of Charley Wilson, at the Half-Moon, Gracechurch street, gives the customers a *cordial* welcome—at least, those who may be said to be con*gini*al spirits. In Goswell-street-road we have a pretty Mrs Jones; in Holborn, a light and sprightly Mrs Carter. Mrs Price, in Villiers-street, Strand, makes her visitors feel that the goods she vends are not dear at any *price*. Mrs Morris, and her daughter, the lovely Emma, hold regnant sway at the Castle, not a hundred miles from Gray's-inn-road; but there is a gentleman residing in Cursitor-street, Chancery lane, who may freely sing—

> 'Of all the girls that are so smart,
> There's none so *fat* as Sally;
> She is the darling of my heart,
> And she lives *just by the* alley.'

The particular solicitude of the neighbouring *bums* is devoted to Sally, for they all strive to *arrest* her attention. To go further a-field, Mrs Pople, of the Tottenham-court-road, is really a remarkably nice person; Mrs Robinson, of Oxford-street, is the very essence of politeness, and our jolly friend, Newman himself, is anything but a 'Pig in the Pound'. Mrs Bull, in Charlotte-street, Fitzroy-square, is both beautiful and good; while the 'wife of Teddy Roe', of Bell-street, Paddington, *wakes* her husband whenever occasion requires. In that suburban locality, the Kent-road, we meet with two lovely girls, daughters of our old friend and sporting associate, Harry England. The way in which Harry has brought up his family is highly creditable to him. But we are really getting too far out of Town; we could go on enumerating charming women, who superintend *palaces* of destruction, in and about the metropolis, till doomsday; but we must cut the subject for the present, otherwise we may be *brandied* for tediousness by some *rum* fellow, and this we do not desire, as *cordial*ity is our sole aim and drift.

THE TOWN
Renton Nicholson, 1838

THE BARMAID

Hail! smiling nymph, of *spirits* gay,
   Although you're often *wineing*,
With pleasure we shall hail the day
   When Hymen's wreath you're twining.

Of witching beauty is thy form,
   Thine eyes of heav'nly blue;
I'd care not should the world prove false,
   If you to me were true.

We have too much gallantry to call her a sinner, though we are free to admit that, being a daughter of that seducing creature, Mrs Eve, it is impossible that she can be totally without sin; but let us hope that she has as little as the frail composition of womankind can be mixed up with, so as to hold together. She is a strikingly buxom person, young and fascinating; and, in saying this, we say quite enough respecting her age, for the ladies, generally speaking, do not like that trifling particular, in their passage through life, meddled with, therefore we are mute upon the matter.

Our sketch is that of a blooming bar-maid in the North of London. There is no doubt many of our readers will recognize her; but if they do not, we cannot help it. She is chatty and agreeable, smiling, unaffected,

195

and pretty, with a perfect knowledge of the fact. She may be said to have been born a publican; her father was in the line, but, being unfortunate, seceded from business some years since. We have little more to say of her, further than to observe that, in our humble ideas of things in general, some Act should be provided to prevent her, as well as most her craft, looking so abominably wicked at many of her Majesty's liege subjects male. We fear, however, that these observations come too late; the petticoat dynasty is too firmly seated, in more senses than one, for us to hope to shake off woman's supremacy, at least in the present reign.

But this is a digression, we must to the humbler walks of female sovereignty, and treat of *bar practice* in its most harmless sense of application. Of a verity some of the *gin-spinners* are excellent judges of the power of personal attractions; those who have not a pretty daughter themselves contrive to get the pretty daughter of some body else; they place her at the bar, and her bright eyes and pretty face bring more *suitors* to her court in a day, than all the eloquence of the legal brotherhood at another bar would in a year.

Progressing towards the West, in Rupert-street, Coventry-street, three *petite* beauties, a formidable array, stand forth and plead the cause of their father, with Portia-like tact and ability. The gorgeous Mrs Emerson, at the Waterford Arms, in the same neighbourhood, leads in every case of importance; but she has sometimes as many as three juniors retained with her. The smiling Betty and the laughing Nelly kindly officiate at busy times.

In the East the bar-maids degenerate; they are fatter and coarser than in the West, and not nearly so refined in their manners; but we must do them the justice to say, that they smile, chat, and occasionally wink, with as much wickedness of intention as any of their sisterhood in other parts of the metropolis.

Then the South, oh, the South! If our gentlemen readers want a specimen of bar-maids in the South, let them go—first of all taking the precaution to borrow a cuirass to protect a certain little jumping gentleman underneath their flannel waistcoats—let them go, we repeat, to the Fountain, in Blackman-street, Borough. Many and many a 'Man about Town' has lost his heart while drinking the potent *waters* of that same fountain.

> Rash youth, from that fountain
>   Turn on thy way,
> Though it lies over mountain,
>   Haste thee, I pray.

London Published by Tregear 123, Cheapside

THE OBLIGING BAR-MAID.

Do you like it mild. Sir?

There dwell at that fountain
  Eyes that are bright,
Spirits the choicest,—
  Hearts that are light!

Leave them, and wander,
  Though dreary thy way;
If you enter, young Cupid
  Will lead you astray.

THE TOWN
Renton Nicholson, 1837

A WAITRESS AT A COUNTRY HOTEL

The dependants at hotels are, to-night, from having a capital specimen before me, vividly presented to my observation; as they are endless in their variety, and in some instances remarkable samples of mortality, they will not, I feel assured, prove an uninteresting theme for speculation.

Various are the opinions offered, and frequently is the subject canvassed, respecting the advantage and superiority of women over men as waiters, and *vice versa;* but I think that, after all the *pros* and *cons*, women are entitled to the preference. When women understand their business, and are not spoiled by an undue familiarity—which is usually, however, the consequence of a liberty given by those upon whom they practise it—they are more congenial to our taste, more home-like and agreeable in their manners, more consonant to the feelings of mankind generally than men-waiters. The willing inclination of the cheerful dispenser of creature-comforts here, without partiality or favouritism, who is even while I write observant of my wants—attempting to furnish, without waiting to be asked for, all the little additions to a repast, which although not costly are not the less acceptable, and from the spirit in which they are provided are always certain of a proper appreciation—is very grateful. I have often wondered how men can at times so far forget themselves as to give utterance to hasty and petulant remarks, to offensive language, to a bearing of austerity and harshness towards this almost (because the parties dare not reply) helpless and mostly deserving class of industrious servitors. This, indeed, is more a subject of regret than of gratulation, though some may seem to pride themselves upon an almost momentary exhibition of their superiority and importance; especially as, without descending to an equality, orders may so be given, wishes or desires may be so expressed, and commands be so pleasantly delivered, as to convey a feeling of pleasure to the respectful and submissive attendant, alleviating, in some measure, the painful consideration of dependence which they who serve, feeling their inferiority of position, cannot altogether divest themselves of. Certain it is, that a man will always, by suavity and forbearance, experience more satisfactory attention, and command a more obedient regard, than by an incessantly irritable and discontented practice of finding fault. Any woman, who can for years, early and late, stationarily and steadily pursue the arduous duty of a waitress, at a well frequented hotel, has more than a few hardships to contend with, and slight and rare opportunities of enjoyment beyond the scene of her labours. She in fact lives daily in subjection, and at the discretion of the various, ever-changing, unceasing diversity of characters which occupy the commercial room; men who embody every variety of temperament, disposition, intelligence, and ignorance, with all the strange and unaccountable biases which go to make up the motley group of human peculiarity, not unfrequently excited and carried beyond itself, by disappointment, chagrin, or perhaps excessive indulgence. Women in this capacity are often compelled to listen to uncalled for reproach, and bound to be respectfully attentive, while writhing under a weight of unmerited censure. She who lives daily subject to such annoyance, almost without enjoying the pure breath of heaven, and hardly ever emerging beyond the threshold of the inn—whose unintermitting occupation, distending the muscles, increasing the size of the ankle and width of the foot, while ascending and descending a flight of steps from the kitchen to the travellers' room and bar, and back again into the kitchen to inhale the sickening repetiton of the steaming, oft-cooked soups and joints, and the more foul tongue of the coarse and vulgar cook—claims at least our respect. She is seldom dejected, however; and her neat and cleanly appearance, and invariable good-humour, constantly cheer us; for although her once rosy tinged and healthy looking cheek is now blanched, and has long lost its colour in our service, it has not lost its power to charm. Yet although her spirit may be willing, her flesh is evidently weak, and indicates not only unceasing labour by day but wearing, wearying, fatigue by night. Until after the ' 'witching hour', she is enveloped in smoke: the air of the room—the only air she breathes—is impregnated with the effluvia of principee, Dutch-cut and Havannah, till she is all but smoke-dried. Well, therefore, does she deserve our sympathy, and well does she merit her hardly earned pittance of threepence per meal, or sixpence *per diem*. Yet she is playful, without descending to immodesty; and there is a pardonable trifling gaiety in her manner, and a humorous tendency in her words and actions, mingled with so much good sense, that the most licentious are kept at a proper and respectful distance, and totally disarmed by her decorous firmness and becoming confidence. She is ever alive, notwithstanding, to our inclinations and desires, and almost before the wish has been expressed she cheerfully supplies our wants.

Such is one specimen of a worthy and respected waitress; and if all are not equally so, let the commercial body take the condemnation to themselves; for a trifling, frivolous bearing, and a looseness of expression have frequently produced a laxity of morals much to be condemned, but which I am happy to find, from the perpetual onward movement, is giving place to a much more correct, moral, and desirable state of things.

THE DIARY OF A COMMERCIAL TRAVELLER
Throne Crick, 1847

THE BARMAN

What ho! thou *hale, stoud* lad of merit,
    We cannot say thou'rt welcome here;
For thousands but imbibe thy *spirit,*
    To lay their bodies on a *bier.*

'Pray, Mr *Town,* don't cast on me
    The gist of other people's shame;
If brandy they prefer to tea,
    'Tis they, not I, as is to blame.

'I know that you are always *rum,*
    And *brandied* so by fame,
That you can give con*gin*ial fun,
    When mirth is on the wane.

'Then blame me not for others' sin,
    But on the fools bestow your patter,
Who spend their *browns* in creaming gin,
    Instead of wholesome teas and *gatter.*

A sturdy-built young fellow is a most necessary adjunt to a gin-shop; in fact, in many neighbourhoods, such an addendum is indispensable, particularly in St Giles's, Westminster, Covent Garden, the back settlements of Holborn, Whitechapel, and by the waterside. Experienced practitioners at 'the bar' state, that a young man, or a lad, though not so attractive to many, is far more serviceable in the business than a blooming

THE BARMAN

lass; and the reason they explain for it is as follows:—There are a vast many sly gin-bibbers in the metropolis, who like to pop in and out of 'the palace' without observation or hindrance. This desideratum they can seldom achieve where a pretty girl serves at the bar, because so many half-witted lads, with side-locks, big sticks, and cigars, congregate around her, to whisper little nothings and soft pleadings in her ear; hence the secret imbibers of *max* peep in at the door, and, seeing how things stand, they mizzle to the next or nearest shop, where a masculine specimen of humanity dispenses the exhilarating though pernicious beverage.

It will, therefore, be seen that the advantage to the *ginist* in keeping a pretty bar-maid is counterbalanced by the disadvantage we have pointed out. There can be no doubt but that the office is one exceedingly inappropriate to the female sex. Nothing can be more repulsive to the delicate nature of women than the scenes of vice which are constantly enacted in the metropolitan gin-shops. Human nature is there placed before their eyes in its very worst form, and the habitudes of the profligate of their own sex displayed, without the exhibition of a corresponding feature of virtue to induce them to look upon the fair side as well as the dark.

Linen-drapers, man-milliners, and others are monopolising the crafts which are unquestionably intended as women's exclusive province. We may now find fault with the fair ones for interfering with that business which ought to be confined to the male sex. In a moral as well as physical sense, nature has not fitted females for such occupations. Any man who introduces his daughter into the bar of a gin-shop commits a moral offence of cardinal magnitude. The language spoken and the conduct exhibited in such sinks of iniquity are by far too gross to describe; however, most of our readers will bear us out in our position, viz., that youth of either sex ought not to be allowed to witness scenes of the description we have alluded to. A man can have but little regard for the morals or chastity of his daughter, who would seek to make money by a display of her charms behind the bar of a gin-shop; yet it is a course too often pursued by many amongst the licensed victuallers, who call themselves respectable.

The late Mr Henneky, a gin-spinning notoriety, was in the habit of spending a great deal of time on the continent. A friend once said to him, 'Why, Henneky, I think that your neglect of business causes your servants to rob you'. 'No doubt it does', replied Mr H,; 'but I can afford to be robbed of five hundred a-year, and then have a very handsome surplus income'. This conveys some idea to the public of the enormous profits arising from gin-palace proprietorship.

The licensed victuallers of London have of late become an overgrown, powerful body; they have got so much money that they actually appear at a loss in what way to invest it. The project most detrimental to their own interests is their steam-boat speculation. By affording people additional facilities for leaving London, they forget that they are injuring themselves, and sending their customers out of town to expend that cash which, if it were not for such facilities, would in all probability be expended at the taverns and tea-gardens in and about the metropolis.

> 'What crowds in summer-time we've seen
>   Go toiling up the hill,
> Which led to the Queen's Arms, to get,
>   For eighteen pence, their fill.'
> 'But now, alas! Those days are past, and all such customs fled.'

But good folk of London town, instead of enjoying the fragrant air of Hampstead, Highgate, Hornsey, or Highbury, on the Sabbath, take their bodies some hundred miles out by steam for the day, and the Londoners hear nor see nothing of them until, upon return, they stagger drunk from the steam-boat to the street, to give the police the trouble of seeing them safely home.

But to return to the subject of our sketch. We may remark that his leading characteristics are speed and civility; he is not unfrequently cellarman as well as barman, and in both capacities, no doubt, finds enough to do. His situation, either in winter or summer, is anything but a sinecure, for a more fatiguing calling cannot be well imagined. In the barman great trust is reposed; it is, therefore, necessary that he should be well paid, and placed above temptation. We are given to understand that they are, for the most part, well remunerated; and, considering that they are a large body, very few dishonest acts are publicly alleged against them.

The licensed victuallers are, generally speaking, a remarkably liberal race of men, both at home and abroad; they are famous for good living wherever they are found. Their fame in this respect, it is said, first induced the Duke of Sussex to preside at their annual dinner.

We perceive, by the public papers, that Mr Gurney prosecuted a barman about a fortnight since, who had contrived to rob him of three hundred pounds in a very short space of time. Surely there must be some mismanagement in this instance. People who so neglect their business inflict a wrong upon the public at large; it is a dereliction of duty highly reprehensible in any master.

THE TOWN
Renton Nicholson, 1838

203

The Warning

DRUNKARDS

A Drunkard is a noun-adjective; for he cannot stand alone by himself; yet in his greatest weakness a great tryer of strength, whether health or sickness will have the upper hand in a surfeit. He is a spectacle of deformity and a shame of humanity, a view of sin, and a grief of nature. He is the annoyance of modesty and the trouble of civility, the spoil of wealth and the spite of reason. He is only the brewer's agent and the ale-house's benefactor, the beggar's companion and the constable's trouble. He is his wife's woe, his children's sorrow, his neighbours' scoff and his own shame. In sum, he is a tub of swill, a spirit of sleep, a picture of a beast and a monster of a man.

THE GOOD AND THE BAD
Nicholas Breton, 1616

A Drunkard is one that will be a man to morrow morning, but is now what you will make him, for he is in the power of the next man, and if a friend the better. One that hath let go himself from the hold and stay of reason, and lies open to the mercy of all temptations. No lust but finds him disarmed and senseless, and with the least assault enters. If any mischief escape him, it was not his fault, for he was laid as fair for it as he could. Every man sees him, as *Cham* saw his father the first of this sin, an uncovered man, and though his garment be on, uncovered, the secretest parts of his soul lying in the nakedst manner visible: all his passions come out now, all his vanities, and those shamefuller humours which discretion clothes. His body becomes at last like a miry way, where the spirits are beclog'd and cannot pass: all his members are out of office, and his heels do trip up one another. He is a blind man with eyes, and a cripple with legs on. All the use he has of this vessel himself, is to hold thus much; for his drinking is but a scooping in of so many quarts, which are filled out into his body, and that filled out again into the room, which is commonly as drunk as he. Tobacco serves to air him after a washing, and is his only breath, and breathing while. He is the greatest enemy to himself, and the next to his friend, and then most in the act of his kindness, for his kindness is but trying a mastery, who shall sink down first: and men come from him as a battle, wounded and bound up. Nothing takes a man off more from his credit, and business, and makes him more retchlesly careless what becomes of all. Indeed he dares not enter on a serious thought, or if he do, it is such melancholy that it sends him to be drunk again.

MICROCOSMOGRAPHY, OR A PIECE OF THE WORLD CHARACTERIZ'D
John Earle, 1628

HIGH AND DRY.

Drunkenness is a sleepy Potion, which seizeth the faculties of the Soul, locking them up in a Lethargy of sin, depriving them of their Natural Function to the support both of the outward and inward man, whereby they come to lose their Active Vertues; it stifles the understanding with fumes of Wine, banishing from it the power of Reason, which distinguish-eth a Man from a Beast; it prompts the Will to all kind of Wickedness, and drowneth that Noble Register the Memory in the Sink of Brutality,

205

forgetting what it should remember, and remembring what it should forget. *Consider then (O man) with detestation this staggering sin of Ebriety, what a* Protean *Disguise it puts upon thee, that couldst thou see thy Monstrous hew in the Glass of discretion, how thou art reeling headlong in the way to Hell, was enough to fright thee into a sober temper: But while thou art snorting in this deathful sin, in this Swinish security (without infinite Mercy) thou maist awake in Hell.*

DUNTON'S REMAINS: OR, THE DYING PASTOUR'S LAST LEGACY TO HIS FRIENDS AND PARISHIONERS. John Dunton, 1684

A Sot has found out a Way to renew, not only his Youth, but his Childhood, by being stewed, like old *Eason*, in Liquor; much better than the *Virtuoso's* Way of making old Dogs young again: for he is a Child again at second hand, never the worse for the Wearing, but as purely fresh, simple, and weak, as he was at first. He has stupify'd his Senses by living in a moist Climate according to the Poet—*Bæotum in crasso jurare aere natum*. He measures his Time by Glasses of Wine, as the Ancients did by Water-Glasses; and as *Hermes Trismegistus* is said to have kept the first Accompt of Hours by the pissing of a Beast dedicated to *Serapis*, he revives that Custom in his own Practice, and observes it punctually in passing his Time. He is like a Statue placed in a moist Air; all the Lineaments of Humanity are mouldered away, and there is nothing left of him but a rude Lump of the Shape of a man, and no one part entire. He has drowned himself in a But of Wine, as the Duke of *Clarence* was served by his Brother. He has washed down his Soul and pist it out; and lives now only by the Spirit of Wine or Brandy, or by an Extract drawn off his Stomach. He has swallowed his Humanity, and drunk himself into a Beast, as if he had pledged *Madam Circe* and done her Right. He is drowned in a Glass like a fly, beyond the Cure of Crums of Bread, or the Sun Beams. He is like a Spring-Tide; when he is drunk to his high-Water-Mark he swells and looks big, runs against the Stream, and overflows every Thing that stands in his Way; but when the Drink within him is at an Ebb, he shrinks within his Banks, and falls so low and shallow, that Cattle may pass over him. He governs all his Actions by the Drink within *him, as a Quaker* does by the Light within him; has a different Humour for every Nick his Drink rises to, like the Degrees of the Weatherglass, and proceeds from Ribaldry and Bawdery to Politics, Religion, and Quarreling, until it is at the Top, and then it is the Dog-Days with him; from whence he falls down again, until his Liquor is at the Bottom, and then he lyes quiet, and is frozen up.

The greatest Drunkards are the worst Judges of Wine; the most insatiable Letchers the most ignorant Critics in Wimen; and the greediest Appetites, of the best Cookery of Meats—For those, that use Excess in any Thing, never understand the Truth of it, which always lies in the Mean.

THE GENUINE REMAINS IN VERSE AND PROSE
Samuel Butler, 1759

FATAL DOSES

One Eliz. Hill of Peckforton, having received the sacrament on Good Friday, went to an ale-house in the afternoon, and then was drunk, and staying late, as she was going home she fell and broke her head on a stone, was carried back to the ale-house, and died the next day.

In July one Lawrence Smith of Peckforton, a proud and profane man, and a hater of good men, especially Mr Hinde, having been at an ale-house near Malpas, and staying late till he was drunk, as he was riding, after a brother-in-law, one Darlington, he fell off his horse, and dashed out his brains against a stepping stone.

This year (1631) five Aldermen of Macclesfield met at a tavern, and drank excessively of sack and aqua vitae, three of them died the next day, and the other two were dangerous sick. Oh that drunkards would learn to be wise.

PROVIDENCE IMPROVED

E. D. Burghall, the puritanical vicar of Acton, begun in 1628, and ended 1663

THE RECKONING

In Inns now and then we feed plentifully, we drink off full bowls, we sing merrily, we dance and skip about: but as soon as the Host brings in the reckoning and calls his guests to an account, they are at a stand, they look one upon another, and at length break forth into these words: would to God we have never come hither! our shot is wonderful dear.

While we are here on our journey, we live in an Inn and unmindful of the reckoning, Feast jovially, carouse till within night, sing, sport and dance. But who will discharge the shot? O people ill advised! We must pay a just reckoning, though a dear one. Tis we have Banketted, Quaffed, and playd the good fellows; tis we have wasted our health, age and substance in riotous company keeping: Now mine Host calls for a discharge, just debts must be paid, Creditours will have satisfaction either from our Purses or Persons.

We have eaten, but with excess, with too much expence and delecacy; we have Feasted, but too often, and at too high a rate: We have fasted, but in a prophane manner and too seldome; we have buried our selves in Wine, we must now digest the surfetting. Wo, because we shall be hungry: eternal Famine, thirsts eternal expects us: O what a Supper after a full, but short dinner! while the damned lived they seem to have licked nothing but salt, so rageing is their thirst in hell.

A PLEASANT AND PROFITABLE TREATISE OF HELL
Hieremy Dexelius, S.J., translated 1668

YOUNG PEOPLE DRINKING

Mr Spectator,

Excessive drinking is become so universal of late among the younger sort, (especially since the vintners have lowered the price of their wines) that unless you interpose your speculations on that subject, it is to be feared the desease will become too epidemical to be rooted out by a single hand.

Our youth, possess'd by a drinking dæmon, seem to have laid aside all their former and more polite diversions of gallantry, to devote themselves to the bottle. Old age indeed may be allowed to supply their want of natural heat with free compotations, and to muster up all their fiery auxiliaries against their phlegmatick enemy the radical moisture; but for young fellows to employ the intervals between business and sleep in handing about the ungodly brimmer, is so preposterous, that I should never have believed it, had I not been convinced of the truth thereof by ocular demonstration: for going the other night to a spacious tavern near the Royal-Exchange, the drawer brought me to a little dirty box, saying, all the rooms above stairs were full, which at another time would have obliged me to go to another house, but being then minded to divert myself with a transient view of the several companies in that noisy tabernacle, I proposed to the drawer to change clothes, and to stay in the box while I went round into the upper apartments, which he readily accepted, being glad of a short intermission from his continual tripping up and down stairs. Having then put on his frock and blue-apron, and taking his snuffers in my hand, which, with a gentlemen d'ye call? introduced me into all the rooms on the first floor, the first of which I found full of beardless-boys, some with napkins about their heads, some without either cap or peruke, and all giving ear to a lewd setter, who, the better to ingratiate himself into their company, was singing a baudy-song

PRECEPT

Young men should practice, sans intermission, *until they can drink four bottles*
without being flustered, then they will be sober people, for it won't be easy to make
them tipsey, a drunken man I abominate ! ! !

to them. In the next room was a parcel of noisy young coxcombs, who
were toasting of healths, and talking by innuendo's of all the celebrated
beauties both in town and country, every one pretending that he had
received favours from some or other of them. In the next room I found a
large company who had formed themselves into small parties; these
were very silent and attentive to the course of the stoppers, which, in the

citycant, signifies cards, for they were at whisk, and after every deal they drank a bumper round, to make amends for the loss of time. In the next room were half-a-dozen of story-tellers and smoakers, who made such a smothering with their mundungus, that put me into a violent fit of coughing, which obliged me to terminate here my review, and I was glad to run down to my dirty box, and wash down the smoke with a glass of sherry, which I ordered my drawer to fetch me.

This growing evil ought to be check'd in its source; and none being more capable than you to stem this tide of wine, which every evening overflows the understandings of our youth, I have sent you these undigested hints, that you may animadvert on them, and remain,

Sir,
Your humble servant,
Abstemious.

LETTERS SENT TO THE TATLER AND SPECTATOR, 1725

THE CAUSES OF DRUNKENNESS

The next person, whom you ought to beware of, is a DRUNKARD; one that takes an unaccountable pleasure in sapping his constitution, and drowning his undertanding. He constantly goes senseless to bed, and rises maukish in the morning; nor can he be easy in body or mind, 'till he has renewed his dose, and again put himself beyond the reach of reflection. I would, therefore, entreat you by all means to avoid an habit, which will at once ruin your health, and impair your intellects. It is a misfortune, that society should be esteemed dull and insipid without the assistance of the bottle to enliven it; so that a man cannot entirely refrain from his glass, if he keeps any company at all. But let it be remembered, that in drinking, as well as in talking, we ought always to 'keep a watch over the doors of our lips'.

21 August, 1755

> Brisk wine some hearts inspires with gladness,
> And makes some droop in sober sadness;
> Makes politicians sound to battle,
> And lovers of their mistress prattle;
> While with 'potations pottle deep'
> It lulls the serious sot to sleep.

Horace

Drinking is one of those popular vices, which most people reckon among their venial failings; and it is thought no great blot on a man's character, to say he takes his glass rather too freely. But as those vices are most dangerous and likely to prevail, which, if not approved, are at least commonly excused, I have been tempted to examine, whether Drinking really deserves that quarter it receives from the generality of mankind: and I must own, that after a strict attention to the principal motives, that induce men to become Hard-Drinkers, as well as to the consequences, which such excesses produce, I am at a loss to account for the received maxim, that 'in good wine there is truth'; and should no more expect happiness in a full bowl, than chastity in the bar of a tavern.

The incentives to this practice are some of them very shocking, and some very ridiculous; as will perhaps appear from the following characters.

Poor Heartly was blest with every noble qualification of the head and heart, and bade fair for the love and admiration of the whole world; but was unfortunately bound in a very large sum for a friend, who disappeared, and left him to the mercy of the law. The distresses, thus brought upon him by the treachery of another, threw him into the deepest despair; and he had at last recourse to Drinking, to benumb (if possible) the very sense of reflection. He is miserable, when sober; and when drunk, stupified and muddled: his misfortunes have robbed him of all the joys of life; and he is now endeavouring wilfully to put an end to them by a slow poison.

Tom Buck, from the first day that he was put into breeches, was always accounted a boy of spirit; and before he reached the top of *Westminster* school, knew the names and faces of the most noted girls upon town, tossed off his Claret with a smack, and had a long tick at the tavern. When he went to Oxford, he espoused the Tory party, because they drank deepest; and he has for some years been accounted a four-bottle man. He drank for fame; and has so well established his character, that he was never known to send a man from his chambers sober, but generally laid his whole company under the table. Since his leaving the University, nobody ever acquired more reputation by Electioneering; for he can *see out* the stoutest freeholder in *England*. He has, indeed, swallowed many a tun in the service of his country; and is now a founder patriot by two bottles, than any man in the country.

Poor Wou'd-be became a debauchee through mere bashfulness, and a foolish sort of modesty, that has made many a man drunk in spite of his teeth. He contracted an acquaintance with a set of Hard-Drinkers; and though he would as soon chuse to swallow a dose of physic, has not courage to refuse his bumper. He is drunk every night, and always sick to death the next morning, when he constantly resolves to drink nothing stronger than small beer for the future; but at night the poor fellow gets drunk again through downright modesty. Thus Wou'd-be suffers himself to be pressed into the service; and since he has commenced a jolly fellow, is become one of the most miserable wretches upon earth.

Honest Ned Brimmer is at present the most dismal object, that ever fell a sacrifice to liquor. It was unluckily his first ambition to promote what is called Good Fellowship. In this undertaking he has in a very few years entirely ruined his constitution; and now stalks up and down in so piteous a condition, as might inspire his companions with more melancholy reflections than an empty bottle. He has quite lost all appetite; and he is now obliged to keep up a weak artificial heat in his body, by the same means that destroyed the natural warmth of his constitution. Rum, Brandy, and Usquebaugh are his diet-drinks: and he may perhaps linger a few months, before he falls a martyr to Good Fellowship.

Having thus taken a short view of the unhappy motives, that induce men to become Hard-Drinkers, few perhaps will think such reasons any recommendation to Drunkenness. Nor can I imagine they will grow more fond of it, by observing what strange creatures they are during their intoxication. *Shakespeare* calls it 'putting a Devil into their mouths, to steal away their brains.' and, indeed, a cup too much turns a man the wrong side out; and wine, at the same time it takes away the power of standing from the legs, deprives the mind of all sense and reflection. It is whimsical enough to consider the different effects, which wine produces on different tempers. Sometimes, like love, it makes a fool sensible, and a wise man an ass; and seems to imbibe a new quality from every different body, as water takes a tincture from the ground it runs through.

Horace has with great pleasantry recapitulated the various effects of wine in a stanza, which I have placed at the head of this paper. One man grows maudlin and weeps; another becomes merry and facetious; a third quarrels, throws a bottle at his companion's head, and could run his dearest friend through the body; a fourth is mad for a girl, and falls

THE PICNIC

in love with a street-walker; while to a fifth, the liquor serves as an opiate, and lulls him to sleep. *Shakespeare* has also shewn this variety of characters with great humour. *Cassio* cries, 'let's to business,' and immediately begins to hiccup his prayers, and belches out his hopes of salvation: Justice *Silence*, who does not speak a word while he is sober, has no sooner swallowed the rouzing cup, than he roars out a catch, and grows the noisiest man in the company. It is reported to have been one of the most exquisite entertainments to the Choice Spirits in the beginning of this century, to get *Addison* and *Steele* together in company for the evening. *Steele* entertained them, 'till he was tipsy; when the same wine, that stupified him, only served to elevate *Addison*, who took up the ball just as *Steele* dropped it, and kept it up for the rest of the evening. They, who have never been present at a scene of this kind, may see the whole groupe

213

of drunken characters, displayed at one view with infinite humour, in *Hogarth's Modern Midnight Conversation*.

Thus excess of Drinking verifies all the transformations, recorded in the fable of *Circe's* cup: and perhaps the true reason, why *Bacchus* is always painted with horns, is to intimate, that wine turns men into beasts. Indeed, if none were to indulge themselves in Drinking, except those, who (like Steele and Addison) could be witty and agreeable in their cups, the number of Hard-Drinkers would be very happily diminished. Most men have so little right to plead an excuse of this sort in vindication of their Drunkenness, that wine either makes them rude, very stupid, or very mad. It is a vulgar error to suppose, that liquor only shews ill qualities, since it also frequently creates them; and engenders notions in the mind quite foreign to it's natural disposition, which are the mere effects of wine, and break out like blotches and carbuncles on the face. The disgustful appearance, which most people make when they are drunk, was what induced the *Spartans* to intoxicate their slaves, and shew them to their children, in order to deter them from so odious a vice. In like manner let the Choice Spirit, who is often seen snoring in an armed-chair in a tavern, or hanging his head over the pot, reflect what a shocking figure he must have made, when he sees the drunken beggar sleeping on a bulk, or rolling in the kennel!

Whoever thus considers the motives, that generally induce men to give into these excesses, and how ridiculous and unhappy they are often rendered by the effects, will hardly be tempted by the charms of a bottle: And, indeed, Hard-Drinking is frequently one, among the many evils, that arise from want of education. The dull country squire, who has no taste for literary amusements, has nothing, except his dogs and horses, but his bumper to divert him; and the town squire sits soaking for the same reasons in a tavern. These are the common herds of *Bacchus's* swine: but nothing is more shocking than to see a man of sense thus destroying his parts and constitution. It not only makes a terrible innovation in his whole frame and intellects, but also robs him of the society of those like himself, with whom he should associate, and reduces him to the level of a set of wretches; since all may be admitted to his company and conversation who are able to toss off a bumper.

These considerations are sufficient to convince us of the evils, which result from Hard-Drinking: but it will shock us still more, if we reflect, how much it will influence our life and conduct. Whoever is engaged in a profession, will never apply to it with success, while he sticks so close to his bottle; and the tradesman, who endeavours to make business and pleasure compatible, will never be able to make both ends meet. Thus, whether health, fame, or interest is regarded, Drunkenness should be avoided: and we may say with *Cassio*, 'Every inordinate cup is unblest, 'and the ingredient is a Devil'.

THE CONNOISSEUR
30 October, 1755

THE DRUNKEN CLERGYMAN CURED

It is related of the Rev Rees Prichard, vicar of Llandingad, but better known, (says Rees in his History of South Wales,) by the name of 'the vicar of Llandovery,' who died in the year 1644, that while a young man he was much addicted to drinking; and he is said to have been cured of this habit by an accidental circumstance, which some have not scrupled to consider miraculous. In his visits to the public house, he was usually followed by a goat. On one occasion, he prevailed on his companion to participate in his enjoyments, and to drink ale till it became inebriated. This one fit of intoxication more than satisfied the goat. It could never afterwards be prevailed upon to repeat the experiment. This incident, though trifling, led the master to reflect on his own condition, and induced a resolution to abstain thenceforth from his old practice.

THE MIRROR, 1833

CURE FOR HABITUAL DRUNKENNESS

You have heard the story of the Highland chieftain, who was advised to put small shot in his bumper glass, to diminish by degrees its capacity for holding whiskey, and thus to wean himself from drinking. The following will teach a trick worth two of this: the name of our modern discoverer is Baron Brulh Cramer, a celebrated German, who has found out a method of making the most confirmed tippler have the greatest loathing and repugnance to all sorts of spirits and strong liquor. The Baron's remedy is not only safe, but powerfully strengthening to the whole body; and the drinker will have the great satisfaction, that while he is acquiring a loathing for strong liquor, he is at the same time improving his health, and adding to his bodily strength. To keep you no longer in suspense, the following is the receipt of the new German remedy for tippling:—Take one tea-spoonful of the tincture of columba, one tea-spoonful of the tincture of cascarilla, one tea-spoonful of the compound tincture of gentian, a wine-glass full of

215

SUCKING THE MONKEY

infusion of quassia, and twenty drops of elixir of vitriol; mix and take twice or thrice a-day, and have a jug of cold water dashed over the head every morning on coming out of bed, and the feet bathed in warm water every night. Continue this for six or eight weeks. Dr Roth, of Swinmunde, has succeeded with this remedy in completely curing many poor creatures, both men and women, who were actually killing themselves by continually tippling and drunkenness. Let us hope it may be equally successful in this country.   THE MIRROR, 1824

216

THE SACK

The E.I.H.[1] has been thrown into a quandry by the strange phenomenon of poor Tommy Bye, whom I have known man and mad-man twenty-seven years, he being elder here than myself by nine years and more.

He was always a pleasant, gossiping, half-headed, muzzy, dozing, dreaming, walk-about, inoffensive chap; a little too fond of the creature —(who isn't at times?) but Tommy had not brains to work off an over-night's surfeit by ten o'clock next morning; and unfortunately, in he wandered the other morning drunk with last night, and with a super-fœtation of drink taken in since he set out from bed. He came staggering under his double burthen, like trees in Java, bearing at once blossom, fruit, and falling fruit, as I have heard you or some other traveller tell, with his face literally as blue as the bluest firmament; some wretched calico, that he had mopped his poor oozy front with, had rendered up its native dye; and the devil a bit would he consent to wash it, but swore it was characteristic, for he was going to the sale of indigo, and set up a laugh which I did not think the lungs of mortal man were competent to. It was like a thousand people laughing, or the Goblin Page. He imagined afterwards that the whole office had been laughing at him, so strange did his own sounds strike upon his *non*sensorium! But Tommy has laughed his last laugh, and awoke the next day to find himself reduced from an abused income of £600 per annum to one-sixth of the sum, after thirty-six years' tolerably good service.

LETTER OF CHARLES LAMB TO THOMAS MANNING
28 May, 1819

[1] East India House

AN EMACIATED LOST MAN

Reached St Alban's at eight o'clock, A.M., to breakfast, after driving twelve miles, and learned that poor Grogram Rummy, from London, in the wine and spirit trade, was in the house. Up to eleven o'clock I never caught sight of him; for I understood that the potations strong of the previous night and midnight had caused him to lie a little longer than usual in bed, and to take, while there, soda water repeated a time or two, and sundry squibs, with water warm and sugarless, of his favourite seldom failing restorative, brandy, to enable the stomach and palate to return to their usual tone.

When up, being unable to take anything solid in the shape of breakfast, out he roamed to add fuel to the already over-enkindled fire, trudging with faltering step from one inn to another, and from public house to public house, where his principal if not entire business was transacted; and immediately finding it requisite to the success of his journey, he would commence his daily draughts, drinking porter or ale with one, spirits with another, wine probably with a third, and something certainly with all, mixing and drinking to suit the humours of his various friends, till flushed a little, better in seeming health than when he left, excited with stimulants, he would return to the commercial room with the view of dining. Alas, no! he could not eat. Of the many things prepared, not one was at all acceptable to his vitiated taste. After discussing in his mind what might be likely to suit his morbid palate, he ordered (in lieu of a basin of good mutton broth) a highly seasoned grill, but was after all unable to touch it. His appearance really alarmed me; for his hand was tremulous, his gait unsteady, his face one mass of corruption, his body full to repletion, his whole system deranged, and his once powerful mind and energetic frame decayed—yes, I might have said destroyed—by that awful forerunner of all diseases, drink! drink! drink!

Oh, what an awful—and, nevertheless, I regret to say, often-occurring specimen of this class of commercial men is the character before us, who to earn a daily bread which he cannot eat, dares to risk a diseased life, and certainly draw on premature death. I never shall forget the vacant and unceasing rolling of his eyes, first lowering, and then again flashing desperation.

His countenance would occasionally, however, light up; but it was only a faint effort, for, immediately relaxing to a placid smile, in apparent unconsciousness, a sullen sadness would suddenly overshadow his once intellectual features, which, previously to his present emaciated state, were regular and good, but are now, from their carmined, distorted, puffed, and carbuncled irregularity, loathsome to look upon. Poor fellow! his hoarse voice, tremulous lips, and faltering tongue, will not long give utterance to his many miseries. His days are numbered; and although I may never meet him more, memory will oft return to the halcyon days of his joyous youth and blooming manhood, when, having received an education of no mean order, and filled a situation of importance, his talents had full scope, and he revolved, the sun of a happy circle. Alas! a chain of events, a whole category of circumstances in quick succession, brought him from his high estate to his present occupation, where, in anxiety to forget the past, he sacrifices too freely at the shrine of the jolly god, drowning his cares in the bowl till he has out-stripped all his former prudence, and from indulgence and excess is only now the phantom of what he was.

THE DIARY OF A COMMERCIAL TRAVELLER
Throne Crick, 1847

GEORGE CRUIKSHANK (1792–1878) AS A TEETOTALLER

'I remember him about 1846', said Mr W. H. Wills, another old friend. 'He was then flirting with Temperance. I wanted him to dine at my house; but he excused himself, saying he should be led into temptation, and he had resolved to be a water-drinker thenceforth'. He did not go to dinner, but dropped in later—much excited; and when his host pushed the water-bottle towards him, he gently added brandy. The guests departed, leaving the hilarious George, with two others, to finish the evening; and when the trio got into the street, they found the old difficulty in restraining Cruikshank's boisterous spirits. After trying in vain for something more than an hour to lead him home, they left him—climbing up a lamp-post! . . .

It was not until after his second marriage that he took to temperance. In his first wife's lifetime he sacrificed to the jolly god rather oftener than occasionally; and surely no man drank with more fervour and enjoyment, nor carried his liquor so kindly, so merrily. Then was the time to hear him sing 'Lord Bateman' in character, and costume improvised from table-covers, table-napkins, and antimacassars—anything he could lay hands on—with the laughing help of his host. He was what Albert Smith called 'great fun' in this song at any time. . . .

On the day of his death, his old friend and fervent admirer repaid his kindness by sketching this loving portrait of him:— . . .

He was, to sum up, a light-hearted, merry, and, albeit a teetotaler, an essentially 'jolly' old gentleman, full physically of humorous action and impulsive gesticulation, imitatively illustrating the anecdotes he related; somewhat dogged in assertion and combative in argument; strong-rooted as the oldest of old oaks in old true British prejudices; decidedly eccentric, obstinate, and whimsical; but in every word and deed a God-fearing, Queen-honouring, truth-loving, honest man.

'This was the famous George Cruikshank, caricaturist, social satirist and moralist, illustrator of books, engraver on steel and copper, draughtsman on wood, painter in oils and water-colours, the doughtiest champion, in his degree, of the temperance cause; and, albeit his "foaming bowl" was for many years replenished only from the pump, the Prince of Good Fellows.' . . .

In one of his Temperance speeches he said: 'I am ashamed to say that for many years I went on following the ordinary custom of drinking, till I fell into pecuniary difficulties. I had some money at a banker's; he fell into difficulties, took to drinking brandy-and-water, and ended by blowing out his brains. I lost my money, and in my distress applied to friends who aided me for a time, but they themselves fell into difficulties, and I was forced to extricate myself by the most extraordinary exertions. In this strait I thought, the best thing I can do is to take to water; but still I went on for some time before I quite weaned myself from my own drinking habits. I went to take luncheon with my friend Dickens (who, I am sorry to say, is not a teetotaler); he asked me to take wine, but I told him I had taken to water, for, in my opinion, a man had better take a glass of prussic acid than fall into the other habit of taking brandy-and-water; and I am happy to say that Charles Dickens quite agreed with me, that a man had better wipe himself out at once, than extinguish himself by degrees by the soul-degrading and body-destroying enemy. . . .

At a meeting held at Manchester, this great artist gave an address on Temperance; in the course of which, referring to the early days of his life, and to the drinking habits which existed at that period, he said he recol-lected gentlemen coming to dine occasionally at his father's house, and he was often surprised on coming downstairs of a morning to find some of them rolled up in the carpet in an extraordinary manner. His own father took too much drink, and shortened his life by it. He shortened his life by the fashion of the day, and left him (the speaker) uneducated. . . . He had watched the effects of drink ever since he had begun to reflect, both among the higher and lower orders. (*Poor Richard's Alamanac*, 1876.). . . .

Having been converted by his own 'Bottle' to total abstinence from fermented liquors, he could be nothing less than an earnest and vehement worker in the cause. He threw himself heart and soul into it; and during the thirty remaining years of his life his zeal never slackened, and he had never made sacrifices enough in it. His impulsive advocacy often took ludicrous forms. He sometimes offended people by his denunciations of even the most moderate drinkers, but he never made an enemy by his *gaucherie* or his downright phrases imported into quiet circles, because the purity of his motive and the well-known impetuosity of his nature excused him. I can remember, in the first year of his total abstinence, meeting him at a ball given in Fitzroy Square, by Mr Joshua Mayhew, the father of Horace and the Brothers Mayhew. He danced and was light-hearted with the youngest; but when at supper the wine began to circulate, he stole round to the head of the table, and, laying his hand upon the shoulder of the venerable host (who was a very haughty and quick-tempered old gentleman), said, in a deep, warning voice, 'Sir, you are a dangerous man'. Mr Mayhew had a glass of wine in his hand, and was about to drink a toast to the health of one of his sons, when Cruikshank's hand fell upon his shoulder. 'I look upon every wine-drinker', Cruikshank added firmly, 'as a dangerous man, sir.' The company, knowing the hot temper of their host, expected an explosion of rage; but it was staunched by Horace Mayhew, who burst into a hearty laugh, and told his father to go on, for 'it was only dear old George'.

In the same way, when dining at the Mansion House, Cruikshank, at the passing of the loving-cup, would go through an extraordinary panto-mime before all the company, expressive of his horror of strong drinks. He would shake his hand angrily at the Lord Mayor, and raise his arms with horror while his neighbour quaffed of the cup. The company humoured the eccentric old gentleman; for, in their hearts, they could not but respect his downright earnestness. He lost no opportunity. Returning home at the head of his volunteer corps, he showed his jaded officers, who had freely taken beer, how fresh he was—on two oranges.

'Ah! you may laugh', he would say, when his friend bantered him about his aggressive protests in society; 'you may laugh, but I can tell you this—the presence of the old jackdaw checked the drinking, if it didn't stop it, and I am very grateful to feel sure of that.' As Mr Sala has observed, 'the veteran sticks bravely to his text'. And well he might, for his temperance renewed his youth. 'He neither smoked tobacco nor drank fermented liquors in his old age; but he was a hearty eater, an early riser, and a vigorous walker, and his reward was that which, according to Gray, is only felt by boys at school—a perpetual "sunshine of the breast".' He was fond of showing this vigour renewed by temperance, at every possible opportunity; for he very wisely regarded it as his most forcible argument. It enabled him, in his old age, to capture a burglar on his own premises. The story runs that when he was following the burglar to the station with the police, he drew him under a lamp, and told him that he could see drink had brought him to this—adding that he himself drank nothing but water. 'I wish I'd ha' known that', said the ruffian, 'I'd ha' broken your head for you'. Cruikshank delighted to show an audience how he could hold a tumbler full of water steady upon the palm of his outstretched hand. At eighty, he was seen in costume at a fancy dress ball at Willis's Rooms, joining heartily in the dance, and letting everybody know that it was 'water that did it'. . . .

On another occasion he drew sharply up before the windows of his old wine merchant, and called out, 'Give me back my thousand pounds!'. . . . Cruikshank could never convert his mother to his views. She lived with him during the latter years of her life, and died under his roof, in the care of a most reverent and attentive son. She had always been a careful, sober body, and would not be coerced because her son could not take his beer or toddy without committing excesses. She had been a handsome woman in her days, her grandson records, and it was picturesque to see the lame old lady, leaning upon her crutch, and wrapped in a plaid,—with her shrivelled features and wild grey hair,—raise her withered arm, and with the old fire declare that she would not surrender her principles. A glass of beer with dinner, and a little toddy at bedtime, she had always taken, and she took them to the end, and George had to submit.

Addressing, on one occasion, a Temperance oration to a Bristol audience, he appealed to his female hearers not to believe that 'nourishing stout' was necessary to nursing-mothers; and he pointed to himself as a melancholy example, saying, 'My mother first lifted the poisoned chalice to my lips'. His aged mother read this in the morning paper. Her wrath was violent. 'What!' she cried, 'am I to be told publicly, at eighty years of age, that I, who always begged and prayed him to be sober, taught him to drink?' Her son did not return home for several days; but he heard of his speech in no uncertain tones when he presented himself to the old lady, who had, in his youth, often physically chastised him for his excesses. . . .

'You will remember', he said, (to Cuthbert Bede) 'how Maclise represented me seated on a beer-barrel, getting my inspiration from pothouse scenes, and pencilling them on the crown of my hat?' 'Yes, I remember: it was in the *Fraser* gallery of portraits. And you have amply proved to the world since then that you can turn to the best account, and for the public good, the people and incidents that you saw in those places.'

THE LIFE OF GEORGE CRUIKSHANK
Blanchard Jerrold, 1883

TEETOTALISM

The Rev Theobald Mathew (1790–1856) was a famous apostle of temperance and Jane Welsh Carlyle describes one of his meetings in a letter to her husband, dated Aug. 9. 1843.

And now let me tell you something which you will perhaps think questionable, a piece of Hero-Worship that I have been after. My youthful enthusiasm, as John Sterling calls it, is not extinct then, as I have supposed; but must certainly be immortal! Only think of its blazing up for Father Mathew! You know I have always had the greatest reverence for that priest; and when I heard he was in London, attainable to me, I felt that I must see him, shake him by the hand, and tell him I loved him

THE VERY REV.^D THEOBALD MATHEW,

Administering the Temperance Pledge.

considerably! I was expressing my wish to see him, to Robertson, the night
he brought the Ballad Collector; and he told me it could be gratified quite
easily. Mrs Hall had offered him a note of introduction to Father Mathew,
and she would be pleased to include my name in it. 'Fix my time, then.'
'He was administering the pledge all day long in the Commercial Road.'
I fixed next evening.

Robertson, accordingly, called for me at five, and we rumbled off in
omnibus, all the way to Mile End, that hitherto for me unimaginable goal!
Then there was still a good way to walk; the place, the 'new lodging', was a
large piece of waste ground, boarded off from the Commercial Road, for
a Catholic cemetery. I found 'my youthful enthusiasm' rising higher and
higher as I got on the ground, and saw the thousands of people all hushed
into awful silence, with not a single exception that I saw—the only
religious meeting I ever saw in cockneyland which had not plenty of
scoffers hanging on its outskirts. The crowd was all in front of a narrow
scaffolding, from which an American captain was then haranguing it;
and Father Mathew stood beside him, so good and simple-looking! Of
course, we could not push our way to the front of the scaffold, where
steps led up to it; so we went to one end, where there were no steps or
other visible means of access, and handed up our letter of introduction
to a policeman; he took it and returned presently, saying that Father
Mathew was coming. And he came; and reached down his hand to me,
and I grasped it; but the boards were higher than my head, and it seemed
our communication must stop there. But I have told you that I was in a
moment of enthusiasm; I felt the need of getting closer to that good man.
I saw a bit of rope hanging, in the form of a festoon, from the end of the
boards; I put my foot on it; held still by Father Mathew's hand; seized
the end of the boards with the other; and, in some, to myself (to this
moment), incomprehensible way, flung myself horizontally on to the
scaffolding at Father Mathew's feet! He uttered a scream, for he thought
(I suppose) I must fall back; but not at all; I jumped to my feet, shook
hands with him and said—what? 'God only knows.' He made me sit
down on the only chair a moment; then took me by the hand as if I had
been a little girl, and led me to the front of the scaffold, to see him
administer the pledge. From a hundred to two hundred took it; and all
the tragedies and theatrical representations I ever saw, melted into one,
could not have given me such emotion as that scene did. There were
faces both of men and women that will haunt me while I live; faces
exhibiting such concentrated wretchedness, making, you would have
said, its last deadly struggle with the powers of darkness. There was one

man, in particular, with a baby in his arms; and a young girl that seemed of the 'unfortunate' sort, that gave me an insight into the lot of humanity that I still wanted. And in the face of Father Mathew, when one looked from them to him, the mercy of Heaven seemed to be laid bare. Of course I cried; but I longed to lay my head down on the good man's shoulder and take a hearty cry there before the whole multitude! He said to me one such nice thing. 'I dare not be absent for an hour', he said; 'I think always if some dreadful drunkard were to come, and me away, he might never muster determination perhaps to come again in all his life; and there would be a man lost!'

I was turning sick, and needed to get out of the thing, but, in the act of leaving him—never to see him again through all time, most probably—feeling him to be the very best man of modern times (you excepted), I had another movement of youthful enthusiasm which you will hold up your hands and eyes at. Did I take the pledge then? No; but I would, though, if I had not feared it would be put in the newspapers! No, not that; but I drew him aside, having considered if I had any ring on, any handkerchief, anything that I could leave with him in remembrance of me, and having bethought me of a pretty memorandum-book in my reticule, I drew him aside and put it in his hand, and bade him keep it for my sake; and asked him to give me one of his medals to keep for his! And all this in tears and in the utmost agitation! Had you any idea that your wife was still such a fool! I am sure I had not. The Father got through the thing admirably. He seemed to understand what it all meant quite well, inarticulate though I was. He would not give me a common medal, but took a little silver one from the neck of a young man who had just taken the pledge for example's sake, telling him he would get him another presently, and then laid the medal into my hand with a solemn blessing. I could not speak for excitement all the way home. When I went to bed I could not sleep; the pale faces I had seen haunted me, and Father Mathew's smile; and even next morning, I could not anyhow subside into my normal state, until I had sat down and written Father Mathew a long letter—accompanying it with your 'Past and Present!' Now, dear, if you are ready to beat me for a distracted Gomeril I cannot help it. All that it was put into my heart to do, *Ich Konnte nicht anders.*

THE PLEASURES AND PAINS OF ALCOHOL

I have tried to be a teetotaller ever since I was a boy; but when these periodical waves, that I have previously described, of appetite and passion

ADVANTAGE OF TEMPERANCE.

TWO glasses of Gin, every day, at three halfpence a glass cost four pound eleven shillings and three pence a year. Which would pay for,

	L	s	d
A Man's Shirt	0	6	0
A pair of men's Stockings	0	1	9
A pair of women's Stockings	0	1	6
Shift and muslin Cap	0	3	8
Printed cotton Gown	0	5	6
A man's cotton Shirt	0	4	0
A man's fustian Coat	0	16	0
A pair of Blankets	0	12	0
A neck Handkerchief	0	1	4
A pair of men's Shoes	0	8	6
A pair of womens Shoe's	0	4	0
A flannel Petticoat	0	2	6
A coarse cloth Cloak	0	7	0
A quilted Waistcoat	0	4	0
Fustian Trowsers lined	0	7	6
A pair of cotton Sheets.	0	6	0
	4	11	3

ALCOHOLIC EQUIVALENTS
(*circa* 1830)

sweep over me, nothing can stem them. You may set yourself against them for days, and even weeks, as I have many times done, but in the end you have to succumb. And the strangest thing of all is that, after this wave has passed over you; in other words, after I have made myself so ill by the consumption of alcohol that my stomach will not even retain water, far less liquor of any kind, when I am laid prostrate, unable to move, and have to be nursed back into health by tea-spoonfuls of beef-tea—I say, the strangest thing of all is, that I cannot explain to myself when again well, how it is that I have been so weak as to succumb to its influence. I believe the true reason is that the first eight or ten days is a period of great enjoyment, something really delightful. I am not referring, of course to sottish drunkenness; I have hardly ever been incapable from the effects of liquor in my life; I allude to a kind of mental exhilaration which begins to be felt soon after one has commenced to imbibe freely. There is no sensation I have ever experienced from any source or cause whatever that yields so much pleasure as during this incipient stage. While it lasts you have, so to speak, the gift of tongues, the command of all knowledge, rare aptitude for invention and for forming new plans and designs, together with marvellous capacity for concentrating thought on a single object; which last, as you may know, was held by Dugald Stewart to be the distinctive characteristic of genius, as distinguished from mere talent. I repeat, by way of emphasis, that the incipient stage of an attack of alcoholism is a glorious experience. Nay, everything that I have accomplished more than my fellows who started life under similar conditions has been conceived during these periods; but—but oh, how dearly I have had to pay for it! No language can describe nor tongue can tell the agony and the torture which has to be endured when the moment arrives that the stomach and the liver refuse to perform their functions, and when sleep deserts your eyes and slumber your eyelids! Many, many times have I wished for death during these periods.

WINE, WOMEN AND SONG
N.D., *c.*1910

Nips

A MARRINER IN A STORME

It chanced that a Merchants ship was violently tossed by a storme at Sea, insomuch that all despairing of safety, betooke themselves to prayer, saving one onely Marriner, who was ever wishing to see two starres. O (saith he) that I could see but two starres, or but one of the two! and of these words he made so often repitition, that disturbing the meditations of the rest, at length one asked him what two starres, or what one starre he meant, to whom he replyed, *O that I could but see the starre in Cheape-side, or the starre in Coleman streete,* I care not whether.

A DRUNKEN SOULDIER

A riotous drunken Souldier, that had lost the sheath of his dagger, carried it naked in his hand: and being demanded by one that knew him, why he bore a drawne weapon so dangerously about with him? he made answere, it was *to stab him that was drunke before him.*

A DRUNKARD AND HIS WIFE

A woman had a husband that used to come home often disguised, and sometimes to lye along on the floore; and stil when she offered to raise him from the ground, hee would not be removed, but answered, the Tenement is mine owne, I pay rent for it, and I may lye where I list. Some few nights, comming home in the like taking, and sitting in a chaire before the fire, hee fell a sleepe: the woman would have waked him, but could not, and therefore went up to bed, in which she was scarce warme, but the Maide cried out aloud, Mistresse, Mistresse, my Master is fallen out of the chaire, and lies in the midst of the fire, which she hearing, lay still, and answered; let him alone, for, *as long as he payes rent for the house, he may lye where he list.*

GENTLEMEN AT A TAVERNE

Some Gentlemen meeting at a Taverne, and being put into a roome two paire of staires high, they called for a pint of wine, which after it was drunke off, they knock'd and call'd, but none either answering, or comming up, one of the Gentlemen threw downe the pint pot, when instantly a Drawer comes up with a quart, and so left them. They following their discourse, and drinking round, soone emptied the Quart pot too. Then they knocke agen, and call, but none answering, downe goes the quart pot, and in a trice comes up a pottle; and after some respit being likewise dispacht, they called aloud and knockt, but none would answer, till at length, they thundred with such violence, that up comes one of the Drawers, whom a Gentleman being angry at such slacke attendance, meets at the top of the staires, and cast him headlong downe to the bottome, at which, all the rest of his fellows, with the Master of the house, began to muster up themselves, and comming up into the gentlemens roome, demanded the reason of that violence done to his servant, and why hee did so. Marry mine Host (saith he) I did it for attendance: for throwing downe a pint, there came up a quart; and throwing downe the quart, there came up a Pottle: wherefore sitting here alone, and no man regarding us, *We flung one Drawer downe staires, in hopes that two at the least, would come up to attend us.*

A SLEEPY DRAWER

A Drawer sleeping under the Pulpit, the Preacher beat his Deske so hard, that the Drawer suddenly awaked, start up and cryed openly in the Church, *A non; a non sir.*

OF WINE

One presented a Drunkard for his New-yeares-gift with these few lines.

Whilst in my Pot or Glasse I keepe my wine,
I bodly dare presume, that they are mine.
But when the Pot I by the glasse devour,
Being drunke the Masters in the Servants power.
I have it not, it hath me; all I have
Is to be made a Prisoner to my slave.
What was my vassall, now I Idoll call;
For I before it must both kneele, and fall.

A GENTLEMAN AND A DRAWER

A Gentleman crost by a Drawer, & conducted into a Roome two paire of staires high, thought thus to be revenged on him. First, he knocks for the fellow, and bids him draw him a pint of wine, I will, I will sir, answered the Drawer; but before he was at the lowest step of the I. paire of staires, he knocks agen aloud for the Drawer, who answered, Anon, anon sir, but came up presently, and asked him what he would have, Drawer, saith he, with the pint of wine bring mee a Spitoon. The Drawer ran downe very nimbly, but the Gentleman knockt the third time louder than hee did before, insomuch that he was forced to come up againe, and entring the Roome very angerly, asked him what he wanted; Nothing, saith the Gentleman, but this, I called thee first up, to bring a pint of Wine, the second time, to bring me a Spitoon, and now I would intreate thee, that thou wouldst not bring the wine up *in the Spitoon*.

A DRUNKEN MAN'S MISTAKE

One Moon-shine night in hard frosty weather, a Water-man that was drunke sate downe on the shoare neere Tower-warfe, at a low tide, and falling a sleepe slept so long till the tide came in, and flowed by degrees even up to his mouth, the moone shining in his face; whereupon suddainely wakening, he sayd, *no more drinke now I thanke you heartily; but a few more cloathes if you please, and then put out the Candle.*

A BANQUET OF JESTS AND MERRY TALES
Archie Armstrong, Court Jester (1611–37)

EPIGRAM ON A CLUB OF SOTS

The jolly Members of a toping Club,
Like Pipestaves, are but hoop'd into a Tub;
And in a close Confederacy link,
For nothing else, but only to hold Drink.

THE GENUINE REMAINS IN VERSE AND PROSE
Samuel Butler, 1759

WARM ALE

A landlord, who boasted much of the goodness of his ale, being requested by a traveller to warm a pot for him, took the liberty of passing a curse on the *stomach* that would not warm the ale; which was met by a rejoinder from the traveller, cursing '*the ale that would not warm the stomach*'.

OXYGEN AND HYDROGEN

While a chymical lecturer was describing the nature of gas, a blue-stocking lady anxiously inquired of a gentleman, what he meant by *oxy-gin* and *hydro-gin*. 'Why, madam', replied he, 'they are nearly alike; only *oxy-gin is pure gin, and hydro-gin is gin and water*'.

BILL SOAKER

Bill Soaker lay stretch'd on the bed of grim death,
By brandy burnt up, and a-gasping for breath;
A friend, in great fervour, besought him to think
On his awful approach to enternity's brink.
Says Bill, 'For such matters I duly have car'd,
And am for a world of *pure spirits* prepar'd!'

A MAN HUNG FOR LEAVING HIS LIQUOR

Stow mentions a custom which prevailed at the hospital of Matilda, at St Giles's, by which 'the prisoners conveyed from the city of London towards *Teybourne*, there to be executed for treasons, felonies, and other trespasses, were presented with a *great bowl of ale*, thereof to drink at their pleasure, as to be their last refreshing in this life'. I believe it was from the circumstance of a malefactor's refusing to partake of this farewell draught, whereby he reached Tyburn sooner than was usual, and just time enough to get hung before a reprieve, which had been sent after him, arrived: hence he was said to have been '*hung for leaving his liquor*'.

THE TOPER AND THE FLIES

A group of topers at a table sat,
  With punch, that much regales the thirsty soul;
Flies soon the party join'd, and join'd the chat,
  Humming, and pitching round the mantling bowl.

At length those flies got drunk, and, for their sin,
Some hundreds lost their legs, and tumbled in;
And, sprawling midst the gulf profound,
Like Pharaoh, and his daring host, were drown'd.

Wanting to drink, one of the men
  Dipp'd from the bowl the drunken host,
  And drank; then, taking care that none were lost,
He put in every mother's son again.

231

Up jump'd the Bacchanalian crew, on this,
Taking it very much amiss,
Swearing, and in the attitude to strike,
  'Lord!' quoth the man, with gravely-lifted eyes,
  'Though I don't like to swallow flies,
I did not know but others might!'

A JOVIAL PRIEST'S CONFESSION

I desire to end my days in a tavern drinking;
May some Christian hold for me the glass, when I am shrinking,
That the Cherubim may cry, when they see me sinking,
'God be merciful to a soul of this gentleman's way of thinking!'

OPTICAL DECEPTIONS

Tom runs from a wife to get rid of his trouble—
He drinks, and he drinks, till he sees all things *double;*
But when he has ceased wine and brandy to mingle,
Oh, what would he give to see himself *single*!

A SPIRITLESS WIFE

'Is my wife out of *spirits*?' said Jack, with a sigh,
As her voice of a tempest gave warning.
'Quite *out*, Sir, indeed', said the maid, in reply,
'For she emptied the bottle this morning.'

OLD TOPING SUSAN

Dead-drunk old Susan oft was found;
  But now she's laid beneath the ground,
As door-nail dead—alas the day!
  Her nose was red, and moist her clay.

From morn to night, of care bereft,
  She plied her glass, and wet her throttle;
Without a sigh her friends she left,
  But much she griev'd to leave her bottle.

THE NOSE

Reader, whene'er thou dost perceive a nose,
That red with many a large carbuncle glows,
Thou may'st conclude, nay, thou may'st safely swear,
That nose was never nurs'd upon *small* beer.

HERBS AND WATER

The late Earl of Kelly, who was not one of the most abstemious, was advised by his mother to copy the example of a person, who enjoyed sound health by living upon herbs and drinking nothing stronger than water. His lordship replied by begging to be excused imitating a person who ate like an *ass*, and drank like a *fish*.

MADEIRA

An asiatic chief being asked his opinion of a pipe of Madeira wine, with which he had been presented by an officer of the East India Company's service, said, 'That he thought it a juice extracted from women's tongues and lions' hearts; for, after he had drank a sufficient quantity of it, he could talk for ever, and also fight the devil!'

TAVERN ANECDOTES. 1825

THE POT OF PORTER

'See how this *pot runs*, look'e, Dick
A jade to serve us such a trick:
Hang it, I'll blow her up sky high.'
'Why, Tom, the *pot don't run*,' 'you lie,
I say it does; why, look here,
The table's puddled all with beer.'
Says Dick, 'confound your stupid tongue,
I'll make you own you're in the wrong;
For can't you see, you squabbling sot,
The *beer runs out, not the pot*!'

THE POETICAL NOTE-BOOK AND EPIGRAMMATIC MUSEUM
Selected by George Wentworth, Esq., 1824

EPITAPHS

Rebecca Freeland at Edwallon, Notts. 1741.

> She drank good ale, good punch and wine
> And lived to the age of 99.

Ann Collins, at King Stanley, Glos. 1804.

> 'Twas as she tript from Cask to Cask,
> In at a bung-hole quickly fell,
> Suffocation was her task,
> She had no time to say farewell.

John Adams, carrier, of Southwell.

> John Adams lies here, of the parish of Southwell,
> A carrier who carried his can to his mouth well;
> He carried so much, and he carried so fast,
> He could carry no more—so was carried at last;
> For the liquor he drunk, being too much for one,
> He could not carry-off—so he's now carri-on.
>
> > Lord Byron

To a Brewer.

> Here lies poor Burton,
>   He was both hale and stout;
> Death laid him on his bitter bier,
>   Now in another world he hops about.

To a Landlord.

> In life a jovial sot was he,
> He died from inebriete.
> A cup of burnt canary sack,
> To Earth from Heaven would bring him back.

To a Country Inn-keeper.

> Here! hark ye! Old Friend! what wilt pass then without
> Taking notice of honest plump Jack?
> You see how 'tis with me, my Light is burnt out,
> And they'n laid me here flat on my Back.

That Light in my Nose, once so bright to behold,
That Light is extinguished at last;
And I'm now put to Bed in the Dark and the Cold,
With Wicker, and so forth, made fast.

And now wilt oblige me? then call for a Quart
Of the *best* from the house o'er the Way;
Drink a Part on't thyself, on my Grave pour a Part,
And walk on:—Friend, I wish thee good Day.

THE DRUNKEN DOG

A German saloon-keeper on Third Street, New York, has another dissipated canine. The dog is slowly but surely drinking himself to death. He not only looks on the beer when it is amber, but risks a sight when it is stale and flat. He watches the trough directly under the ice-chest where the beer kegs are placed, and when the trough becomes filled, the intemperate animal will lap it up. He refuses water, and drinks beer morning, noon, and night. After drinking heavily he will go to sleep, and the first thought on waking up seems to be of beer, as he goes directly to the trough and satisfies his thirst. He is becoming quite corpulent, and is a confirmed old drunkard. His only apparent amusement and enjoyment in life are to drink and to sleep.

A MISUNDERSTANDING

When the presiding judge saw how unimportant the case seemed to be, he suggested that the counsel should get his client (rather deaf) to compromise the matter, and to ask her what sum she would take from the defendant to settle it. The counsel thereupon shouted in the ear of his client, 'His lordship wants to know what you will take?' The good woman immediately replied, 'I thank his lordship very kindly, and, if it's no ill-convenience to him, I'll take a little warm ale!'

BEER WARMS THE HEART

Dr Michael Hutchinson, who collected £3,249 for rebuilding All Saints' Church, Derby, in 1730, was so industrious and successful in this labour of love, that when the waits fiddled at his door for a Christmas-box, he invited them in, treated them with a tankard of ale, and persuaded them out of a guinea!

FROST AND ALCOHOL

In 1468 the wine distributed to the soldiers in Flanders was cut with hatchets; in 1744–45 the strongest ale in England, when exposed to the air, was covered with ice one-eighth of an inch thick, in less than fifteen minutes.

IN PRAISE OF ALE
W. T. Marchant, 1888

ARIZONA NON-STOP

Sir Norman Birkett gave Green Room Club diners an amusing sidelight on his recent experience of American hospitality.

When the New York Bar entertained him, a man from Oklahoma remarked: 'In my State, we have drinks between drinks'. Whereat a man from Arizona rejoined: 'In *my* State we have no such distinction'.

THE EVENING NEWS
16 June, 1947

THE TAPPER'S TACTICS

Sir,—An accomplishment necessary to a publican is an ability to outwit the tapper, that ubiquitous gentleman who finds himself simultaneously possessed of a raging thirst and no money. At some expense we soon learn to recognize the type and are prepared for the stock approaches, ranging from the gambit, menacing, to the appeal, heartrending. Twice within a week, however, I have been almost nonplussed by new tactics. One man offered to deposit his spectacles with me as an earnest of his intention to repay a modest loan, and the second overwhelmed me with his dentures. I feel that the free provision of security against short-term loans is an unheralded aspect of the magnitude of Mr Bevan's bounty which should not go unrecorded.

I am, Sir, yours, &c.,

WALTER SEELEY

'The George', Millwall Dock, E.14.

LETTER TO *The Times*
26 May, 1949

THE TOUCHY IRISH

'Sirs,—I have been a member of this Club for a number of years, and during my membership have been in the habit of ordering, when thirsty, a large *Irish* whisky at the charge of fivepence per glass. A few days ago I happened to discover that the charge for a large *Scotch* whisky is sixpence: a difference to which I desire to call your attention, since I consider it as casting, implicitly, a slur on the nation to which I have the honour to belong.'

THE PALL MALL MAGAZINE, 1898

THE FAREWELL

INDEX

INDEX